BEYOND WALLS AND WARS

Art, Politics, and Multiculturalism

BEYOND WALLS AND WARS

Art, Politics, and Multiculturalism

Edited by Kim Levin

MIDMARCH ARTS PRESS
New York

Library of Congress Catalog Card Number 91-068502
ISBN 1-877675-11-3

Cover photo: *Liberating the Berlin Wall, Brandenburg Gate, November 9, 1989*; courtesy of the
German Information Center, New York.

Published in 1992 by
Midmarch Arts Press
300 Riverside Drive
New York, New York 10025

Printed and bound in the United States

Contents

Introduction

The theme, "Beyond Walls and Wars: Art, Politics, and Multiculturalism," was chosen in that brief ecstatic interlude between the toppling of the Berlin Wall and the burning of the Kuwaiti oilfields. It was a moment of euphoria, a moment that somehow echoed the hopeful utopian beginnings of this waning century, not the brutal middle. None of us could have imagined that history would soon provide the spectacle of a short but terrifying war in the Middle East, a retrograde coup followed by the rapid dissolution of the USSR, and an uncivil ethnic war splitting apart what had been Yugoslavia. But history moves fast in these electronic millennial times. While the United States chapter of the International Association of Art Critics, known as AICA (Association Internationale des Critiques d'Art), organized its 1991 Congress in a bicoastal effort, the volatile world began to unravel at the seams.

The Congress was held in Santa Monica, California, in October 1991. It was the 25th international AICA gathering, but the first to be held in the United States. Founded in 1948 under the UNESCO charter, with international headquarters in Paris, AICA now has national chapters in nearly 60 countries and over 2500 members worldwide. Delegates from 35 of those nations attended the 25th Congress. The papers presented were neither abstruse theoretical tracts, nor detailed monographic studies, but brief essays, often amplified by slides, bringing the ideas of working art critics from around the world to an international audience of their peers.

Critics and artists had long debated notions of the end of modernism, theorizing it nearly to death, but suddenly events in the real world, too, seemed to signal the end of an era. Both communism and capitalism had come into sharp focus, not only as complementary opposites, but as uniquely modern economic systems. "In its deepest sense, the end of Communism has brought a major era in human history to an end. It has brought an end not just to the 19th and 20th centuries, but to the modern age as a whole," remarked Vaclav Havel (at the World Economic Forum in Switzerland, February 1992). The widespread dissatisfactions and deficits in the United States suggest that our modern system has malfunctioned, too. And, though the term "postmodernism" has become a catch-all replacement (to the point of cliché), we do not yet have the slightest notion what the configurations of the postmodern world will be.

Perhaps our conference bit off a bigger chunk of issues than any mere gathering of art critics could comfortably chew. Multiculturalism. Ethnicity. Censorship. Post-Totalitarianism. Post-Colonialism. Postmodernism. Politicized Art. Aestheticized Politics. Engaged Criticism. Our deliberately open-ended theme consisted of more than one bite. And more than one vantage point. We wanted it to be relevant to critics from all continents. The issues addressed by our speakers — from Eastern as well as Western Europe, South America, Africa, the Middle East, the new Russia and the old U.S.A. — ranged from the roles of African-American and Native-American art on this continent to the appropriation of Western European art in Africa, and African art in Latin America. Speakers explored the problematic relationships between modernism, colonialism, and totalitarianism, and the effects of politics on art and art on politics. They spoke of advanced aesthetics in places that were long ago marginalized and pushed to the peripheries — by Francophilic modernism as well as European conquest or American dominance. For the first time at an AICA Congress, delegates from nearly every country in Eastern Europe were able to participate.

One critic, from the Islamic edge of Europe, told me that the concept of postmodernism was very important to artists in her country because it allowed them a way to enter the international discourse of art, whereas modernism had assiduously shut them out. Another critic, from what had been one of the most repressive countries in the Soviet bloc, remarked that where he comes from everybody is already a survivor of modern utopia. As some of the papers reveal, artists and critics from parts of the world that endured those utopias may well be more sophisticated about the relationship of art objects to ideology, politics, societal memory, and the amnesias of history than are most of their American or Western European colleagues. While we in the West were questioning the individualistic western Self and its ties to consumer society, along with modernist notions of authorship, originality, and uniqueness, artists and writers in places like Poland and Czechoslovakia were making the posters and choreographing the strikes that led to actual change. Critics and curators in Moscow were manning the barricades. While we sought to escape from an alienated individuality, they struggled to revive an individualistic and autonomous art in adverse collectivist circumstances. While we in the United States were discovering the need for a politicized art and criticism, they were suffering from a past of overpoliticized aesthetics.

And so, as some of the papers in this volume reveal, while we may like to think that we all meet on the same intellectual track, it is more likely a series of not quite parallel paths along which we are traveling in opposite directions. As other papers imply, postmodernism is not a universal panacea. Multiculturalism has different implications in Canada than it does in South Africa; cultural identity provokes questions of assimilation in the Netherlands, while it invokes the indignation of stereotyped expropriation in Senegal. At the moment, the issues and concerns that occupy critics around the world appear to coincide because — converging from a multitude of different pasts — we have all reached a crossroads. We share the perplexities of being witness to a collapsing era. But the problems and solutions elsewhere are not necessarily the same as ours.

The 25th Congress signaled that it is time, within the ranks of art critics as well as out in the real world, for multiplicity and inclusiveness rather than exclusion — for diversity without divisiveness. And for a new consideration of the relativities of our own stance, whatever that stance may be. It is time for art and criticism from the former totalitarian countries to enter the international dialogue: we in the West have much to learn about the other side of modernism, the obverse of the avant-garde. It's time to listen to critics from former colonized nations, whose artists have experienced the exploitative underside of modernism, and whose traditional and 20th-century art has been either appropriated or ignored by the West. And it's time, though most of our Asian colleagues were unfortunately absent, to consider the hypermodernism and ultramodernity of the new Asia.

Most of all, it is time to realize that there is no such thing as the "Other." For much of this century, hardly anyone seemed to notice that the apostles of modern art were always male, always Western, always white. Everyone else just tried to fit into the system and keep their differences as inconspicuous as possible. As the tenets of the modernist paradigm have slipped away, social identity — cultural, ethnic, racial, sexual — has become a major issue in art. In the United States, which may some day recognize its own true identity — not as a white, Anglo-Saxon "First World" superpower, but as a truly polymorphic, multi-ethnic, multiracial, multicultural nation — we are gradually realizing that the "Other" is most of us.

That this Congress took place in the United States in October 1991, just one year before the 500th anniversary of Columbus's accidental "discovery" of the New World, was nicely symbolic. At our own transitional, conflicted, uncertain time, on the brink of unknown global changes, issues of survival rather than progress have come to the fore. Instead of celebrating obsolete modern notions of "supremacy" and "progress," we indirectly commemorated 1491: the final year the original civilizations and ecosystems of this hemisphere survived intact, unmolested by European "Others." The history of 20th-century art — like the whole Western history of civilization — has been, up to now, enormously biased and grossly incomplete. One usage of the word "postmodern" is to express the idea that art and criticism have come out of their lofty aesthetic towers to redress our century's damages and wrongs. Another is that voices previously inaudible are beginning to be heard.

With the exception of one speaker (Aliane Badiane from Senegal) and two discussants (Dave Hickey and Catherine Cooke from the United States) who spoke extemporaneously, this book contains the complete proceedings of the 1991 Congress's five symposium sessions. It includes the keynote address by California artist and activist, June Wayne, and the guest lecture by Serge Guilbaut, author of the controversial book, *How New York Stole the Idea of Modern Art* (1979). Also included is a paper that would have been presented by the president of the Cuban section of AICA, had her U.S. visa arrived in time.

Delivered at this international gathering of working art critics, the 42 papers engage the theme of Art, Politics, and Multiculturalism in ways that are relevant to diverse national situations. They report on the state of contemporary art and criticism, and the various effects of politics on art in other longitudes and latitudes besides our own. Some bring news from places that were until recently *terra incognita*, such as Bulgaria, Romania, Estonia. All offer evidence, not only of the decentralization, but also of the de-peripheralization of contemporary art, and the vitality of aesthetic ethics and intellectual consciousness in places the "art world" has been oblivious of. These papers are reports from the field, as it were, provisionally mapping some of the peaks, valleys, and quagmires of the new terrain of engaged art and criticism.

The modern age, whose worldly demise Vaclav Havel noted, was an era of doctrines and ideologies, "an era in which the goal was to find a universal theory." A common denominator is no longer the aim. In the current revulsion against ideals of universality, we seek differentiations, specifics, localized relevance. Perspective — whether viewing the uneasy relations between art and politics, or anything else — is shifting and relative, aligned to the temporal and spatial position and cultural identity of the observer. One by one, these papers offer evidence of common concerns and differing angles of vision. Together, they announce that the postmodern, post-colonial, and post-totalitarian (or "post-catastrophic," as some critics from the former Soviet empire have labeled it) community of multicultural art and criticism has more facets, more nuances, and more complexities than anyone had previously expected. It is vaster and more various than we have yet imagined.

— Kim Levin
President, AICA U.S.A,
April, 1992

Acknowledgements

I wish to thank Ann-Sargent Wooster and Josephine Gear for their generous help with the editing and fine-tuning of these papers, and for their many good suggestions. I wish to thank Monique Fong and Lara Ferb for translating those papers that had been presented in French, and Felix Cortéz and Lanny Powers for translations of those that were in Spanish. I also thank Lara Ferb for her time, effort, and assistance as the papers were edited and re-edited. Editing the written versions of English that was, for many speakers, a second language, was a sometimes daunting task. (What to do with a perfectly expressive but nonexistent word like "ensplittenness?" How to retain the essence of a sentence whose foreign grammar had obscured its sense?). Wherever it was necessary, I tried to coax sentences and words into readable English as gently as possible, and without altering the meaning. I hope I have managed to do so without distorting or diluting anyone's ideas.

As for the event which led to this book, I am grateful to: Phyllis Braff, who helped me shape the symposium; Merle Schipper, Congress Chair and Special Events Coordinator, who worked closely with me to organize the XXV Congress, as did administrative assistants Rodney Sappington and Mindy Williams; the Lannan Foundation and also Michael Tanaka and International Conference Systems for making possible simultaneous interpretations in Spanish, English, and French (the official languages of AICA); the Getty Trust for a travel grant that enabled speakers from Eastern Europe and other developing nations to participate; the Soros Foundation, Yugoslav Press and Cultural Center, LOT Polish Airlines, Jessair, and Air Afrique for additional travel assistance; and Ed Rubin, whose research and coordination was crucial. Also, I want to acknowledge Peter Frank for his suggestion that the theme of the Congress could be summed up by the words "Walls and Wars."

— K.L.

Walking Backward into the 21st Century

by June Wayne

It is an honor to address the International Association of Art Critics. I worried about accepting the invitation because I am an artist, and artists and critics are not always comfortable with each other. By the nature of the pecking order in the art world, we need each other. But we also feed upon each other. Which is the cannibal and which the missionary? It depends. Every time I have an exhibition, you have the upper hand. You are the surgeon; I, the patient. I arrive at your dissection table willy-nilly, hoping for a painless outcome but fearing a death certificate — which can be quite unsettling when one is very much alive.

Some critics avoid knowing the artists personally. They believe it undermines their objectivity. Others feel that they can't know too much about an artist if they are to understand the work from every aspect. But artists understand that critics are essential to our survival in the present art ecology, so we are self-conscious with you and maybe a little artificial, in the sense that one rearranges one's face to have a photo taken.

For my own part, I have always had friends who are critics and some of my most valued conversations came from interchanges with them. So I took the invitation to speak here as a melting of the artificial barriers between your art and mine, a *détente*, as it were, that I hope is an augury of things to come.

Many of you have come to Los Angeles for the first time. Whenever I return here I am struck anew by what a quiet colossus this city is compared to the noise levels of New York, Paris, London, or Berlin. And how huge it is, maybe a hundred kilometers in any direction; and mostly one and two-story buildings that cast no shadows. Our sunsets are feverishly iridescent thanks to the wide spectrum of pollutants in the air, and the Pacific Ocean sends the wind to shove the smog inland toward the mountains, so Santa Monica and Venice are definitely the best places to do your breathing while you are meeting here.

We have almost no public transportation, but we do not walk: the distances are too great. We drive a car to meet our friends by appointment, so we have a lot of privacy. We can be as single-minded as termites chewing through a wooden porch. And like termites, we can swarm whenever we get the urge to do so, because there is always something going on — a scene. Every kind of artist: visual, musical, literary, filmic, theatrical, lives here, and since the '20s this place has been significant for its avant-garde contributions to art, architecture, and design, a fact only now being recognized.

What is not as widely understood is that Los Angeles is a scientific center in the basic sciences. The Jet Propulsion Laboratory at California Technical Institute is the world-wide nexus of the space craft voyagers to other planets and to the galaxies. So if you are looking at the ocean at dawn or dusk, and if you are lucky, you may see the vapor trail of a misfired rocket — in a calligraphy of hubris writ across the sky, thanks to a defective computer chip. It is this aspect of Los Angles that proved critical to my art which is so entwined with quantum physics that I call it quantum aesthetics. In reviewing my city for so many of you who come from abroad, I hope I have revealed that this artist is as objective as any critic.

This audience, taken together with your colleagues who could not come, has written and spoken millions of words on art history, aesthetics, structural theory, and the socio-political implications of every kind of visual art, whether it be a square of color, a vacant canvas, a monumental sculpture, or a painting of a typhoon. Kilo for kilo, writings on contemporary and historical art probably equal or exceed the weight of the art itself. The art historians among you comb the past as carefully as the lifeguards in Santa Monica comb our beaches, and many an artist in many a culture is being retrieved from the void. Some of you specialize in contemporary art, and you bring word of artists who have begun to bloom. In turning your light to one or another artist, however, it seems to me that the aesthetic assumptions of the past still dominate the taste, criteria, and discourse we engage in.

Over the last twenty years, feminism and multiculturalism have expanded the content of art, and arts professionals of every kind have been sensitized to a broader spectrum of images. But I see no comparable interest in the nature of the art world itself, nor even a broadening of our understanding of how it works. Its table of organization and its territorial imperatives parallel any other commercial sector. Even the radicalization of the content of art, as in protest art, has not interrupted or deflected our fixation on the past and the immediate present as the enduring model of the community of the arts. That we could do things better and differently in the future seems outside our ken, even outside our capabilities.

This conference takes place during international upheavals of mammoth proportions. Nations around the world are exploding like volcanos and their parts are still hurtling through the air. We don't know how they will reassemble themselves or what the next map of the world will look like. But it is painfully clear that the oxygen of freedom that some people long for also feeds the flames of nationalism and religious hatreds. Freedom has many definitions, it seems, definitions that conflict with each other and that certainly conflict with what freedom means to the creative community. Day by day, on television or in the press, one can follow the efforts of competing governments, corporations, religions, juntas, guerillas, idealists, ecologists and just plain opportunists scrambling to capture those fragmented chunks of nations wherever they finally land. The scramble is so vicious that it hurts to watch it.

But there are some great moments as well. For me they include the appearance of intellectuals whose vision of the future grew out of years of thought, commitment, and even imprisonment. They are influencing the course of current events by being the artists they are and doing what artists do — implement a new vision, a vision projected forward, a vision rejecting the dark side of the past. Obviously one thinks of Vaclav Havel and Nadine Gordimer. One must think of Andreas and Halina Sakharov as well. Each spent years of preparation for these times and each had a clear vision of the kind of future they wanted to bring about. Each was capable of strategic thinking, and they fashioned their tactics to implement it. I find no such clarity of vision or of purpose in the arts community of the United States. We do not image the future as anything but a duplicate of the past, just bigger. (These remarks are not intended to apply to other countries because I don't know enough to be able to do that.)

In essence, we react. We do not act. When government at any level attacks a work of art or an artist, we defend. And in the last three years we have had a lot of practice in defending. We have grown some very good, informal networks among art organizations and individuals; but they are networks triggered at the time and place chosen by our enemies. Since we do not shoot first, we take the first hit; being wounded is how we discover that trouble has arrived again. We've overturned some regulations that censored artists, but the same issue simply reappears again in another guise. This is the case in the Helms amendment now incorporating censorship of the arts into the appropriations bill passed by large majorities of the House and Senate.

It seems to me that the arts in this country, and probably in all countries, must move to another level of development, to consider how to restructure the art world itself — which means to restructure how it fits into the larger functions of the nation. If we are asked what kind of changes we want to make, we must do the work that it will take to give a coherent answer.

The arts, as a good in themselves, are of marginal interest to every government. Because creative people are unsettling to every status quo, they are inherently suspect. Every hegemony prefers as little change as possible and tolerates only such change as enhances its own stability. But for creative people, the only meaningful status quo is change itself. The impulse toward change is a creative constant, synonymous with the creative life itself.

Every power structure, big or small — monolithic or not — led by presidents or kings or dictators, corporations, churches, universities, unions, even social clubs, somehow must "manage" the creative component in its population. When a system becomes too coercive, its population becomes creative about evading it, or resisting it, and might even overthrow it entirely. Thus governments find it imperative to know when, where and how to encourage creativity in one discipline while discouraging it in another. The Egyptian dynastic rulers encouraged a certain amount of scientific development, but for centuries required artists to work within such a rigid canon that their individuality could only be expressed subliminally in handling the same images over and over again. One might express this more concretely by noticing that the Russian mathematician, Pontryagin, flourished by spouting anti-semitism: meanwhile the Sakharovs languished under house arrest in Gorky. Naguib Mahfouz, the Muslim Egyptian novelist, became a Nobel Laureate but Salman Rushdie has been condemned to death. Robert Motherwell received The National Medal of Honor in Washington D.C. even as Robert Mapplethorpe was excoriated. Yet had this been the '50s, it could have been Motherwell drawing the fury of the McCarthyites, for whom Abstract Expressionists were subversive tools of the Kremlin.

Whether in the East or the West, I believe the arts have much in common; the differences are a matter of degree and local configuration. The arts are quiveringly vulnerable to official policy, which we see in sharp relief when a poet is invited to perform abroad, or when the invitation is suddenly withdrawn in some behind-the-scenes barter of non-art issues by governments. In the '60s, Betty Kray, of the YMHA Poetry Center in New York, and later the American Academy of Poets, told me, "watch the poets if you want to be ahead of the news. They signal a change in the political weather — not by their poetry but as pawns in the power game."

Until recently, the artists of the West were envied by artists behind the Iron Curtain. Over the years, mostly in Paris, I met a few Yugoslavs, Poles, Romanians and Czechs who managed to escape to the West, and now, thanks to glasnost, some Russian artists have entered the western art market. For them it provides an ecstasy of possibilities and has drastically altered their lives for the better. But it is by no means certain that their success will endure. Now they are in the same market as the rest of us, subject to its fits and starts of trends and tastes.

I have the impression that the artists they left behind look to some new form of entrepreneurship, perhaps some form of democracy that will buy them the materials they need, the audience they long for, and the freedom to create as they please. But the Western model of an entrepreneurial art world will disappoint them. Its best days may be over. It isn't working for us just now, and I don't think it ever worked well for artists in spite of the star mentality it engendered. We have been, whether we admit it or not, a collection of cottage industry types who, should they become successful, must then become the centers of manufactories, with teams of assistants to assure a sufficient production of saleable objects.

In this country, the economic base of the arts is disintegrating, much as certain kinds of earth liquify during earthquakes. Some museums are going broke, and trying to quietly sell some of their art to keep the doors open. Others have cut their hours, their services and their staffs. The death rate of galleries is deplorable even as collectors buy at bargain prices or do not buy at all for lack of confidence in art as an investment. I need not remind many in this audience of the job market at the College Art Association's annual meeting, of the hundreds of applicants who are interviewed for a single opening for which the university lacks the funds to complete the hire. Even ancillary services of framers and shippers are in trouble. Yet this crisis was predictable at least ten years ago. Why were we unprepared?

No one does for the art world what the Rand Corporation does for the Department of Defense, or the Brookings Institution does for corporations. Nobody does for the arts what Amnesty International does for victims of atrocities by governments. Nobody does for visual artists what PEN International has done for writers and what PEN has done for all the arts in the last couple of years. The climate in the United States has become hostile toward the arts. We have fought some mighty battles with the Congress and have grown a network of resistance which has won us time and some minor victories, but not the war. We should be moving toward a new assertiveness but we don't know how. The work on which to base our objectives has not as yet been done. I'm not talking about making a list of demands: I'm talking about redesigning the ecology of the arts. We must try to achieve a new practical structure for the arts, and in so doing remind ourselves of the comments of Vaclav Havel about the inutility of arguing principles, right and wrong, with any center of power.

In the book *Disturbing The Peace: A Conversation with Karel Hvizdala* (NY: Alfred Knopf, 1990), the foreword describes a letter Havel wrote on April 8, 1975. Therein he described "a new model of behavior": when arguing with a center of power, don't get sidetracked into vague ideological debates about who is right or wrong; fight for specific goals and be prepared to stick to your guns to support good lobbyists' work. But Havel's tactic derived from his larger intention. It might have been a mutable intention, but it was nonetheless defined: to bring democracy to his country.

I believe the arts need a change of mind-set. We need a futurist mind-set in the generic sense — like that of Buckminster Fuller, not Boccioni. Future-thinking is a way of problem solving and it can be applied to aesthetic socio-political problems. We need to understand the ecology of the arts, map its parts, and come up with reliable data and tangible objectives. We need a prestigious voice that can be heard. In short, we need a Center for the Study of the Ecology of the Arts. I see it as an overarching futurist center that documents and assesses the problems of creative people, crossing from country to country and noting concurrencies of issues. Such a Center would help us design a better model for the future of the arts. In so doing, the subsets of particular crises could be dealt with more quickly because they would be anticipated. Such a Center would not be a substitute for the battles we are fighting, but it would give us the long term strategic, tactical and structural options that we now lack.

Yet I have reservations about my own proposal. I don't trust institutions with their own buildings. They develop their own imperatives and become battlefields for competing interests, as happened at UNESCO. They attract professional conference-goers and the dead-wood representatives that organizations send to do the necessary eating. In short, I do not want to see another table of organization made up of paper shufflers and pecking orders that diffuse accountability. What would please me more, at least in the beginning, is a chain of guerrilla futurists — thinkers with access to such specialists as they might need, and meeting intensively for a week at a time, several times a year, in various places where the "natives" can be studied. I would feel more comfortable with a network of futurists, who might produce a model of what a better ecology would be like once they understood the ones we've got.

Of all the players in the art game, it is the critics and the artists who have the most in common. You are every bit as marginal as we are, perhaps more so in certain ways. Perhaps we could get such a futurist mind-set going. Practice it a bit among ourselves. Our talents are complementary and they can be synergistic. By our gifts and our intentions, we intuit, observe, explore, invent, propose and persuade. We are powerfully motivated people, self-starting and capable of enormous exertion to make a point. And you, especially, are skilled at argument and research. The question is whether critics as well as artists can give up walking backwards into the 21st Century. Dare we think of where we need to go? Dare we face where we have been? Over the years I have addressed pieces of the puzzles and problems we live with, accepting them as "normal" when they were merely usual. I could see solutions for many pieces of the ecological dysfunctions of the art world, but did not try to make my findings known because to do so would have robbed me of the time to follow my own art.

But this seems to me to be the right moment to raise these questions and you the right audience perhaps to hear me (meanwhile forgiving a certain awkwardness in how I express myself.) It may be that none of you will take seriously that we can plan for a better future for the arts and to so manage our present crises as to expedite it. In that case I predict (being a futurist) that sometime, somewhere, one of you will hear an echo of this speech and a light will go on. You might even say — so that is what she meant!

Part I:
Art, Politics, and Ethnicity
in a Multicultural World

The Situation "Beyond" as a Situation "Behind"

by Luchezar Boyadjiev
(Bulgaria)

The situation beyond "walls" and "wars" is a situation that could be described as "context in search of a text." It is a situation where the movement of the contextual synchronization is producing a text. It is this text that we are part of here at this congress. The text expresses a collective utopian desire for a normal and unified world.

The dream of normalcy and unification will undoubtedly get explicated as an ecstasy of communication. But communication does not necessarily mean understanding. Understanding presupposes subject-object relations which in itself raises suspicions as to the reciprocity of exchange.

The text, if completed, might become a "wall," a new type of definer-divider in a new world.

I. BEYOND WARS AND WALLS there lurks the perspective of "walls" between form and meaning and still more "wars" between the greatness of form and the ideological convertibility-inconvertibility of meaning.

The new split between form and meaning in this situation could be exemplified by one possible interpretation of the career of the Bulgarian-born American artist Christo (Javashev).

One immediately visible characteristic of the plastic form in Christo's works — preparatory, as well as final stage — is its absolute classical greatness. It is so fluent and perfect in terms of execution, coordination of materials and hierarchy of changing viewpoints, that it is almost apersonal in its totality. The astonishing thing is that when his recent works (mainly preparatory ones) are compared stylistically with his early and student works (preserved in some museums and private collections in Bulgaria) it becomes obvious that they are both equally based on the strong traditional academic education Christo received while studying at the Academy for Fine Arts in Sofia. Thus, it could be said that Christo the draftsman, actually "stayed" in the East.

On the other hand, it could also be claimed that his "wrapping" concept, as developed and practiced in the West, is equally strongly based on his practice as a student-member of the summer youth brigades in the mid-1950s in Bulgaria. As is a well-known and by now a proven fact, the art students from these brigades were sent to help the peasants from the cooperative farms along the route of the Orient Express to "artistically" arrange their farmyards. The art students arranged the machinery in a dynamic way, repainted the decrepit buildings in joyous colors, and covered the backyards with gigantic murals, depicting powerful socialist peasants in the process of jubilant labor activities. Thus an illusion of success and affluence was produced and it was meant for the eye of the foreign (Western) traveler on the train. As it turned out later, this "technique" of substitutions became paradigmatic for the entire practice of construction of the socialist/communist utopia as a reality. For it was undoubtedly built, at least on the level of language, as a symbolic shell. Words, metaphors, and illusions substituted entirely for things. Material reality was only functional through its symbolic, not its economic, productiveness. Real utopia was only possible as an illusion and Christo at first participated in its construction.

One can see that later in the West, Christo uses similar utopian procedures. First, he creates the project and it is entirely arbitrary. Then, he creates the public which is already participating in the realization of the project by force of its expectations. Then, the project is realized by force of the sheer willpower of the artist now acting as a "leader of the masses." And finally, it transforms totally some portion of the pre-existing "natural" reality. There is the metaphor and the dream (and utopia is always a dream at first), then there is the technology for putting them into practice, then there is the radically redesigned reality. Christo's realized projects are just the same "temporarily" real utopias as "real communism" turned out to be. And I think that is why Christo occasionally claims with a touch of irony that he still is a good Marxist.

But however identical the substance of these practices of his as plastic form and procedures may be, there are relevant differences in their meanings, i.e. functions, in the East and the West. His simulated avant-garde activities in helping build real utopia in Bulgaria were later transformed by the force of the cultural context of the West into authentic avant-garde subversiveness. Christo's projects in the West fulfill an anti-utopian function once they are realized. If, in the context of communism, Christo used to transform real objects into the reality of utopia, then in the West (maybe without actually intending to) he must be unmasking through his actions the existing reality as a utopian one. For his wrapped objects (boundaries, territories, etc.) reveal their new, transformed identities as just things — monumental shapes stripped of any symbolic value. And isn't precisely this displaced, pushed-aside symbolic value the reality of the world he is working in and with? Isn't Christo making visible the arbitrariness of the "real" in the West? Isn't the suggestion of his art that what is consumed in this world is not at all material?

II. BEYOND WARS AND WALLS it is possible to achieve an international consensus on the question of how good or bad a given artist or a work of art is, but it is not advisable to look for (because it is hardly possible to get to) a consensus on why we do or don't think of an object as a work of art. This is so because a consensus in the realm of art is possible only for as long as we stay in the context of art as it is traditionally defined. But the consensus is impossible if we think out of the specific contexts of the different cultures and realities of the recent past. Here the historical approach gets in the way of understanding. Which is so much the better — a postponement of understanding gives more chances to develop distinct identities.

Again Christo's case could serve as an example. His art and concepts are *authorless* in the sense that he is not creating an imaginary world of his own. But when we think of the two different contexts — East and West — in which he has been functioning, it becomes apparent that in them there are two very different types of absence of the traditional author's function.

A. The culture of the former East, the world of "real socialism," is a collective speech culture. Its logic is the logic of becoming, as if by itself. The function of the author is totally overtaken by the supreme authority of the Party and its apparatuses which double-up the social to the full. There it is as if the technology, which is constructing the reality of utopia, is working all by itself. The simulacrum of the ideology is sucking in all reality until its final annihilation. The vast majority of artistic acts are performed in the non-specialized spheres of the social. Actually each act of the supreme political power in the speech culture is an "artistic" one by intention.

The collective speech culture is necessarily interiorized in every creative act. Here *the author is not dead*. Here *the author simply cannot ever be born*. Here the demiurgical pretensions of the creator are only possible as a parody of the creativity of the social as a totality.

The speech culture of socialism knows nothing external to itself. In contrast to the prostheses or the technical simulacrum, the social simulacrum is a simulacrum squared. Simulacrum of the simulacrum — which is not limited by anything. It is not that the manifestations of a reflexive culture here are suppressed. It is that the very conditions of its appearance are eradicated ontologically, so to speak. Here, the rule is the *potlatch*, the symbolic exchange. This culture, being the culture of the utopia of production, produces only collectivism. And the effectiveness of the collective bodies is the effectiveness of their internal burning, which does not go on to produce a product. They are so intensive internally that they simply have no strength left to be productive on top of that. They are their own sole product. They live in a state of ecstatic sociality. And this sociality is becoming a text in itself, which interiorizes all features of authorship. The work of art is only possible as a text which has written in it the very impossibility of the individual author to be born.

Had Christo stayed in the East as a conceptualist, his ultimate act as an "author" would have had to be the *wrapping of a spaceship* and its subsequent *launching into outer space in a wrapped state*.

B. If we indeed call the above described culture of "real socialism" *a utopia of production*, then we can call the culture of "real capitalism" *a utopia of consumption*. Here the market guarantees the conditions of consumption. It does so through, for instance, the institutions of the authorship, the signature, the frame, the archive. But it does so without the help of reflection. The market is not anti-reflexive (as is *potlatch*) but is hyper-reflexive. And hyper-reflexiveness is identical to the annihilation of reflexiveness by its own force and action. Here the author is dying (or is already dead, as Roland Barthes has it) because of his or her overproductiveness, overintensiveness, overexhaustion in the act of "writing."

Here the author is dying because of the commodification and, in the end, the self-consumption/annihilation of his own "authorness." The state of *the death of the author* here is comparable with the state of the *not-ever-to-be-born author* there only in terms of the always already manifested *absence* of the individual author's function in both cases. But this is a synchronic, not a diachronic statement. Which could be verified only if we think in post-historical terms — if we can claim that the utopia of production is dead as much as the utopia of consumption is dead. If this is so, then it could explain why Christo has not yet performed in the West something which might make him here an author in the traditional sense.

He has not yet wrapped himself. He has entered the situation of the death of the author as an author not-ever-to-be-born. This is probably his good fortune. Because it is not necessary to die for something that is not even born yet. It is probably his genius of intuition which prevents him from wrapping himself — for this act of the birth of the Author Christo would be the "wrapping-up" and death of the Legend Christo, with all implications following from this in the market and the real Western world in general.

III. BEYOND WARS AND WALLS you experience the end of "progressive" history and the proliferation of the poetics of after-the-end existence-Art. But this is so only if you are an Eastern European by birth and place of residency. Otherwise you experience it at least once removed and it only counts as an art (not existential) experience. This creates new "walls" by itself — the Eastern European experience and culture are being commodified. The case of the Russian *Flash Art* is one example. But I realize that my speaking here now is also contributing to the process — because it too is an image, a representation. That's why I will limit myself to saying just a few words about the situation of advanced art in my country.

Advanced art there is the art which tries to break free from the situation of the not-ever-to-be-born author. This art deconstructs the immenseness of the collective sociality. Unlike the original deconstructors, though, who worked away on the excesses of reflection, the artists in Bulgaria (and perhaps not only there) are trying to dissimulate the ecstatic consciousness of the collective body in socialism. Their deconstruction is more of a primary reconstruction of the individual as a possibility for reflection.

This is work on the establishment of an embryonic reflexiveness, of a minimum of reflexive culture. Actually, reflection is a doubling-up of the world in the apparatus of reflection. But in order to have something to be doubled-up, it has to be created (or re-created) first.

Thus some artists in Bulgaria are performing work on the reconstruction of the distance from the world, of the meditative position and of the culture of the gaze (of seeing). Still others are reproducing the void of the author's function in Bulgarian speech culture as precisely this and not some other concrete form of void. Theirs is an art using the simulationist paradigm, which brings them closer to some of the trends in the West. Within this paradigm the differences in the East-West situation become less pronounced because here there are only two types of the ecstatic — the market and the symbolic ones — that are on a collision course. It is here that the similarities between the ideological simulacra in the East and the market commodity in the West are easiest to locate. And it is on the level of this type of art alone that there appear the problems of the actual compatibility and exchange within the world art market. Regrettably, the market might again prove to be the lowest common denominator in the East-West communication.

IV. Beyond wars and walls you can see that Jean Baudrillard was wrong when in, his book *America* (1986), he wrote:

A. "What is thought in Europe becomes reality in America. Everything that disappears in Europe reappears in San Francisco."(1991 Verso Edition, p. 84). Baudrillard is wrong here on two counts:

1. What is thought in Europe becomes reality not only in America but in Eastern Europe as well (see Utopian Socialism-Marxism-Leninism-Stalinism-Socialism-Perestroika and the whole problematics of achieving utopia). For in Eastern Europe utopia was achieved just like in America, although these were two very different kinds of utopias.

2. After the 1989 events in Eastern Europe one can also claim the opposite — what is thought of in America (the death of modernism and the "birth" of postmodernism were conceptualized here but were never played-out in real life) becomes (or has already become) reality in Eastern Europe. Communism as the ultimate paradigm of political modernism was killed off successfully a long time ago by the so-called socialist revolutions. They established at the same time postmodern situations which in their turn dissolved into a past-postmodern vacuum of reality — i.e., the end. The world as image has broken down.

B. "To see and feel America, you have to have had for at least one moment in some downtown jungle, in the Painted Desert or on some bend in a freeway the feeling that Europe had disappeared. You have to have wondered, at least for a brief moment, 'How can anyone be European?' " (ibid. p.104-105). Of course now Europe as it was has disappeared. But Baudrillard was wrong here, too, because after 1989 and the first "natural" death of a real utopia in Eastern Europe, the first such death recorded in human history, you might ask "How can anyone *not* be European?" If the death of one real utopia was possible, then maybe real utopias of other types could also die?

V. Beyond wars and walls you can also see that Jean Baudrillard was incredibly right when he wrote:

"Ours is a crisis of historical ideals facing up to the impossibility of their realization. Theirs (in America) is the crisis of an achieved utopia, confronted with the problem of its duration and permanence."

Excluding Eastern Europe from Baudrillard's "ours," I can say that my "ours" is the crisis of the total collapse of all reality — symbolic, as well as material. This puts us in a position to have experienced for real the negative resolution of both of the above-mentioned crises. And this gives us in Eastern Europe certain privileges since we have advanced knowledge on some of the alternatives facing the rest of the "civilized" world.

Christo, *Dada emballé*.

These alternatives could be summed up by using again a text of Jean Baudrillard's — "The Precession of Simulacra." If we agree with him that the world as we know it is after all only an image without origin, we can illustrate the state of this new world-image in Eastern Europe after the breakdown of the previous one in the following way:

First, to remind you, Baudrillard describes the successive phases of the image as:

1. it is the reflection of a basic reality
2. it masks and perverts a basic reality
3. it masks the absence of a basic reality
4. it bears no relation to any reality whatever: it is its own pure simulacrum

So, after the end of the utopia of communism as a social reality, we in Eastern Europe are completely in the fourth and last phase of the world-image — we are producing production on all levels of society and culture. Or to paraphrase the French author who did not even know how prophetic he was:

phase 1. fact, no power
phase 2. fact as power
phase 3. power as fact (i.e. real utopia)
phase 4. POWER, NO FACT

But otherwise, returning to the above-mentioned passage, Baudrillard made a terrific point which allows us to say: If Western Europe can understand Eastern (formerly socialist) Europe, then perhaps the whole of Europe will be better able to understand America (U.S.A.) or at least California. And vice versa.

The "other" of Europe is no longer America. It is Eastern Europe now that is the other of both America *and* Western Europe, if we must still use such a distinction. For Europe *was* a whole — politically one part giving legitimacy to the other. The problem of Europe now is that it cannot allow itself the luxury to divide again, this time strictly culturally, for the benefit of its own "progress" from now on.

Eastern Europe as a deviation from the Western norm is no more. Now it is Western Europe and America that deviate from the norm according to which the world-image is transforming itself.

Multicultural World as Cultural Paradigm

by Katalin Keserü
(Hungary)

It took me a long time to decide which of the four conference themes I could contribute to. The third theme, Post-Colonial and/or Post-Totalitarian Art, might seem to be the most appropriate for a critic from Hungary. However, an art critic or an artist living in a post-totalitarian society is just as dependent these days as he or she was before, only his or her dependence has become economic and tied to the West.

Can we, then, speak of a post-colonial situation and, in connection with it, of postmodernism? In my country, postmodern architecture dates back to roughly the same time as Charles Jencks's legendary date,[1] although, for reasons having to do with ideological and economic difficulties, it came into being instead of modern architecture. This being so, I could not contribute to the third theme, Post-Colonial and/or Post-Totalitarian Art.

The second theme, the Politicization of Art and Criticism, would not have been a good choice either. For over twenty years now, art criticism in Hungary has painstakingly kept out of both practical politics and ideological debate. This is understandable if we recall the dictatorial art policies of recent decades. The fourth theme, Censorship and Art, has lost its relevance for present-day Hungary. In any case, censorship always influenced public manifestations of art rather than art itself.

So I was left with the first theme, Art, Politics and Ethnicity in a Multicultural World, which is a typically American one. The situation in Europe is radically different. With the exception of gypsies, we must speak of European nations rather than European ethnic groups. In Europe there are some genuine nation states, but there are also pseudo-nation states created by political fiat, and there are national minorities. There are also regions whose characters are defined by distinct (new or old) artistic traditions. These regions and nations became equals in the sphere of art, thanks to the vernacular trends around the turn of the century.[2]

At the beginning of this century, non-European (tribal or peasant) art and works made without the specific aim of creating art (childrens' drawings, visions, etcetera) began to be described as artworks. This new valuation itself arose from the nonacademic character of artworks and the artistic culture of the non-industrialized, non-developed regions or nations in that age of anti-academicism (secessionism). Generally, this anti-academicism grew from a search for primary meanings, functions, features, and methods, dealing with the relationship between art and culture, as well as the vernacular of visual arts. In several cases this coincided with living local/ regional traditions among people engaged in traditional rural activities.

The common regional character of the Northern, Eastern and Central European countries derived from the semi-feudal situation — social, political, and historical. The art and culture of the peasantry became a vernacular, preserving ancient cultural forms. It was, at the same time, a basis for the new national culture. In this way, vernacularism was in places identical with national movements in art, especially in countries with limited political independence: it could emerge with the support of national cultural politics. This was a special trend of vernacularism, because the interest in regional cultures yielded common characteristics in works of art which were neither merely stylistic nor definable within the customary historical categories of art styles. Therefore, regional cultures created a new paradigm in art. Substantial changes ensued in the value system, creative method, and function of art, which differed from the so-called Grand Art. As a result of this general vernacular movement, different types of art — defined by Pierre Françastel and Lajos Németh as the ritual-magical, classical-autonomous and subjective-romantic — with diverse functions, born in diverse civilizations and social strata, became equal, as did the ethnic cultures which produced them.

Although there was an awareness in different countries of how similar the vernacularisms based on peasant traditions were, the style (kinship of forms, techniques, symbols) was not tagged as regional, whereas for the first time in history, true regionalism — based on national foundations — was considered to be the major style, instead of provincial variants of a major style. Each country regarded its region richest in cultural traditions as the source of its art (Karelia in Finland, Dalarna in Sweden, Kalotaszeg in Hungary), and its art as vernacular. In a broader sense this was reflected in the network of new artistic relations as well. Pilgrimages to the traditional centers of Europe gave way to a mutual interest among Scandinavian, Eastern and Central European countries. The point of reference had changed and so had the sphere of influence. One or two highlights had been replaced by equivalent patches of color on the map of Europe, and the hue of a region previously on the periphery now had the same value as that of a former center. This regionalism, which thus created a homogeneous style, meant an exodus from so-called modern civilization, as a variant of "secession." It meant an alternative.

In these countries too, the regional style existed side by side with art fed by the stylistic innovations of the art centers; there was a coexistence of various types of art (grand art, peasant art). Regionalism was thus not all-exclusive but one of several simultaneous style types. Hungary, for example, was multicultural — to use a present-day term. Present-day terms are, of course, the products of the present situation, which is political rather than cultural on this side of Europe. The region is different, too, created artificially by historical-political determination.

In what follows, I try to reconstruct this "regional style," taking Hungary as my starting point. The culture of the whole political region was basically determined by the ideology of the Soviet Union. The first Soviet fine arts exhibition in Budapest laid down the guidelines. It declared that art had to be Socialist Realism. In 1949 this demand meant the artificial and belated adjustment to a center, yet with the obvious aim of creating a regional style. However, the tools and models were predetermined: Soviet Socialist Realism and monumentalist Mexican painting of the 1930s, despite the fact that they had no connection whatsoever to any East-Central European artistic traditions. Besides, there were no real artistic connections among the countries pitted against each other in the name of socialist internationalism.

Instead of the pseudo-regional Socialist Realism, the avant-garde traditions oriented to the Western contemporary artistic centers emerged victorious in the 1960s in East-Central Europe. Regional connections between countries can be detected; they result from the unofficial initiatives of artists. Depending upon where the official cultural policy was the most tolerant at any one moment, artists migrated to Poland, Czechoslovakia or Yugoslavia.

Among the regional traits of the emerging East-Central European neo-avant-garde, one can list the general use of the term neo-avant-garde, the political overtone implied by the category, and the specific East-Central European interpretation of avant-garde (claiming that it was related to sociopolitical movements), as well as a tendency to generalize the political-historical character of iconography. This, of course, differs from the activist variant of Western art trends.

In my view, the most remarkable feature of this neo-avant-garde is its dual outlook: on the one hand, it joined the international currents, which implied the survival of culture in these countries (survival requires constant renewal); and, on the other, it referred to the local situation and traditions. This duality has a past in Hungary, reaching back to Romanticism.

The absurdity of socialism, which prohibits in reality what it proclaims in ideology, is evidenced in the absurd dadaist way of the neo-avant-garde. Regional meaning and historical background are the sources of forms and features, as in György Galántai's series of "sole" statues.[3] The story behind Galántai's sculptures is that they were made at the Dunaujváros Ironmill, a monster established during the period of aggressive industrialization of the socialist dictatorship. Yet, because of Galántai's avant-gardist method, which looks not only inward, but outward at international trends, his sculpture is international and regional at the same time.

Another example of this double outlook is based on a different tradition of Hungarian art, referring to nature and its universal meaning. Géza Samu discovered a peasant crafts tradition with his monumental instruments such as *Big-Mons-Fly*, finding a natural language which belongs neither to the visual meta-language nor to historic symbols of culture (such as the horned devil). He created a sophisticated enviromental art, pseudo-magic and pseudo-ritual, a non-conceptual kind of Land Art in which art mani-

György Gazàntai, *Man*, 1968.

György Jovànovics, *The Second Step*, 1977.

fests itself as part of nature. His present works are finely proportioned, stripped branches with tapering ends, covered with bark or feathers, and painted. In his *Mutations*, miscellanies of plants, birds, animals, and humans, and other environments, Samu presents the aesthetic as something inherent in nature, which is what cultural anthropologists (*e.g.*, T. Sebesk) do: they treat art, a form of consciousness, and human activity in general as part of nature, and uphold life itself as the underlying principle. And that is a universalist idea. These works of art show how regional cultures, ahistorical in character, can — with different nuances — become sources for contemporary universal trends in art.

The third type of art in the region is characterized by the universality of autonomous art, independent of center, periphery, or regional relations. This grand art was, at least in Hungary, constantly engaged in a battle with provincialism and regionalist currents. If it is incomplete, it is because of this struggle and because of its "home-made" character due to lack of sufficient patronage. What might specify it as regional is its incompleteness. Art history is expected to step beyond the limits of regionalism in evaluating this universal art and facilitating its unfolding. But in the 1980s, the neo-avant-garde continued to be ignorant of the past decades of Central European art. It was deliberately (in the East) and cautiously (in the West) ignored, while internal cultural policies continued to renounce it.

With the category of regionalism, the West lent a specious prop to our thinking which, like a tall fence around the emerging Eastern art market (around the alliance between the finally legalized neo-avant-garde and current art intent on breaking into the West), leads again to the non-recognition of autonomous art. This state of affairs is reinforced by the collapse of art publications and the prospective flood of Western books in the former socialist countries, which will banish local (both regionalist and universalist) art and art historical works to oblivion.

One of these "Ost-Modern" characteristics is the historicism in iconography, the historical viewpoint. It is reflected in the constant postponement of social changes, a corollary of which is that certain themes and genres retain their significance. This is also a tradition of the Hungarian avant-garde.

My reason for connecting concepts such as art, ethnicity and politics is the so-called recent Europeanization of the "socialist" countries. These nations and the West prefer Westernization without reckoning with local fundamentals. But the present definition by Western art historians of East-Central European art as "regional" appears to be highly artificial. By the same token, it would be instructive to see if the art of the West is regional, and, if it is, what makes it so? History? Geography? The market? And into what regions is "Western" art to be subdivided: American? West European? Or smaller regions? It should be explored whether a network of regional arts really exists, without which "region" is merely a polite term for "province." The West, meanwhile, continues to regard itself as universal.

It may well be that the restoration of identity to East-Central European art requires a familiarity with its regions. One possible way would be to declare the region "mutual," and to get to know one another here, with support from art history. Regionalism in this sense should not mean a type of art, but a cross-national organization and store of knowledge. This is the only way for multicultural countries to interpret regionalism.

The idea of a multicultural world is the cultural paradigm of our day. It signals the need to withstand the forces pushing civilization simultaneously toward assimilation and annihilation, and the need to make the intellectual switch-over to enable us to support cultures for their own sakes in their original places of birth. This is vital, because the existence of nations and individuals is tied to their cultures. Global culture, as Levi-Strauss put it, essentially has no mutations: hence no possibility of survival.

To so enrich the image of a multicultural world could be a more important political act than the deeds of politicians. Discovering and illuminating the special characteristics and artistic values of nations and local areas, among them the art of the Central-East-European region, is a mission for art critics.

NOTES:

[1] "In 1972, many slab blocks of housing were intentionally blown up at Pruitt-Igoe in St. Louis. By the mid-1970s, these explosions were becoming a quite frequent method of dealing with the failures of Modernist building methods: cheap prefabrication, lack of personal 'defensible' space, and the alternating housing estate." Jencks, Charles *What is Postmodernism?* NY: St. Martin's Press, 1987, p. 16.

[2] This is appreciated by contemporary art history, especially since it was outlined at the Dublin conference of the Association of Art Historians in 1990.

[3] The "sole" statues were begun in 1975, just after the freezing of the first political reform attempts. Some pieces (two tiers of steps, stabile, marking time) represent contradictory structures of the stubbornly immovable status quo. Those who thus interpret these playful anachronisms must be familiar with the very opposite meaning of stepping in Hungarian iconography: revolutionary marching was represented by one-time avant-gardists during the first Soviet republic in Hungary in 1919. (Victor Madarasi's romantic picture of Felicia'n Za'ch is a prototype.)

Poland: Searching for New Values

by Anda Rottenberg
(Poland)

The change of the paradigm of art, observed throughout the whole world around 1980, occurred in Poland in a particularly distinct manner, made even more credible and vivid by the circumstances of political life. When the "Zeitgeist" exhibition opened in Berlin, Poland was already in a state of martial law. What most explicitly characterized the nature of Polish art during this period was a shift of criteria from the aesthetic to the ethical. The choosing of a given moral stand became more important than an artistic statement. It became apparent that the line dividing Polish art ran not in accordance with the heretofore accepted qualitative categories but often crossed them outright. A different yardstick is applied, after all, for estimating an attitude than for critiquing a work of art. It also became obvious that although art expresses the whole outlook of the artist, in creative praxis there were only a few artists for whom questions concerning the limits of art dealt with the limits of freedom. Artistic life in Poland for quite some time ceased being identified with the life of art at all, or, speaking more strictly, with its natural transformations. The Polish art scene had always been extremely complicated, involved in ideological controversies inherited from the past, and burdened by the "patriotic syndrome" which dated back to the Romantic era; after World War II, it also became entangled in the postulative cultural policy pursued by the state.

The political context affected Polish art until the present. There was, for instance, a time — the years 1949-1955 — when abstract art was banned. Then, following a brief period when it was permitted — between 1956 and 1959 — its presence at exhibitions was restricted by the authorities to 15%. It became necessary, therefore, to wage a battle, and so each abstract painting became a political act. It is from that period that the legend of Tadeusz Kantor as the unyielding champion of the autonomy of art started to grow. This longing for autonomy often concealed a striving for a partner-like presence in world art and for co-creating its image; a feeling which, after all, remained in accordance with the postulates of the avant-garde from the very beginning of the century. Regardless of the type of art pursued, Polish artists shared a conviction about participation in Western culture, rooted in tradition. This was the source of anxieties as to whether the level of Polish painting was sufficiently "French." It was also the source of a frenzied "catching up with the lessons of history" after years of perfecting the obligatory Socialist Realist portraits of Stalin and Dzierzhinsky; hence, the fear of whether Poland had become the scene of "informal" or Pop Art, Happenings, or Minimal art. Were we not already too late?

And often we were. The animosity towards realism that was injected in the 1950s — towards that "mirror walking along a street" — together with a constant lack of consumer goods, did not create conditions favorable to the emergence of Pop Art. Pop Art, after all, was also a mirror, albeit of the carnival variety — a distorting mirror which reflected the face of prosperity. The battle for abstraction continued during subsequent decades, and ended with a questionable success: in the years of intense social tension (1968-1970-1976) paintings devoid of meaning became a convenient refuge from reality, an "artistic art" which proved to be very useful for the authorities. It became necessary for a new generation to appear, one which had not experienced Socialist Realism, in order for art to submerge itself in "life." This was, however, a conceptual submergence, produced by the rebellious wave of 1968.

This wave rose in Poland in March of that year — slightly too early, and once again not synchronized with the rest of Europe. When the political "Spring" was celebrated in Prague and Cohn-Bendit led the students into the streets of Paris, Adam Michnik was already sitting in prison together with tens of other "rebels" — who today are parliamentary deputies, senators and Solidarity leaders. Did we become partners in the European art world? Conceptualism — more a trend of thought than a current in art, developed so buoyantly in Poland primarily because it did not require a large financial outlay, and its matter was intellectual substance. It appeared during the temporary prosperity of the Gierek era — based on loans — which made it possible to calmly recede into the domain of self-examination, to research the language of art, to trace the fleeting nature of its symptoms and to construe elitist oases of art. But it also became possible to try public intervention, to seek contact with life and the people "in the street," as did Wojciech Krukowski and the Academy of Motion (established at that time), or to go even further and enter the political domain, as in the staging of the *Red Bus* (1975).

In that performance, in the headlights of cars standing on a snow-covered space between the Stalinist Palace of Culture and the main shopping center of Warsaw, surrounded by Christmas-rush lines on a bitterly cold December night, silent, panting figures hurriedly unfurled and cast away into the darkness the words of a poem written on white sheets: "We, who eat meat once a week. . . ." At that time, "meat" was a dangerous word, subject to official censorship.

Somewhere, strikes were brutally put down, political trials were conducted, the Committee for the Defense of the Workers (KOR) came into being, secret investigations were carried out, mysterious assaults took place, and the first underground publications were issued outside the official censorship system. Some people were engaged in art, others in politics, just as in every normal, or almost normal society. But when Solidarity appeared on the scene in August 1980, political life became so attractive that it totally outdistanced art, which still defended its autonomy and enclosed itself in self-examination. Symptomatic of the attitude of the artists in the early 1970s was the arrogant *Self Portrait* by Tomasz Osinski (1973), which imitated the outsize portraits of equally arrogant officials displayed on the walls of public buildings. In 1981, Osinski showed another painting, a realistically executed portrait of Edward Gierek — a person blown away by the winds of history — depicted in sweet candy hues on a 1:1 scale. The circle had closed. This conceptual composition predicted the coming changes, which were accelerated by the end of 1981 with the presence of tanks on Polish streets.

The country was divided by a sharp demarcation line which initially signified a struggle for the retention of values won by Solidarity in 1980, and in due time marked a trench-war waged for the sake of principles. This general schizophrenic state also affected artistic life. On the one side, there was still the official "court" art, supported by the mass media (which remained a state monopoly). On the other side was the unofficial, rebellious art, functioning on the borderlines of public life — in churches, private homes, and those few galleries which refused to succumb to political pressure. Inasmuch as the first group was excessively displayed, the second found itself in a latent state which is so easily mistaken for a total absence of life.

This "latent" life of art during the period of martial law assumed different forms: displays were held in private homes; "artistic pilgrimages" consisted of visits to a network of homes and studios in various towns; exhibitions which could be carried in a single suitcase were shown throughout the country. The authorities were boycotted and the artists turned toward the Church which, in this aberrational configuration of social forces, became a "refuge for the majority." What was at stake were not only patronage and the possibility of free expression or the organization of exhibitions in architecturally interesting spaces. After the breakdown of secular ideology, Christian universal truths became factors of a strong social bond. Thus, under the patronage of the church a meaningful number of exhibitions and meetings were held, with the participation of artists, writers, journalists, critics, musicians and actors, some of whom had never before presented their Catholic outlook.

In the course of time, however, attempts were made to seek areas for art which would be independent from the Catholic patron too. Interesting new "generation" galleries were established in Poland. Several existing state galleries — Foksal, Dziekanka and Labirynt — managed to retain their own programs. Many others were unable to defy the pressure and succumbed. As always, and everywhere, this mainly depended upon people's personalities. The sharp criteria of division gradually blurred and there arose the need for summaries. The most important from this point of view was a group exhibition entitled "The Expression of the '80s," held in 1986 in the Sopot City Art Gallery.

The very title of the display indicates the trend pursued by the youngest generation. During the first half of the '80s, Poland witnessed a virtual explosion of expressive art and was the scene of a triumphant return of painting; the pressure of the latest experiences finally had shattered the previously acknowledged artistic values. Significant shifts occurred in the comprehension of the function of art, the mission of the artist, and the circle of his or her interests. The common trait of this entire (greatly differentiated) generation of young artists was their unwillingness to identify themselves with any sort of group, artistic or political, functioning in Poland after 1981. The spontaneously created alternative pattern — collaboration or the Church — which even exerted an impact on the very nature of art, became difficult for the majority of young artists to accept. After numerous attempts to fit into this schizophrenic situation, it was obvious that they could not and should not identify themselves with a movement in which authentic experiences and dilemmas too often took an insufferably melodramatic form and whose symbols were so clearly unambiguous that it became a temptation to oppose them. The capacious formula of the trans-avant-garde proved to be salutary; it made it possible to shed the uncomfortably tight costume of the hero and to ridicule the servile one of the conformist. Only the clown costume seemed to suit the situation. This otherness, which was manifested in clothes, involvement in punk-rock music, and an unusual lifestyle, became an important element of clowning which concealed to a greater extent our own Gombrowicz than did superficial borrowings from the Western, mainly German, stylistics of certain compositions. These borrowings, by the way, were rejected by the most interesting representatives of the generation, who were able to endow their statements with an original and unique form.

During recent years, the political situation in Poland and in almost all of Eastern Europe changed so rapidly and radically that the facts presented above are already part of history. Polish art, as the outcome of social distraction and permanent poverty, has managed to survive successfully. What the underground movement consisted of is now the mainstream of a new official "court" art, shown in most of the main state galleries. What had been shown in churches finds it place in the National Museum. The only difference is that portraits of Lech Walesa have replaced those of former communist party leaders.

And it suddenly occurs to us that there still exists the same margin — as always filled by artists who attempt to identify the boundaries of art with those of freedom — regardless of the political system.

Multicultural Identity and the Problem of Self-Knowledge: Environment, Gender, Race, in That Order, or Strange Fruit Hanging from the Popular Tree

by Joe Lewis
(United States)

A number of years ago, a close friend came to me and said, "Joe, you are always talking about parody and cultural inclusion, but you won't talk to me about my paintings because they are abstract and not politically motivated."

If the world were a town of 1,000 people. . . . There would be

564 Asians
210 Europeans
86 Africans
80 South Americans, and
60 North Americans

Of these people:

500 would be hungry
700 would be illiterate

In contemporary society, on the *Philo[sophical]-lipservice* plane, cultural diversity has become a desirable if not inevitable lofty and sublime fashion. Yet, in spite of all the altruistic chest beating and accompanying songs of radical change, decades of European philosophical minority rule (the modernist canon) has taken its toll on both the meaning of multicultural ideology and the people advocating its inclusion in the mainstream.

"I have come to believe that if history were recorded by the vanquished rather than the victors, it would illuminate the real rather than the theoretical means to power: for it is the defeated who know best which of the opposing tactics were irresistible."[1]

The Ultimate Conspiracy Story

Plato's cave was actually a time machine. Aristotle, Socrates and Plato went back in time to the library at Alexandria, translated the most important texts into Greek, and then torched the repository. They returned to their own time, presenting the assembled texts as original. Unfortunately, Socrates, who believed that clear knowledge of the truth was essential for a sound life, had a change of heart, and told his confederates he was going public with the deception and plagiarism. This would not do! His colleagues had him arrested for not going with the flow, and, corrupting the morals of society. Juried and found guilty, Socrates carried out his sentence by taking his own life. And "they," supporters and detractors both, watched the truth disappear into stone like hemlock.

Out of the law of averages, I would imagine, there must be a few stone-faced modernists who believe there is something to be garnered from contemporary other-than-western-cultures. I use the phrase "contemporary" because anything of merit from the aforementioned cultures of historical importance has already been deconstructively appropriated and recontextualized.

"The fact of a plethora of art forms and styles representing societies, states, and peoples of the world with few or no barriers of space and time has struck many thinkers as a new phenomenon, sometimes referred to as post-modernism." Ironically, "viewed as the end of history, indicative either of the breakdown of standards of quality or as a promise of pluralism and equality, postmodernism is treated as the outcome of economic and political forces that have to come to dominate cultural developments more generally. Indeed, the breadth and quality of art forms have never been matched."[2]

But the appearance of these strange fruits is not what makes many of us uneasy as we look into the future. The demise of a ruling cultural philosophy has everyone worried. Especially now, when political and cultural upheavals hang from the globe like cheap imitation knock-off watches sold on Fifth Avenue. We are not blind. We are watching it happen. We are uneasy because everyone knows what can happen.

To many, the advent of cultural diversity is more about the notion of decline and disintegration than of sublime genesis and development. Frankly, many seem more prepared for the worst case scenario than any other possibility, especially multicultural respect or mutual understanding. Why? Because our cultural heritage was built with an exclusionary strategy. There is no precedent for what is about to come into our lives.

It is not meritorious cultural experience that has created the gnome that stalks each of us during our slumber-filled and/or waking hours but the omnipresent concepts of absolute power and control which are truly the stakes we are playing for — and playing for keeps! Who is going to control all of this stuff (establishing societal values, extended community trust, and the creation and development of new aesthetic criteria) once the inevitable happens?[3] Who is going to *"have the power"* over those intellectually astute primates — I meant to say — former primitive peoples? I would like to note, both the Chinese and Japanese cultures were included in the group of primitive societies until the early 20th century, when they were removed from the likes of Africans, Micronesians, and aboriginal people.

My recurring nightmare is finding out that the new ministers of culture during the next phase of global multicultural development will resemble the entertainer Vanilla Ice.

NOTES:

[1] Deren, Maya, "Divine Horsemen," Documentext, p. 6, 1991.

[2] Zolberg, Vera, *Constructing a Sociology of the Arts*, London: Cambridge University Press, p. ix, 1990.

[3] By the year 2000, more than 1/3 of the population of the United States will consist of people of color.

Afrocaribbean Presence in Modern Cuban Painting

by Adelaida de Juan
(Cuba)

The countries that José Marti named "Our America" (such is the title of his famous essay published in *La Revista Ilustrada de Nueva York* exactly one century ago) articulate, regardless of their cultural unity, three zones: Amerindia, Afroamerica and Euroamerica. Brazilian anthropologist Darcy Riberro has proposed them as examples of what he has called, respectively, testimonial, new, and transplanted peoples. I will deal with two artists representative of that new people, Afroamerican, Afrocaribbean, that is Cuba. Our *mestizo* being (essentially forthcoming from the fusion of Iberic and African ethnicities and cultures) is not, in the words of its Cuban scholar, Fernando Ortiz, "unsubstantial hybridism, nor syncretism, nor decoloration, but simply a new substance, a new color, a refined product of transculturation." This last term, created by Ortiz as a substitute for "acculturation," was agreed upon by Bronislaw Malinowski. Present throughout the Caribbean, transculturation, especially notable in music and dance, will become a profound basis for the determination of features differentiated from those of the oppressors throughout the centuries.

A paradigmatic case of the conscious incorporation into a plastic expression of universal protection of the *mestizo* essence of our people will be found in the vast works of Wilfredo Lam. Born in Cuba in 1902, and after many years in Europe, his definitive expression will be found back in Cuba; the starting point is in such pivotal works as *The Chair* and *The Jungle*. Lam is by then familiar with African art in European museums; he also knows of the assimilation of its expressive values by avant-garde artists. But above all, an important event has taken place: his return to his native land. Let us recall that he did some notable drawings for the Cuban edition (1943) of Aimé Césaire's *Cahier d'un Retour au Pays Natal*. Lam's re-encounter with his original background will certainly be decisive for the outcome of his characteristic work. In fact, Lam's painting is not, at any time, descriptive of representative elements of liturgies, idols or ceremonies. With few lines and brushstrokes he places some details that function as evocative starting points; his images suggest rather than define. Each object has become independent of its totalizing context and is sufficient in itself so as to just indicate the indispensable for the imagination of the spectator in order to provoke participation.

The symbology in Lam's work refers to one of the "African surnames" studied by Ortiz. Carnal themes include femininity as a constant feature, especially in the maternal breasts. On more than one occasion, Lam has created an extraordinary feminine figure whose face is a mask or a stylized indented instrument. The masculine presence is fundamentally indicated by strong, sharp horns. In both cases, the human being does not appear with the totality of its realist, traditional contours. But the symbolic element *par excellence* in Lam's work will be found in his use of the foliage element, which is of course a constant presence in our lands. In his painting it acquires a supreme degree as it overlaps his most characteristic features: among sexual symbols, masks and scissors. The vegetation interweaves: it advances and recedes, it is a background and comes to the fore — vegetable and animal, creation and destruction, myth and reality.

This allegorical character of the imagery uses signs that go back to a faraway African source re-elaborated in our lands and will become manifest in various ways. Transmutations of sacromagic nature will become visible: they are evidence that the symbols in Lam's painting allude to pre-iconic times. They are also evidence of his capacity to recreate a classical imagery that functions in a reality differentiated from its original source. This is an example of the metalepsis studied by Ortiz as a transvaloration in a horizontal direction: we could recall *Crucifixion* (*Gaceta del Caribe*, 1944) where Catholic symbols are organically transmuted into symbols that originate in the transcultured Cuban reality. Once again, it is the *mestizo* character that comes to the fore with the enrichment of new and imaginative interpretations.

Three decades after Lam's definitive work, a newly promoted group of artists, with quite different backgrounds and formation, begins to exhibit and thus joins the uninterrupted development of modern Cuban art. Quite soon one artist will be distinctive; an artist who, like Lam in the '40s, will search for — will find, as Picasso aptly put it — his expressive creation in the African roots of our nationality. Manuel Mendive (1944) will also have an initial academic training (in his case, only in Havana); soon after he will step out in order to develop his own way of painting that radically differs from Lam's. He uses, in order to transmute the African contributions, a voluntary primitivism that is far from being a lack of technique; it is his

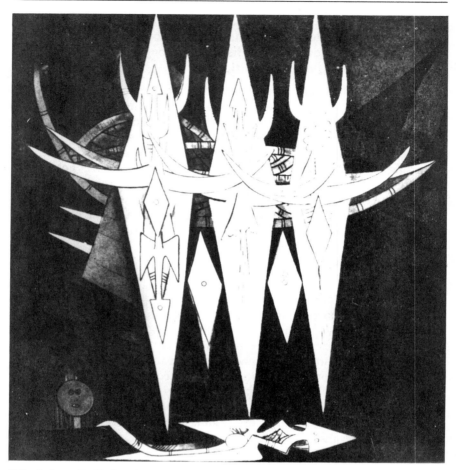

Wifredo Lam, *Untitled*, 1956.

choice of themes and his own symbolic world. Mendive continues a tradition deeply rooted in our country, that of his immediate familiar way of life. Far from abjuring the background of his home where the continuity of ancient Yoruba cults is an everyday reality, Mendive enriches it with the artistic techniques he has assimilated. These are precisely the tools he uses in order to create new plastic worlds where the transcultured African roots find new expressive manners.

Water is for Mendive what vegetation was for Lam. It is present not only in paintings that have to do specifically with Yoruba deities connected to the ocean and the rivers, but also in many other themes. It refers, by extension, to the water that defines the island; it is also the water that, from time immemorial, has signified the constant and fluid being. From 1968, Mendive's painting will open up to a more everyday reality that joins the mythological allusions that had been up to then his main theme. It is, as the Cuban poet Nancy Morejón has pointed out, an imbrication of "the quotidian with the mythological." Daily life is felt very intensely by the painter. We then see the constant presence of complementary and contra-dictory elements. Time and again, Mendive reminds us, in feast, party, and sex scenes, of the presence of death. It can take the form of the spirit covered by a long white cloth that sits in a rocking chair in the midst of the dance, or it may rise from the waters of the sea wall where couples embrace. Allusions to death appear constantly in the double faced figure that is Elegguá, one of the more constant deities of our *santería*. Elegguá opens and closes the roads, controls laughter and tears, life and death. This is one of Mendive's constant reminders; this is one of his ways of overlap-ping a personal mythological symbology with his own personal life.

These realities are obviously defined by his country's historical moment. Mendive introduces, in a natural way, his feelings as part of his people. History will also be seen in a double fashion. The artist will look back-wards in order to relive those moments when our African ancestors be-came part of the island's life, in painful slavery scenes and in scenes of their struggle. In this last aspect of liberation's struggles, the painter's eye joins past and future. A valid testimony is the series of works centered on *Che, Martí with Ová* (goddess of the cemetery).

An Historical Overview of Syrian Painting Since Independence (1946)

by Hassan Kamal
(Syria)

Twice in the past Syria has fallen under foreign domination: that of the Ottoman Empire from the 16th to the 20th centuries, and a French mandate in the 20th century that lasted only 25 years. During these periods of foreign domination, circumstances were not conducive to the development of plastic arts. Upheavals and instability in the land prevented such development. But despite these obstacles, Syrian artists met in groups to discuss their problems and help one another as much as possible in order to enrich their knowledge and experience. Works of the period prior to Independence, found in some homes in Damascus, were a major discovery for us.

After Independence, however, the situation changed and the competent authorities reorganized activities in many fields, including the arts. Those who were in charge of education succeeded in supplying teachers with thoroughly thought-out programs, designed to give younger generations a feeling for the arts. Thus the arts became one of the major subjects taught in teachers' colleges, so that they, in turn, would make instruction in the arts a national mandate.

Gifted students were given scholarships and sent to Egypt and to Italy where they were able to advance their knowledge of art. Upon their return, they were given important functions in art education so they could communicate the fruits of their experience to a new generation, and thereby contribute to improving the status of the plastic arts in Syria.

In 1960, the Ministry of Higher Education established several schools at the University of Damascus, including a school of Fine Arts. Additionally, the Ministry of Culture established a number of centers for applied arts in Damascus and in other large cities, as well as in specialized secondary schools.

In 1956, as soon as I returned from Paris, where I had been studying at the Sorbonne at the Institut d'Art et d'Archéologie and L'Ecole du Louvre, the

D. Algarm, *Portrait*, 1879, Collection Musée National, Damascus.

Ministry of Education made me curator at the Museum of Modern Art in Damascus, established that very year. The question remained of where to find works to nurture the new institution. I followed two roads: on the one hand, I bought some works directly from artists; on the other, I organized official exhibitions to which artists were invited. From the beginning, I had decided to organize major exhibitions twice a year: in the spring and fall. These shows enabled us to select the best works, while encouraging the best artists to arrange for solo shows of their own.

That was one part of my work. However, in the meantime, Syria signed many cultural agreements with friendly countries that were more advanced in the arts. Clauses in these agreements provided that artists could travel to these countries to study or to establish contacts with artists there. The Syrian artists could familiarize themselves with new art forms and modern trends. Thus their eyes were opened to a world which they had not known even existed. The new climate enriched their experience and was soon reflected in the work of each of them as well as in the development of art in general.

Whatever obstacles there may have been, modern art is now thriving in Syria.

Today, most museums in Syria have important collections of modern art that offer an overview of the works of such pioneers as Mahmoud Hammad, Adham Ismail, Nassir Chaura, Elias Zayyat, Fateh Moudarres, Nazir Nabaa, Turky Mahmoud Bey, Ghassan Sibai, and many others. The works of several of these artists are now in museums and private collections throughout Europe.

Though modern art as we know it appeared in Europe toward the end of the last century, its roots go deep into the culture of the East — the cradle of all major civilizations. In Syria, at the archaeological site of Al Moureibet, the oldest mural in the Near East — a black and red work on a white background going back 11,000 years — was discovered together with stone and clay figurines which seem at first sight to have been created by Henry Moore. There are numerous other examples at such well known archeological sites as Mari, Ebla, and Ugarit. The Euphrates Valley played a major role in the history of modern art, supplying it with a fertile ground for developments to come.

Translated from the French by Monique Fong

The Hyphenated Experience:
African-American Art Enters the Mainstream

by Linda F. McGreevy
(United States)

As we enter the last decade of the century and begin a new millennium, the American experience is undergoing reappraisal. Our constitutional belief in the inevitability of economic and social equality is falling prey to the realities of capitalist competition. And, in the wake of this increasing inequity, we are becoming both cynical and realistic about the homogeneity of our cultural identity. By accepting the multiculturalism that animates American life, we must reject as outmoded the concept of the "melting pot." America's system is no longer seen exclusively as a filtering and equalizing process resulting in a generic "American" type. In an economy and culture of choice, the spirit of postmodernist revisionism has resulted in acknowledgment and celebration of our disparate heritages. We have become distinctive hyphenated Americans, grouped by genetics — as Italian-American, Hispanic-American, African-American — or by predilection — Gay-American, Pro-Choice American, Politically-Correct American — proud of our differences and ready to promote them.

But the attempts of each group often fail to penetrate "mainstream" American awareness. Resistance born of fear of change and difference takes the guise of repressive rightist polemics, and follows age-old patterns of prejudice, feeding on the ignorance born of a failed educational system and widespread intellectual passivity. The accelerating re-ghettoization of ethnic groups condemned to marginality, both cultural and economic, has led to further misunderstanding of the contributions made to the American psyche by such venerable hyphenated groups as the African-American population. One of our earliest immigrant — uniquely *forced* immigrant — groups and paradoxically both the least and most assimilated, the African-American cultural contribution has been primarily confined to the fields of entertainment and sports. The visual artists have fared less well, finding that their work remains largely unappreciated in their own country.

It is difficult for African-American artists to express their complex identity, given the historical repression of their origins and the segregation of their communal experience. Threatened by the impoverishment of their society and stripped of their history by pre-revisionist historians, African-American artists have nonetheless bridged the void, translating the ethnic experience into art. With the acceptance of multiculturalism a small window of opportunity has opened within the art world for these messages. Postmodernist receptiveness has multiplied opportunities in both stylistic and situational realms.

There are a number of African-American artists pursuing a variety of stylistic choices ranging from history painting to conceptual installation, who are aided in their search for mainstream recognition by the presence of Black History month, a favorable — if temporally ghettoized — situation that dictates public accessibility each February. In these and other such institutionalized "windows," artists have begun the translation of ethnic experience for mixed audiences sorely in need of the lucid exposure given by such avatars of the movement as Adrian Piper, David Hammons, Faith Ringgold, Robert Colescott, Houston Conwill, and Howardena Pindell. Their work succeeds because they utilize formally overlapping pictorial strategies ranging from lyrical abstraction to mergers of craft and folk technique tinged with personal and often politicized irony.

The gritty urban environment forms both the source and locus of David Hammons's streetwise art, a combination of scrappy Arte Povera materialism and site-related or site-specific installations. From his Harlem neighborhood he collects refuse, embellishing trees in empty lots with discarded liquor bottles, or arranging the bottles in elegantly loopy configurations adaptable to museum and gallery. The ironies inherent in Hammons's work, which toured the country in a retrospective titled "Rousing the Rubble," are explicit in pieces redolent of despair and self-destruction. In the *Higher Goals* installation in Brooklyn, one of several such fragile and ironic references to basketball and its singular seduction, the message is implicit. These totemic objects point to an avenue to the mainstream, but one still closed to the majority of its targeted minority, who must sight their goals elsewhere. His irony, however, is most overt in *How Ya Like Me Now?*, Hammons's white-face portrait commenting on Jesse Jackson's controversial political aspirations in 1988, which was intended for a public site in the nation's capitol.

Faith Ringgold's work is known for its explicit political content. Although she has abandoned the flag paintings that marked her entry into the art world in the late '60s, she continues to explore political issues. Her installation for the American Bicentennial in 1976, *The Wake and Resurrection of the Bicentennial Negro*, had a perversely celebratory air. In this piece and in her more recent series of painted quilts, she draws on the long-denigrated domestic arts, weaving the rich oral traditions of her Harlem neighborhood into an elevated form more acceptable to the hierarchy-bound art world. These fictional tapestries meld reality and fantasy, the African-American oral tradition and contemporary expressionism, with 19th-century craftwork into the soft, protective surfaces of coverlet-paintings such as *Street Story Quilt*. The personal tales written across such works are so familiar that the translation Ringgold seeks comes easily, even in such critical pieces as the two-part *No More War Quilts*, which embed the painful reminiscences of veterans within camouflage patterns.

Activist artist/philosopher Adrian Piper has a long history of confrontational work, which cannily utilizes language and photography to subliminally investigate the complex realities of her explosive topics. Racism, sexism, and classism lurk in the rooms Piper installs with scaled-up drawings, cut-out photoboards, and random piped-in sounds. Her piece for the Directions Series at the Hirshhorn, *What It's Like, What It Is*, pointedly attacks the now-I-see-you, now-I-don't syndrome hidden within our conflicted ideology of opportunity. Her strategies are tied to the philosophical interplay of illogical language, to word and image disparities.

Piper's installation *Safe*, which occupies an intimate space in the exhibition of the current Awards in the Visual Arts competition, is a series of reassuringly middle-class, upwardly-mobile familial groups printed with simple declarations that further the feeling of security and inclusion. But the contemporary figures in *Safe* seem assimilated, shorn of the mark of difference, their heritage identifiable only by skin pigmentation. Their social marginality is made the more incomprehensible by their apparent cultural centrism.

More traditionally narrative conflations are presented in Robert Colescott's works. The heretofore hidden history of the African-American is the *raison d'être* for Colescott's ambitious cycle of history paintings collectively entitled *Knowledge of the Past is Key to the Future*. These congested narratives, simultaneously educational and critical, include the pertinent *Some Afterthoughts on Discovery*, which links slavery to conquest, and *General Gordon Romancing the Nile*, which implicates British colonialism.

In didactic scenes like *Pygmalion* from 1987 and the 1990 *Identity Crisis*, Colescott explores complications brought about by the collision of aes-

Adrian Piper, *What It's Like, What It Is #2*, mixed media installation for The Hirshhorn Museum and Sculpture Garden, 1991.

thetic standards and genetics, tangling his images to reflect the complexities of the subject. While Piper utilizes ubiquitous photographic imagery whose banality masks her criticality, Colescott subverts by compactly massing banal objects of desire and coating them in a seductive candy coating of traditional oil paint.

The stereotypical image of the African-American was once thought to be the sole domain of Colescott's work, but several artists have dealt with the theme. Hammons's series of body prints and assemblages, "Spade," also toys with the negative associations hovering over a simple term. Piper pierced the heart of the problem in her poster, *I Embody*, locating the fear of the powerful "other" that lies beneath racism and sexism.

Houston Conwill's installations and performances have focused on the use of his African-American heritage, but his cultural history has been made participatory in performance-oriented ritual re-creations, meant to aid healing and unification. His great wheels, titled *Cakewalks* after slave dances of the same name, are aligned to cardinal points of geographic significance for African-American culture. These historicist circles are accompanied by texts, pyramidal reliquaries, and other celebratory objects that bring traditional African formal strategies into an American context in a ceremonious and uplifting manner. Inspired by a sense of commitment to history, culture, and community, Conwill's continuities assure us of a positive identity.

This search for a dignified, if hyphenated, identity rooted in ethnicity, has led to works which explore the nature of the self. Ringgold's first quilt, *Echoes of Harlem*, produced with her mother, Willi Posey, in 1980, resembles Hammons's series of body prints and hair sculptures. In both cases the results are dependent upon the materials and interactions that comprise personal identity. When that identity is not only threatened by marginality, but is wiped clean by accident — as occurred with Howardena Pindell after a near-fatal car wreck — reconstruction can commence only with the help of family and community. In her allusive, amoeboid shaped series, "Autobiography," Pindell has literally reconstructed her history through a fragmentary collage technique. Postcards she had sent to others on her travels were cut and interwoven on the scarred surfaces of her unevenly stretched canvases. The postcards were embedded in glittering debris as memory triggers. Once Pindell's own body is traced on that surface, the imprint of the self is assured, and art can truly be used for healing. As in Hammons's 1974 body print, *Pray for America*, personal identity and ethnicity are vital parts of the variegated system that comprises the American experience.

Time in Art

by Márcio Doctors
(Brazil)

My original idea, which I called "Radicalness of That Which is Real," was to deal specifically with the great Brazilian artist Lygia Pape, whose work is fundamental to the understanding of contemporary Brazilian art.

I decided to change the theme for two reasons. The first is that, just like artists, we critics should seek an absolutely private vision of reality. A singular interpretation is possible only if we remain faithful to our own concerns. Without sincere investment in his or her beliefs, a critic cannot further his or her work. I have not stopped believing in the importance of Pape's work. Quite the contrary, it was precisely a central aspect of her production which influenced my change of mind, i.e. her transversality.

Lygia Pape is an artist whose fundamental commitment is to swimming against the tide. She seeks a strategic position which will reveal the alternate: the other. This is not a negation within the classic Hegelian dialectic. Rather, she accomplishes a dialectic of affirmations. Confronted by a thesis, she presents another, without necessarily aiming at a synthesis. During her journey into the visual arts, she plays a game of "positivations," which allows her a vision that is always alternate. She splits reality. She undoes the search for a unique meaning. She drains the idea of essence. She reveals the contradiction, the paradox and the multiplicity of that which is real. In other words, she cuts reality obliquely and makes us see through the cracks. She does not seek the answer but rather the question. She is radically committed to doubt and refuses to be imprisoned in a recognizable territory by art history and criticism. Instead, she misleads, confuses, deterritorializes. I call this strategy transversality.

This same commitment to doubt and to deterritorialization led me to preserve the meaning I discovered in the work of Lygia Pape. I believe that the relationship between art and politics, the topic central to our meeting, is at the heart of the search carried out by this Brazilian artist. I will apply her strategy to a wider discussion of the force of art, as I perceive it.

As a child, I learned from my paternal grandfather that the Jewish people were divided into three groups: Cohen, Levi and Israel. The Cohanim, who did not constitute a tribe, were responsible for the liturgy and retained religious power. The rest of the people were divided into 12 tribes, 11 of which had defined and demarcated territories and were obliged to reserve a portion of their income to sustain the twelfth tribe, the Levites who had no territory. Freud analyses this question well in "Moses and Monotheism" and emphasizes the strangeness of the formation of a group that has neither territory nor direct political-religious power, but which nevertheless exercises a determinant importance in the formation of the Jewish people. It is they who remind the people, in time of crisis, of the meaning of Judaism that is to be preserved. The Levites are the guardians of the word of God, that is, of public consciousness reiterating the fundamentals of the Jewish universe. Therefore, they have an active political role, albeit not a permanent one, as it is not connected to immediate circumstances, but rather to ethical values. The fact that they are deterritorialized endows them with the necessary detachment for a clearer view of the situation.

The connection I would like to establish between transversality and deterritorialization lies within the concepts which I will apply to my discussion of art. Jorge Luis Borges defined Argentinians as Europeans in exile. As a Jew and as a Brazilian I borrow his subtle perception. My move in the game of the central nations is the presentation of a peripherical view springing from the deterritoriality and transversality of my condition. Our societies' use of time is central to the question.

The difference between the use of time by economic and political systems on the one hand, and by art on the other, outlines their relationship. Art, like the Levites, is a deterritorialized force, crossing political and economic systems, maintaining its autonomy and capacity to enable us to see and perceive alternate relations between human beings. Art and artists are able to do this, because they avoid the structure of time imposed by economic systems on the majority of individuals.

These are disturbing and delicate political and ideological times. The tearing down of the Berlin Wall has erased the boundaries between East and West, between capitalism and communism. The capitalistic system, which claims to be the guardian of democracy, feels victorious and intensifies its values. Capitalism feels its adversary, in spite of egalitarian rhetoric, has been incapable of providing for the well-being of its people. Whereas democracy affirms the right to be different as the basis of the political expression of liberty, the dictatorship of the proletariat stresses the right of the majority to be equal as the political translation of freedom. Politics offers a strange and complex mathematics, seeking to balance difference and equality.

Now that the East-West border has been erased, another arises between the North and South hemispheres. In the South, Brazil has developed a society tied to the values of Western capitalism. However, like Eastern Europe, it is unsuccessful, as most of its population lives in poverty. Perhaps this has come about due to a perverse mixture of the ideology of free initiative and totalitarian power structures. In fact, Brazil has had democratic experiences, but these did not contribute to actual improvements for its people. The problem is more profound and wide-ranging and involves the world's distribution of political, economic, and cultural power. I believe the fall of the Berlin Wall will enhance the gap between South and North, rich and poor.

However, I do not wish to dwell on an eminently political analysis, since this is neither the appropriate place, nor I the appropriate analyst. My political comments are aimed at showing that the question of liberty (a constant theme in art since the Renaissance) is not limited to direct power structures. Neocapitalism, as a step towards genuine liberty and creation, is a mere illusion. Both the communist East and the capitalist West have failed to attain them, as they emphasize the concept of efficiency. They have this objective in common, though in different ways: both administer the life time of their citizens guided by the dogma of production.

Contemporary man is a slave of time, a slave to the structures of state and production. We are dominated by time and let ourselves be captured by its logic. Time hovers unpunished over our heads, as if it did not belong to us. Modern societies have made time their God. Men and women relate their lives to the time and the logic of production, which are imposed upon them as a fact of nature. This perverse allocation of time has an alluring side, since it anesthetizes death, filling its emptiness. In the most advanced technological societies, those that create free time for their members, this question is both more accentuated and more concealed at one and the same time. Here art becomes a leisure-time industry, rather than a thought structure. The outcome is melancholy. Man is detached from the great joy: the experience of the eternity of time, its vigorous and monumental presence. Only art is capable of creating this time, made of presences and permanences.

Time is twofold. When bound to the myth of absolute liberty, therefore

Lygia Pape, *Divisor*, environmental work, 1968.

unattainable, time captures individuals in an order where logic is speed. But, as Paul Virillio tells us, absolute acceleration leads to disintegration. Imposing increasing speed on time wipes out the contours of form. It undoes matter, undoing consciousness of death. When, however, time is bound to a circumstantial and relative concept of liberty, it becomes attainable. This is the time created by art, enhancing the consciousness of life in the living: its limit, death. It produces "presentifications"; material extensions of the sensitive body. Time ceases to escape and is retained by the process of consciousness that the making of art awakens.

Art reveals a time structure which should be our guide as we come to discover the relationship of art and politics. Furthermore, let us consider art as a force capable of engendering from its creative process forms of joy and even other forms of organizing life. Our time of speed has separated art and life and besieged liberty. To the true artistic action, this division is false. It is exercised by those who wish to territorialize art and to imprison it. Art is an eminently transversal and deterritorialized exercise. We critics should be aware of this, and constantly restate it.

Art is the only structure of thought-action that, on the basic of an absolutely singular experience, attains universality. Whereas science observes the multiplicity of phenomena to infer general laws, or philosophy builds thought systems seeking to underpin the multiplicity, art is set and founded by the living experience of the multiple and the different. These are the very same forces that move the current of time. Found in an absolutely singular structure, art generates sensitive aggregates which affect other individuals, creating a circle of sustained meaning. This leap from the particular to the universal is sustained by the creation of absolute differences, which is fundamental to art. This capacity is art's ability to shake political structures.

Like a river, time in art is ever present, ever changing. Nothing could be more penetrating nor further reaching, politically.

Translated by Judith Miller

Art and the Language Question: Words Pressed Against the Pane

(Northern Ireland)

Irish art has been both praised and criticized for having a literary bias. It is true that there is an easy relationship between poet and painter in Ireland. The name *Rosc*, chosen for our international exhibition held in Dublin, means "poetry of vision" in Gaelic and testifies to the literary thinking of the original organizers. It is curious then that Irish artists have not produced the manifestoes so beloved by modernists.

Things are changing however. The shift from modernism to postmodernism in Irish art has been marked by a more conscious search for a personally tailored idiom that is much more ambitious conceptually and contextually than the art-making of a previous generation: the soft lyrics once sung have given way to a new agony in the garden. There is now a more open examination of the Irish cultural tradition — the political troubles acting as a raw catalyst. Text has become important either as carefully considered titles, or words superimposed on images, or words and slogans worked up from the landscape or townscape itself.

Michael Farrell is historically important here. Towards the end of the '60s and early '70s, the political troubles in Northern Ireland had begun and Farrell's work, which until then had no political connotations, began to respond to the tragic situation in Ulster. His *Pressé Series,* which had been purely formal abstractions, began to take on meanings that put the formal elements of Farrell's visual vocabulary to the service of more significant and compelling content. The squirts of "pop" juice now became blood, the once sterile language of the *Pressé Series* became the passionate "Pressé Politique," as anonymity gave way to personal identity.

Variations on this theme continued to become more and more reflective on what it means to be Irish and an artist rather than merely an artist. In *Une Nature Morte à la Mode Irlandaise* (1975), we witness newspaper headlines of various tragedies chopped up by the now fulminating "Presse" elements and the deadly appropriate pun in the title on the concept of "nature morte."

In an interview in the *Irish Times* in 1977, Farrell reflects on his artistic change:

> "I became interested more in the literary aspects and less in the formal. It put me in a terrible jam, and rethinking the whole basis of my work took a long time. I've withdrawn from the international stream of art to a more human and personal style than before. I found in my big abstract works that I couldn't say things that I felt like saying. I had arrived at a totally aesthetic art with no literary connotations. I wanted to make statements using sarcasm, or puns, or wit, and all of these I could not do before because of the limited means of expression I had adopted."[1]

Farrell was by then living in Paris and in this new domicile he chose to deploy Boucher's painting of Miss O'Murphy (herself an Irish emigrant living in France and one-time mistress of Louis XV) as a potent symbol for his artistic and personal concerns. In one work in this series the artist lays out Miss O'Murphy like a piece of meat in a butcher's window, signifying the various butcher's cuts "gigot, forequarters, le cut, knee cap." Thus, he both puns upon the name of the artist of the original painting, Boucher, and poignantly comments on the savagery of the political system and its victims in the North of Ireland, (knee-capping is a customary punishment carried out by the I.R.A. for informers and the like). The artist himself has said of these paintings: "They make every possible statement on the Irish situation, religious, cultural, political; the cruelty, the horror — every aspect of it."[2]

Another source of influence has been a series of English artists who showed at the Orchard Gallery, Derry, during the 1980s. These artists, among them Kit Edwardes, Tony Rickaby, and Terry Atkinson, juxtaposed imagery and text. One work by Edwardes, shown in 1983, was in the form of an altarpiece, which contrasted pictures of English football heroes (World Cup Stars 1966) with drawings of saints and martyrs. This change in cultural deification and values was offset by the statement: "That which is phenomenal in British history is the extent to which a people, insular, uninterested in domination and expansion, have yet spread the pattern of their thought and rule over the world."

In another work, Edwardes used buildings, representing one level of reality (vested interests, power), alongside group photographs of World War II soldiers (human values), with the caption: "They resist unconsciously, and they resist in their sleep." His concern was government and state manipulation in a capitalist society. Religion was also examined, particularly on a psychological and sociological level.

Language, image, meaning, and their interrelationships were also the concerns of Terry Atkinson, a founder-member of the conceptual Art and Language Group of the late 1960s, whose work was exhibited in Derry in September, 1983. The work shown spanned the years 1977-83. Themes ranged from the human and political aspects of World War I to the exploitation of the Third World by the West, the Falklands War, the Middle East Crisis, and media and news presentation.

Atkinson's style was what might loosely be termed German Expressionist, and his intention was clearly didactic. As an artist, he demands a lot from the onlooker. In the catalogue he developed in essay form his ideas about art, particularly the relationship between art and expression. Art is not simply a matter of sensory aesthetic experience or awareness that elicits an emotional response from the viewer, Atkinson maintained, but has to do with thinking. He blames the modernist tradition for this separation, which makes art and language incompatible. He states, "The artist 'feeler' has come to enjoy such a premium in precisely the context of downgrading thinking. And, making concrete this division, has been . . . sensitive craft skills and technical competence set over and against intellectual competence."[3] He sees image and statement/text as the solution to this dilemma. In one work, for example, two cats recline on a table with a view of the dawn sky through a large window, somewhat in the style of Edvard Munch. The caption reads, *Property Ad 1: Two fat cats on a peninsular breakfast bar at dawn in front of a picture window. Beautiful views, a natural idyll. £750,000 — cats not included. This property is especially suitable for persons or families who like watching the dawn break or for insomniacs.* Here one's response changes from a sensory experience to reflection upon issues such as consumerism, materialism, and advertising.

Again, in the series "Blue Skies," one is expected to change gear from visual feeling to literary thinking. The blue dominates the battered face of a black boxer whose head is covered by a towel as he listens to music via earphones while a pet rat runs in a curious ladder device. The caption reads, *Blue Skies VI: After retaining his title, the champ, his cuts already healing, meets the media at his exclusive island retreat whilst listening to Rock n' Roll, and with his pet rat running. For the fight the champ received 700,000 dollars.*

Works of this nature, dealing with philosophical propositions and word associations, can all too often fall uneasily between significance and obvious pretension. The work of these artists doesn't rest easy, but has an honest seriousness, inviting the viewer to reflect not only upon social and political issues, but the nature of art activity itself.

It is interesting to compare Atkinson with Dermot Seymour, whose lurid, ominous, and displaced Drumlin borderlands are also myth-laden. Seymour uses words to explore conundrums, complexities, and bizarre juxtapositions; nothing seems to be what it is. If the Ulster problem is about territory, then it is also about insecurities. Seymour brands and marks his absurd menagerie of sheep, cattle, and "pookas" so that they only stray into his pictures just as partisans mark and territorialize the Ulster countryside. But it is his titles that set off the riddles.

Titles like *A Freisan coughed over Drumshat on the death of the Reverend George Walker of Kilmore* and *The Queen's own Scottish Borders observe the King of Jews, appearing behind Sean McGuigan's sheep on the fourth Sunday after Epiphany* all evoke the land question. In *Who fears to speak of '98* the dominant symbol of Harland and Woolf is relocated on Napoleon's Nose (a local term for part of the Cave Hill visible from Belfast). Here, free Presbyterianism stands over the free thinking of Henry Joy McCracken and his associates. According to Seymour, being Protestant is not being allowed to think for yourself. Frustrated behavior results and the soldier beetle drops from nowhere.

Ideologies scare the artist and here Seymour differs markedly from Terry Atkinson. Atkinson's contrived titles arise from ideology — Marxist thinking and dogma; Seymour's arise naturally from the townland. Convoluted local historical references, anecdote, and myth are interlaced in the titles like tatted lace. The complications of our society come out like "pookas" at night. A crossroads is not just a junction; it is where someone was shot, a patrol ambushed, a 300th anniversary celebrated — or where traffic is monitored or surveilled.

In Ireland, surveillance is a kind of national voyeurism where no one is sure who is the watched or the watcher. It is an infinite regression of an image within an image within an image, like the structure of a Flann O'Brien novel or the open, circular mode of traditional Irish music.

In Willie Doherty's work, questions of word and image are central. Doherty's art stems from a desire to redress certain photojournalist images of the "war-torn city" kind. But there is much more at stake than a "how we see ourselves" antidote. The artist deals with concepts of the land, Irishness, self, and otherness. To do this, he presses words against the pane. Some of his images are appropriated from a second-hand reality given by reportage. The overprinting of words pulls them back into a new, existential state, where contradictions, ironies, and subversions are at work. As Victor Burgin advises:

"It seems to be extensively believed by photographers that meanings are to be found in the world much in the way that rabbits are found on downs, and that all that is required is the talent to spot them and the skill to shoot them. . . . However, the naturalness of the world ostensibly open before the camera is a deceit. Objects present to the camera are already in use in the production of meanings, and photography has no choice but to operate upon such meanings."[4]

In *Fog Ice*, nature usurps a covert activity. Who is the viewed and who the viewer? The Yeatsian swim is at work again in *We shall never forsake the Blue Skies of Ulster for the Grey Mists of an Irish Republic*. Here again nature is the ironic equalizer. The view is looking southwards down the River Foyle, toward the Republic, from a grey and misty Northern Ireland.

But a good slogan does not worry about actual weather conditions. Doherty has continued this interest in the contradictions of place, territory, and orientation in works such as *West Is South; East Is North* (1988) and *The Walls*. He has also examined historical identity and nationalism in works such as *Stone Upon Stone* (1986) and *Lost Perspectives* (1988). Text in these photoworks is direct and spare. It hangs like movie subtitles in a kind of atavistic hold. Working by physical encounter and contemplation, the words must be experienced in a physical space. All these images are in monochrome, appropriate to the conceptual charge.

In 1988 Doherty turned to color in response to Paul Graham's photographs in *Troubled Land*. In *Dreaming* and *Waiting*, he deals not only with the romance of the pictorialist landscape, but also with the process of myth-making and the travelogue. Chris Coppock has observed:

"Doherty's work has been compared with the work of Richard Long and, certainly on a formal level, owes much to the preoccupations of Long and other exponents in the photo-image/text field. But this is where any similarity ends. Doherty's passion for Derry, a city steeped in contentious history, is of a fundamental nature. While Long scours the world, Doherty locates himself in an environment that he has known intimately from birth. The relationship of image to text is nourished by a highly subjective response, which channels modernist techniques in an attempt to articulate a personal localized polemic. In this sense Willie Doherty's very particular vernacular perhaps offers a resistance to cultural travel. This form may be accessible but the dialect deceptive."[5]

The influence of various artists who have shown at the Orchard Gallery is clear. The central question Coppock raises is, does Doherty's work travel beyond the pale? Is it too heavy a dialect to be understood elsewhere? The sensual intuition of subversion at work will be caught. Is that enough?

Words and text form a kind of material and moral land survey in Chris Wilson's work. Maps, territory, light intrusions — images of growth and decay — mark, measure, and incubate the holy ground of Wilson's collages. These gothic-hothouse abandoned interiors have atavistic taproots of deep penetration. Plantations, family ties, and religion plot Wilson's urban territorial maps.

Angela Kingston, in a recent catalogue essay, has observed:

> "When he draws the bare earth, it is as though he is a farmer working a piece of land, attending to the matter at hand with a pleasurable respect. At each stage of his work, he seems to be striving to substantiate the ground he is working on — paper can seem so ephemeral — whilst at the same time gaining a practical knowledge of the fabric of the world."[6]

Wilson's mapping technique is a measurement of transformation and acceptance. In his earlier sculpture he explored substance as an idea. In *Potato Table* (1985), a table, or perhaps more accurately, a tabula, is made of potatoes. A staple of the Irish diet with its obvious socio-political references becomes the material for what is usually an inanimate piece of furniture. This is not an eating table, but something much more ritualistic.

The use of reversals underpins much of Wilson's subsequent work. *Harvest* brings back the potato as an offering from an absent congregation to an absent deity. Again, Angela Kingston says,

> "There are memories, perhaps of churches and chapels overflowing with produce at harvest time, and packed congregations singing rousing hymns: does the spilling of potatoes in an empty, echoing church represent a moment of mournful longing for values, faith and community? Or was that dull thudding, as the sack was upturned, about futility and anger in the face of change?"[7]

Wilson cites French poetry with its searching for attachments as an interest. But John Hewitt seems a more relevant association. Frank Ormsby points to Hewitt's restless fix as an Ulsterman:

> "To be native to a province colonized by one's ancestors, at home and yet 'alien,' a city man who loves, but must struggle to relate to, the country, someone aware of . . . gaps that are finally unbridgeable, is to be perpetually unsure of one's place."[8]

The obliteration of language is an issue, too. The playwright Brian Friel, in *Translations*, demonstrates that what is lost in the act of translation can never be regained. And, since cultural identity is laid into language, it is not surprising that language can become the cause of violent interaction

Willie Doherty, *Last Hours of Daylight, The Bogside, Derry*, 1985.

Dermot Seymour, *The Queen's Own Scottish Borderers Observe the King of the Jews,
Appearing Behind Sean McGuigan's Sheep, on the Fourth Sunday After Epiphany,* 1988.

between colonized and colonizer. Seamus Deane, writing of Friel's *Translations*, cautions, "On the hither side of violence is Ireland as Paradise; on the nether side, Ireland as ruin. But since we live on the nether side, we live in ruin and can only console ourselves with the desire for the paradise we briefly glimpse. The result is a discrepancy in our language; words are askew, they are out of line with fact. Violence has fantasy and wordiness as one of its most persistent after-effects."[10]

Rita Donagh in *A Cellular Maze* reacts to the idea of the physical and graphic presence of "H" blocks on the landscape. She also considers the location of the "H" blocks in proximity to Lough Neagh, with its association to ancient mythology. Donagh also used the idea of the six counties as a territorial unit, or what she calls the "shadow of the six counties" — a shadow on the lung. The presence of the British?

Exploring grids and various projections in a series of drawings, she led one to the "Long Meadow." Usually one sees aerial photographs of Long Kesh. Here we see blocks diagonally set across the canvas like a still from a German Expressionist film — light creates the intense mood of this air raid.

Many artists who have responded to Ireland as a psychic landscape have deployed maps, networks, and text. Sarat Maharaj, writing on Rita Donagh's use of the map, stresses that nothing ever is what it seems. Donagh teases out and plays upon a particular feature of the map: the fact that, if it gives us what we tend to take for granted as an accurate account of the "world out there" . . . it also looks radically unlike what it represents. We rarely think of the two things in any way at odds with each other: the particular convention of representation involved has so much become second nature to us.[11]

In Ireland, a particular relationship between words and image is, in many ways, endemic to the culture. Witness, for example, the government's banning of direct interviews with Sinn Fein representatives, so that we get a curious form of image and dubbing. And, of course, there is the word, the text and the Bible in Protestant fundamentalism. There are also the literary structural models of writers like Joyce, O'Brien, and Beckett. But what all the Irish artists considered in this essay share is the use of words as ways of investigating what is invested in the cultural mapping of the psychic landscape.

NOTES:

[1] Farrell, M. See monograph by Cyril Barrett, Douglas Hyde Gallery, 1979 and *Irish Times* interview, 1977.

[2] Farrell, M., *op. cit.*

[3] Atkinson, T. See Orchard Gallery catalogue, 1983 and *Mute II*, Orchard Gallery, 1988.

[4] Burgin, V. *Thinking Photography*. Macmillan, 1982 (introduction).

[5] Coppock, C.,"A Line of Country, Three Artists from Northern Ireland," catalogue essay, Manchester, Cornerhouse, July/Aug 1987.

[6] Kingston, A., "Chris Wilson, From the Growth of the Soil," catalogue essay, Arts Council, Belfast, Sept/Oct 1989.

[7] Kingston, A., *op. cit.*

[8] Ormsby, F., editor, *Poets from the North of Ireland*, Blackstaff Press, 1979.

[9] McClatchy, J. D., editor, *Poets on Painters, Essays on the Art of Painting by Twentieth Century Poets*, Berkeley and Los Angeles: University of California Press, 1988.

[10] Dean, S., *Celtic Revivals, Essays in Modern Irish Literature*, London: Faber and Faber, 1985.

[11] Donagh, Rita, catalogue essay, Central St. Martins, April 1989.

Art and Politics — Experiences from Czechoslovakia

by Petr Wittlich
(Czechoslovakia)

In the twenty years between the occupation of the country by the Soviet Army in 1968 and the "velvet revolution" in November 1989, art in Czechoslovakia developed in a rather strange manner. That whole period was marked by a strong dualism of values, a dualism which in such a crystallized form existed at that time only in the USSR. On the one side, there was an official Union of Artists, made up of prominent ideological people of the so-called normalizing Communist regime, artists, who as early as the 1950s "were fighting" for socialist realism and now saw that here was their last chance to gain power and fortune. Also included in the Union were many average artists, who earned their living by producing various concoctions of classical modern art.

On the other side stood a large group of intergenerational artists, literally disregarding the official strictures, living their own lives, pursuing their own activities and moving on the edge of political illegality. These attitudes were sharply defined, especially in the 1970s. However, in the last two or three years the isolation of this group was reduced as they achieved some concessions and were able to exhibit. The orientation of this so-called alternative culture was naturally anti-official and anti-bureaucratic, promoting creative freedom for the artist. In spite of a remarkably broad spectrum of individual expressions, there was a certain joint strategy, not only in practical cultural policy, but also in the general conception of the content of art. This art was not formalistic. L'art pour l'art-ism does not belong to the tradition of Czechoslovak art. On the contrary, there is almost always a tendency toward involvement, though of a purely artistic kind.

As this art did not want to get involved in the existing social structures, it looked elsewhere for the horizon of its influences. Just as Antigone in ancient times insisted on the supremacy of the "natural" law over man's order, this art looked for a point of view that would rid art of its dependence on the mechanisms of social codes — this in a country then fully dependent on the dictate of the central political power. An artist belonging to this group could take advantage of its solidarity, yet in principle he or she was an individual searching for identity by trying to break through to the sources of creativity and originality. The aversion to social hypocrisy provoked aggressive expressionism, a liking for quasi-brutal treatment of materials and an attempt to shock with neo-romantic reminders of natural calamities. The most interesting Czech artists of the 1970s often turned their drastically gained experience against themselves.

In general, however, this alternative art endeavored to choose, as a counterpoint to the spoiled social reality, the eternal law of nature, understood cosmologically as a matrix of elementary relations. Several of the artists, who in the 1960s were in contact with neo-constructivism or minimal art, gave their works a transcendental content exceeding the limits of object phenomenalism.

Besides this sublime art, often pathetically elevating the relationship between Man and Nature to a metaphysical and mystic concept and to the myth of a cosmic whole, it was — especially by the 1980s — the grotesque that found the greatest application, parodying the contemporary state of human relations which in the late communist society completely caricatured its proclaimed high ideals. Even here, however, the absurdity of the situation offered a much larger and more important scope and turned it into a most attractive form of alternative culture. In the grotesque was a paradoxical remedy for the social situation. I believe that Czech cartoonists and other artists greatly contributed to the bloodless process of our November revolution, as they had made of it a far-reaching and effective cultural phenomenon long before the revolution.

It is well known, even abroad, that it was above all students and artists who paved the way for the return of democracy to Czechoslovakia. All the more interesting may be the question of their position today in post-Communist Czechoslovakia. At the same time there is also the question of how to evaluate the artistic strategy of "alternative" art today — whether it should be re-evaluated in the new social context or even totally abandoned.

The people in today's Czechoslovakia generally realize that the time of great changes has come, when virtually all forms of existing social and economic behavior must be changed. They had to overcome the first shock of a 35% rise in prices within one month at the beginning of 1991. Culture, too, was in for its first shock when it lost the usual state subsidies. The prices of printed matter rose drastically, as well as the rent for exhibition premises and art materials — often by more than 100%. Theaters that were the platforms for democracy in November 1989 now yawn emptily and manage with difficulty to keep their heads above water. All these troubles, however, have not disturbed the morale of Czech artists resolved to tread the new road. They realize, like most of their fellow citizens, that there is no return; that economic and social reforms must be completed.

It is of course, not only a matter of material difficulties, but a question of the content of the work of art, its deeper sense. In fact, it is only now that — in the theory of art and art criticism — we can openly discuss basic concepts such as postmodernism and deconstruction. In Czechoslovakia these concepts still sound rather new and are associated with a certain legalization of the previous alternative art, which had been, if only from a generational point of view, rather heterogeneous. Pluralism is a recognized characteristic of the contemporary situation in art. Moreover, there is enough good will to understand multicultural expressions.

It has been a traditional problem for artists living in the Czechoslovak lands — even in the time when no Czechoslovakia existed — to reach a certain balance between worldliness and the preservation of national identity. On the whole, they have so far managed to maintain this dynamic balance, perhaps due to the fact that they are somewhat isolated from the international art market

It is still difficult to foretell to what extent Czechoslovak art will be drawn into the international market. Prague still has very few private galleries; in the future these private galleries should prove more effective than Union and State institutions. It is also possible that the international market is oblivious because it does not know much about Czech art, with the exception of some well-known emigrants, such as Jirí Kolár or, more recently, Magdelana Jetelová. The answer to whether Czechoslovak art will preserve its identity or adapt to contemporary international vogue and standards does not rest so much with economic opportunities and pressures as with the decisions and intentions of the artists themselves.

This, I believe, can be considered a favorable moment, especially if the Czechoslovak artists can quickly shake off the fatigue plaguing them after the great tension of the time of revolution, and if they refuse to be broken by economic difficulties. One concept widespread in Czechoslovakia is the dream of a united Europe that would go far to overcome the stagnating division into power blocs, and would serve as example of cooperation among nations and perhaps as a model for the whole world. Naturally, we all hope for good relations among nations, made possible by the collapse of totalitarian régimes and the iron curtain, yet sometimes a myth emerges

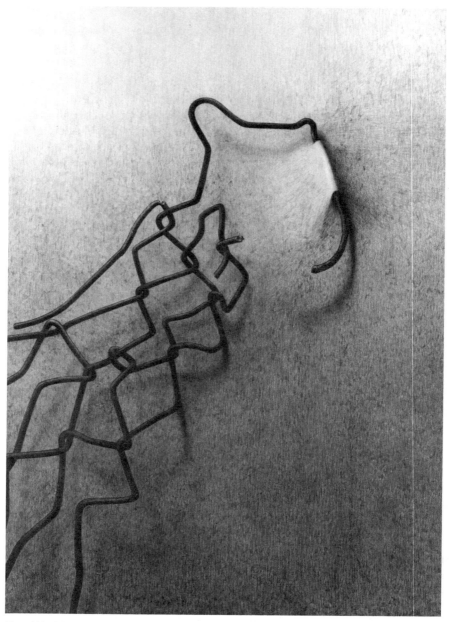

Pavel Nešleha, *Study of the Objectness*, 1982.

of a large body, such as we knew in the past in its socialist or communist version and which in spite of high ideals had devastating effects on us all. I would not like to treat all these ideals as identical, but it must be said quite frankly that the utopia has never come true. The actual result of such ideals is usually a kind of uniformity, and I have the impression that perhaps even a certain uniformity of a pluralistic type is possible.

The mentality of artists in post-totalitarian countries is today rather complicated. On the one hand, they are naturally attracted by the variability and freedom of Western art, whose sub-surface ties and existential patterns they hardly know, and on the other hand they realize that they have been through an extraordinary life and art experience which they should not cast aside but really evaluate and make use of in their work. The problem is not so much the individual expression of this experience, which may even be quite original, but rather a certain complementary aspect of the views and style of these expressions, something that could be presented on the international scene. The totalitarian regime drove real artists into isolation and paradoxically developed their individualism. Today these artists search for a common language, but it is up to them to decide: Will they repeat the words of the international artistic Esperanto or contribute something of their own to the international discourse? We can only hope that the new shoots of this enrichment of world art are not crushed by blasé international judgment before they can take root and develop.

Zaostalí Group (Zdeněk Berau, Bedřich Dlouhý, Hugo Demartini, Pavel Nešleha), installation, 1992.

How Latin American Artists in the U.S. View Art, Politics, and Ethnicity in a Supposedly Multicultural World

by Shifra M. Goldman
(United States)

> *What if suddenly the continent turned upside down? what if the U.S. was Mexico? what if 200,000 Anglo-Saxons/ were to cross the border each month/ to work as gardeners, waiters/ 3rd chair musicians, movie extras/ bouncers, babysitters, chauffeurs,/syndicated cartoons, feather-weight boxers, fruit pickers, &/ anonymous poets?/ what if they were called waspanos, waspitos, wasperos or waspbacks?/what if we were the top dogs?*
>
> — Guillermo Gomez-Peña

Three themes are married herein: the naming and mapping of America; the coming celebrations, or anti-celebrations, of the Columbus Quincentenary; and the significance of "multiculturalism" for second-classed ethnic groups of artists. All these themes are addressed in terms of art production by Latin American artists residing in the United States.

On the eve of the 1992 "celebration" of the Columbus Quincentenary, and two years before the 70th anniversary of the Monroe Doctrine, which gave political leverage to the U.S. concept of Manifest Destiny, it seems urgent to start this presentation with a consideration of the name "America." Not its "etymology" in the corrective solution given by Florentine navigator Amerigo Vespucci to Columbus's notion that he had arrived on Indian soil (thus misnaming the continent's indigenous populations), but its political/social usages. When Chilean conceptual artist Alfredo Jaar first came to the U.S., he, like many other Latin Americans, was shocked to discover that the United States had appropriated this continental designation as its national identification without allowance for the other countries which also inhabit the Americas. Jaar's testimony indicates that he considered himself an "American" (of Chilean nationality) as a matter of course, without thought or further embroidery; but he discovered in New York that he was an outsider, a foreigner in *this* America. The question was not one of semantics, but of hegemony; the usage reflected real power relationships. Challenging this appropriation with images and texts, Jaar located *A Logo for America* (1987), a computerized Spectacolor lightboard, in the public space of New York's Times Square, long known for its profusion of neon light signs and a famous moving light-strip of daily news headlines that dates back at least to the 1940's. To counter-appropriate U.S. electronic technology in order to redefine First and Third World interaction displays a fine sense of irony. "This is not America" and "This is not America's flag" are superimposed respectively on a map and the flag of the United States; Jaar also spins the continental map of America — North, Central, and South — on an axis of the letter "R."

Jaar is neither the first nor the only Latin American to employ an imaginative geography to reframe the American discourse. In 1936 the Uruguayan constructivist master, Joaquin Torres-Garcia, published a drawing which inverted South America to emphasize its autonomy from European aesthetic, and to justify the right of southern artists to recoup the northern pre-Columbian cultures regardless of where the artist was located in the continental scheme.[1] (A similar argument has recently been made by a Cuban critic concerning African sources.) Another aspect of the mapping process is the comparison between the 16th-century Mercator map "created basically to abet the imperialistic endeavors of European navigators in their discovery, colonization, and exploitation" of Third World regions; and the 1974 Peters map, which shows the Northern hemisphere to actually be half as large as that of the Southern,[2] thus reversing the earlier order. The Peters projection (upon which Jaar has inscribed an image of Western toxic waste dumped in Africa) visually symbolizes, by its very creation and dissemination, the beginning of the West's loss of its dominant position vis-a-vis those countries it has considered peripheral and marginal.

Remapping projects have long interested other U.S.-based Latin Americans, like Chileans Juan Downey and Catalina Parra. Downey's fascination with maps that demonstrate the flow of invisible energies across space and the distinctions cartographers make between topography, national boundaries, travel, and communication networks, is illustrated in his large drawing *Two Maps* (1985) and *World Map*. In 1981, upon her arrival in New York, Parra collaged text from *The New York Times* with clippings of football players that raise the specter of the football stadium in Santiago which the Pinochet *coup d'état* turned into a concentration camp and killing field in 1973. The enclosing frame (whether intentionally or not) suggests the long narrow shape of Chile turned horizontally, while the text _The Reunited States of America_ emphasizes the close relationship of U.S. power (symbolized by the _Times_ headline) to disastrous events in South America. Distances are eclipsed on this political map which unites two American states.

Brazilian Jonas dos Santos emphasizes the complicity of both Americas in the destruction/salvation of the ecological and human environments. Focusing on the Amazon rain forests and their aboriginal inhabitants who bond with each other without shame, the artist mirrors himself in performance with two horizontally-reversed maps within the installation of _Brazil via New York: Oxygen Share_ of 1989.

Multiple are the ways in which Latin America artists globally have addressed the question of the Spanish conquest, and of successive neoconquests up to the present. Obviously some of the works mentioned earlier can be seen as overlapping this related discourse. New York artist Fernando Salicrup fictionalizes the gentle pre-Hispanic Taino Indians of Puerto Rico peering through the leaves like shy wild creatures in his painting, _Once More Columbus_, or _Before Discovery_ (1976). Argentine Leandro Katz puts an ironic spin on the conquest with his 1982 installation, _Friday's Footprint_. Based on the 18th-century British allegory _Robinson Crusoe_ by Daniel Defoe, the novel is as impregnated with colonial ideology as any one can find. Set in South America near the Orinoco River, the wrecked mariner Crusoe survives on an uninhibited island for twenty-four years. He lives alone in rude comfort until he discovers the naked footprint of a "native" whom he names "Man Friday" and whom he rescues from cannibals. Friday is converted into a companion and servant. The cannibals (who miraculously made _no_ appearance for a quarter of a century) are again defeated, while Crusoe and Friday find the means to return to England. _Crusoe_, said a book reviewer in 1948,[3] is a manual of the qualities that have won the world from barbarism — courage, patience, ingenuity, and industry — qualities much admired in the industrializing capitalist world for many centuries.

Recast from the Renaissance to a later period, the story seems to repeat that of Shakespeare's _Tempest_: Man Friday takes the place of Ariel as a native servant devoted to his master, while the cannibals represent the coarse and unfaithful Caliban, an anagram constructed by Shakespeare from the word "cannibal."

This is not the moment to review the literature, but Latin American intellectuals have been involved in a central (often metaphoric) discourse about identity since 1900, stretching from the essay _Ariel_ by Uruguayan

José Enrique Rodo to Cuban Roberto Fernandes Retamar's (1971)[4] *Caliban* — or Man Friday — in which Shakespeare's monster is taken as a more appropriate symbol of America's people. *Caliban* allegorically rejects the colonialism that Columbus brought to the New World; while Man Friday, in Katz's installation, is superseded by another image. Directly above the footprint is reflected an extremely sophisticated stone carving from the Maya civilization. Neither pliant servant nor barbaric cannibal, Katz seems to say, was the true condition of the autochthonous American peoples. Both the footprint and the epithets were European constructions. Puerto Rican Rafael Ferrer makes more direct references to the Caliban persona: in his tent installation, *El gran canibal* (the Great Cannibal), of 1979 he erects a pseudo-primitive residence on whose surface games with words reflect the European/American semiotic encounter.

Multiculturalism is an idea whose time has been coming since the early 1980s, when the feminist and civil rights movements for Blacks, Latinos, Asians and Native Americans, generated in the 1960s and culturally activated in the 1970s, achieved a certain visibility. Demographic changes across the U.S., resulting from revised immigration laws which brought increasing numbers of Third World peoples to North America, made the handwriting on the wall much clearer. By the mid-1980s, a series of blockbuster exhibitions of modern Latin-American art, related to the art market, prompted me in 1988 to compare the "art boom" to the Latin American literary boom. Two recent books — one a 1990 catalogue for "The Decade Show: Frameworks of Identity in the 1980s"; the other, Lucy Lippard's *Mixed Blessings: New Art in Multicultural America* (1991) fixed this phenomenon and its exciting new conception in the public eye. No longer would North American art be dominated by white Anglo/European males; the cultural, national, and gender diversity now characterizing the United States must be given equal place and time. To which we said "Hurrah!"

Unfortunately, multiculturalist discourse coexisted with the most conservative/reactionary political agenda imaginable as the Reagan/Bush administrations increasingly signaled a return to 19th-century codes and the subversion of all gains made since the days of Franklin Delano Roosevelt and the New Deal. Racism, sexism, anti-semitism (against Jews *and* Arabs), ageism, homophobia, xenophobia, and censorship accompany joblessness, homelessness, and deepening poverty at home, and militarism and imperialism abroad. Increasingly, the U.S. population is polarized and fragmented as the ultra-right leads its attack on all fronts.

Leandro Katz, *Friday's Footprint*, installation, The Whitney Museum of American Art, 1982.

Alfredo Jaar, *A Logo for America*, computer animation sequence on spectacolor lightboard, Times Square, New York City, 1987.

In the arts, many of the groups under attack have made a certain amount of common cause. Thus "The Decade Show," at the Museum of Contemporary Hispanic Art, the New Museum of Contemporary Art, and the Studio Museum of Harlem (all of New York) represents a true multiculturalism, however chaotic and unfocused. Lippard's *Mixed Blessings*, while generally accepted, has been criticized for compiling only artists of the Third World. The problem with these sprawling outlays, however, is that while the concept is utopian, the reality is not. The true hybridization and cross-culturalism that can rally different viewpoints and aesthetic configurations around common issues, that can realistically define a multicultural American continent with comprehension of the confrontation that is taking place (and must take place) between the forces of power and the disempowered, has not yet occurred. As a result, the hegemonic power is able to confuse and disorient this new inclusive democratic surge represented by the term multiculturalism. The symbolic and *Realpolitik* social meanings of multiculturalism are obscured: some use the term as a synonym for the discarded "minority" designation; others as a tool for a new neo-colonialist maneuver to contain, divide and defeat. The idealists don't always understand that inclusion is not sufficient — that access to power, decision making, and funds must be included. A retranscription of past cultural history is simply not sufficient.

NOTES:

[1] The Torres-Garcia drawing was published in his magazine *Circulo Y Cuadrado*, 1936, brought to the author's attention by Mari Carmen Ramirez-Garcia.

[2] Grynstejn, Madeleine, 'Alfredo Jaar,' La Jolla Museum of Contemporary Art, California, 1990, p.35.

[3] Benet, William Rose, *Reader's Encyclopedia*, 2nd edition, NY: Thomas Y. Crowell Co., [1948], 1965.

[4] Published in Havana in 1979 as *Caliban y otros ensayos*.

Art and Politics

by Marcel van Jole
(Belgium)

Art is not politics
Art is art. — Ad Reinhardt

In my role as a European observer of the contemporary art scene at large and in the light of the present theme, I would only bring to the fore a few non-structured remarks on art and politics and the intricate relations between both, not only because I think that these do not fit into a schedule or have binding causal relations linking them to each other, but most of all because I do not wish to associate with any of the "parties" in this conflictual relationship.

After the breakdown of the "iron curtain" and the implosion of the communist dictatures in Eastern Europe, the traditional leftist neo-post-Marxist discourse seems to have lost most of its credibility in the West. The post-'68 syndrome, some sort of social critique based on a curious mixture of syndicalism, ecological considerations and such, which led to a politicization of the artistic discourse *à la* Hans Haacke, seems to have lost its relevance.

It seems to have been replaced, in America at least, by less utopian political ideas and visions of our society. Our economic system is questioned on its (in)human implications, not on its political foundations as such. In line with the ideas of postmodernity, artists now seem to have found peace with the idea that art mainly operates in the artistic circuit and that politics belongs to the realm of politics. At least the museum building has once more become the center of artistic discourse, as opposed to the "art-on-the-street" and "art-in-the-land" mentality of the late '60s and '70s.

However, all in all, recent art is characterized by a growing concern with values that are more humanist than politico-economical. This appears for instance, in the "Truisms" of Jenny Holzer and in the poster-like works of Barbara Kruger. The remarkable fact that Holzer represented the United States of America at the Venice Biennial of 1990 shows that her work and, per extension, the stance she adopts, meet with some degree of official recognition.

The content of her statements in the form of "Truisms" cannot be traced to any of the known traditional leftist, rightist, or other discourses, but has affinities with the feminist critique of the past decade and with other emancipation movements. This is also evident in the work of Barbara Kruger. Because they refuse party politics and prefer a broader scope, but more because of the irony and references to the visual language of commercials, they stand closer to the work of Andy Warhol than to "politically conscious" artists `a la* Haacke.

After the turmoil caused by new censorship proposals advocated by Helms and Hatch in the wake of the Mapplethorpe incident at the Corcoran Gallery in Washington, a large number of American artists have tried to come to terms with this most thorny of issues. The AIDS crisis also mobilized many artists, cf. the participation of Gran Fury in the Venice Aperto and the involvement of artists as divergent as Laurie Anderson and David Hockney in ACT UP fundraising. The work of Felix Torres-Garcia and Zoe Leonard, both featured in recent Belgian group shows, seems to have this disease as its main subject. In 1987, AMFAR International started a campaign in the U.S.A. that soon became the most important one ever organized in the art world: Art Against Aids; first in New York, then in Los Angeles, later in San Francisco, Chicago, and Washington D.C. Under the active patronage of Elizabeth Taylor, Art Against Aids collected over 6 million dollars for the benefit of programs in the struggle against AIDS all over the world. In 1991, the first campaign outside the U.S.A. was held in Basel, Switzerland, after comparable events organized by other organizations, such as the Frankfurt rally presided over by Jan Hoet. Typically, these events do not question the status or the nature of art as such; they certainly do not subscribe to an aesthetics that blurs the differences between the function of art within a given society and the nature of art, as was the case in the conceptually oriented research of the late '60s-early '70s. This new form of campaigning uses the newest and most efficient marketing techniques, escaping the endearing pseudo-bohemian post-hippy syndrome of the earlier home-spun variety in favor of a markedly urban and realist approach.

The response to these campaigns was considerable and proves the growing engagement of artistic circles in attacking this alarming problem and finding adequate solutions. As yet, other eminently modern and urban social problems such as drugs or the homeless, have not been dealt with in the same thorough manner, probably because the arts community is less directly concerned. But most artists clearly took a stance regarding issues of sexism and women's liberation, homophobia and gay liberation, the new censure and artistic freedom, racism and cultural pluralism.

Typical of the influence of the provocative art of Andy Warhol and its ambiguous relation to social critique is the extremely obnoxious art of Jeff Koons and his ilk. On the one hand they seem to flirt shamelessly with the excesses of the commercialization of art; on the other hand they carry this socio-political evolution to its ultimate paroxysm.

The problem of the homeless, as it comes to the fore in the work of artists like Jeff Wall, who is also amazingly influential in Europe, is also treated and visualized on the basis of its (lack of) humanist dimensions, not as an illustration of a (Marxist) analysis of history and society.

Overall, as appears from the above paragraphs, we could state that the art of today, as it originated in the United States and quickly spread all over the world, does have political connotations, but these are no longer a translation or a visualization of a preconceived political dogma or program (i.e. a Marxist one). The enormous importance of multicultural exhibitions like *Les Magiciens de la Terre*, the fact that women outnumber men on the contemporary New York art scene, and that non-Western and Black artists have added new inspiration to an otherwise tired and over-referential so-called postmodern scene, plus the identity claims of Gay-Lesbian and Jewish artists (both of course have always been over-represented on the cultural scene according to their demographically small numbers,* but not as such), and the use of non-traditional materials like electronic publicity on Times Square: all point to a renewed and more inspiring osmosis between the arts on the one hand and social critique on the other. The tyranny of political dogma is replaced by a pluralistic and realistic emancipatory discourse.

Multiculturalism in Ontario, Canada

by Gerald Needham
(Canada)

We need more clearly to focus our lenses and straighten our mirrors, so that we can see ourselves as we truly are . . . the most successful multicultural nation in the world.

— Gerry Weiner,
Canadian Federal Minister of Multiculturalism

Whether Mr. Weiner's claim is accurate or not there is no doubt that Canada's multicultural policy is unusual in its importance and is a very distinctive one in its role in the arts. After World War II, modern Canada, which had been founded by French, Scots, English, and Irish and which had admitted other peoples rather reluctantly, actively encouraged emigration from all over the world and took in many of the displaced people from Europe. Even in recent years, when high unemployment has led to a reduction in immigration, many refugees are taken in.

Toronto, the city I live in, has particularly attracted immigrants and there are numerous districts devoted to specific ethnic groups. The largest is the Italian (Toronto is said to be the seventh largest Italian city in the world) and there are a number of quarters where all the signs are in Italian. When Italy won the World cup in soccer five years ago, Toronto almost came to a stop for a day! There are numerous Portuguese who often share districts with the Italians, and there is a very well-known Greek section that began after World War I. I live on the edge of the Polish area, which also has a Yugoslav enclave. A local restaurant features the cuisine of the Mauritius Islands. There is also a very large population from the former British West Indies, and very confusingly there is a large Indian population, not North American Indians, but people from the Indian sub-continent, not to mention those same Indians who had gone as indentured laborers to East Africa and the West Indies. There is a very considerable Chinese population which is a mixture of refugees and rich Chinese from Hong Kong.

I could go on and on with almost all the countries in the world, but I just want to give a sense of the situation which led the Canadian government in the 1960s to examine the new ethnic nature of Canada. A Royal Commission recommended that Canada should be bilingual but multicultural.

A multicultural policy was created in 1971 and in 1972 a Minister of State for Multiculturalism was appointed.

In the province of Ontario — and like the states in the United States, the Canadian provinces have very considerable powers — there is also a minister responsible for multiculturalism. His or her title has changed frequently with changes of government or cabinet shuffles; presently it is Minister of Culture, but the multicultural component is understood. Money is given by both federal and provincial governments for a variety of social and cultural programs and events. As far as art goes, it is only one small part but not insignificant, and what is significant is that many of the subsidies in various areas are not determined by a jury, but by ministerial decision.

What is multiculturalism? The terminology in Canada is opposed to the idea of a melting pot; we have a "multicultural mosaic." The whole forms a kind of wonderful San Vitale, but the individual parts remain distinct ("distinct" and "mosaic" are the two key words). The policy has generally been favorably received, especially in the city of Toronto. There has been a remarkable acceptance of the many different peoples, and while racism exists, of course, it is very little compared with what one might have expected. A great deal of color has been added to what was a rather grim Scots Presbyterian Town. Restaurants may point to one of the reasons why Torontonians have welcomed strangers. Scots cooking in public places was not something to bring joy to the heart!

To turn to the art of multiculturalism itself. You see a statue in a Toronto public park of the outstanding Ukrainian poetess, Lesnya Ukrainka, who lived from 1871 to 1913. It was erected in 1975 and it represents a conservative artistic approach with the idealized features and the classical dress. When one looks at the back of the base we find an acknowledgment of the financial aid of the Federal Minister of Multiculturalism. Most of the funds would have come from the Ukrainian community, but the government contribution was probably very important. There are quite a number of monuments erected by ethnic groups in Toronto to honor heroes and heroines and to commemorate the victims of history. The dramatic abstract sculpture put up by the Polish community has no acknowledgment to the Minister of Multiculturalism. It was probably unacceptable, as it has a political significance. It memorializes the 15,000 Polish military officers massacred at Katyn. We Canadians have had great difficulty in accepting that anything evil happened in the Soviet Union, though this is beginning to change now, and in this particular case the Soviets themselves have now acknowledged the killings.

This monument may suggest that Polish taste is more advanced than that of the Ukrainians, but a 1985 statue of Pope Paul II shows that this is not necessarily the case. This work also was not supported by multicultural funds as far as I can ascertain, presumably because of its religious significance. I have selected these two sculptures to make the point that the effects of the multicultural policy are not necessarily only direct. The whole emphasis on the importance of ethnic groups has encouraged them to have pride in their traditions, to assert themselves and to undertake activities on their own.

Another important area for art is the subsidizing of exhibition catalogues and books on artists. A book on a Polish artist, Eugene Chruscicki, states on the copyright information page that the publication was aided by a grant from the Ontario Ministry of Citizenship and Culture. It is quite lavishly illustrated with color plates, and we find portraits, historical scenes, particularly of Hussars charging on horseback, folk dancers, nudes and church decorations. Chruscicki's style is representational, often somewhat loosely brushed, similar to the style we often find in accomplished amateur artists. The author writes (and we must remember the painter was born in 1913 and died in 1984), "Chruscicki painted female nudes in a variety of poses, some reminiscent of the figures of the Renaissance. Indeed, he had a tendency, especially in his earlier pictures, to exaggerate the subjects' voluptuous appeal." This description is a fair one and indicates the artist's somewhat conventional concepts.

A second book, enigmatically entitled *EKKT*, has as subtitle *1956-1990, Art Album, Society of Estonian Artists in Toronto*, and is in fact a record of 64 artists of Estonian origin who have exhibited with this group. Each gets a double-page spread with biographical details in English and Estonian, and three reproductions, one of which is in color. There is a great range of styles, and a number of the artists fall into what we might regard as amateur status, although the number of artists is remarkable for such a small national group. Of interest to us is the beginning of the book where reproduced photographically are letters from Gerry Weiner, the Federal Minister of Multiculturalism, the Premier of Ontario, the Minister responsible for multiculturalism in Ontario, and other political figures. All these letters are full of praise for the contribution of the Estonian artists to Canadian culture. We come here to the heart of this paper. Politicians are keenly aware of the importance of the ethnic vote, and clearly this funding is related to vote getting. As I mentioned earlier the funds are usually dispensed from the ministry and the question of artistic merit is not a major criterion.

Especially in the past year, the whole question of multiculturalism has been vigorously discussed and there is no longer a general acceptance that it is a good thing. There exist two aspects: the political/social and the artistic. There have been criticisms that the policy leads to ghettoization, that children of immigrants need to learn English or French and to learn the ways of Canadian society in the work world and the political world. One thing that has been felt deeply is that if people choose to come and live in Canada and become Canadian citizens they ought to accept the principles of Canadian society or choose a different country. For example, the continuation of national hatreds from other countries is quite inappropriate. The blowing up of an Indian airliner with the deaths of 500 men, women and children by Sikhs living in Canada is a dramatic example. People feel that if this is what heritage programs encourage, we are better off without them. The war between Serbs and Croats has also produced sad consequences in Canada from people who consider themselves Serbs or Croats first, and only secondly as Canadians. Needless to say, many people of Yugoslav origin entirely reject the continuation of historic hatreds, and are happy to be in Canada away from them.

Artists bring up different questions about multiculturalism. With diminishing funds for the arts, they ask how money is allocated. Even within ethnic communities there have been criticisms of "multicultural" art. In the Ukrainian community, for example, writers have questioned the concept of Ukrainian culture as being just a matter of folk costumes, folk dances, beautifully decorated Easter eggs, and paintings of a romantically idealized Ukraine of the past. Artists and writers demand that support should be allocated on the basis of artistic merit, not ethnic pieties. These questions have come to a head recently in Ontario with the election of a new government formed by the New Democratic Party, a socialist party.

The former Minister of Culture, Rosario Marchese, has suggested that the Art Gallery of Ontario and the Royal Ontario Museum should focus on the community rather than culture in a traditional sense, and that the Art Gallery of Ontario should begin to program exhibitions from the Chinese and Portuguese communities located around the Art Gallery. He has said, "We have to admit we have a cultural bias in terms of what we mean is excellent, so I am arguing that we have to look at excellence a little differently. If it is important to a community, is it excellent? I would say yes. We say it's wonderful because it expresses that community." Mr. Marchese was criticized by the art writer of a newspaper, *The Toronto Star*, who stressed that the function of the museums and of institutions like the Canadian Opera Company was to promote culture, which is the name of

Artist Unknown, *The Katyn Memorial*,
Toronto, 1980.

Mykhaib Chershniovskij, *Memorial to
Leslya Ukrainka*, Toronto, 1975.

Mr. Marchese's office. He wrote, "The fact that something is important to the community and expresses the community does not make it art."

The art critic, Christopher Hume, was criticized in his turn by Annamarie Castrilli of the National Congress of Italian Canadians for his ignorance of the concept of multiculturalism. She went on to say that in spite of multiculturalism, "our institutions in Canada still largely reflect two predominant cultures (the Anglo-Saxon and French)." Without taking sides, one might point out that the Art Gallery of Ontario contains pictures and sculptures by Italian artists from the Renaissance, Baroque, Futurist, and contemporary periods. It is not intrinsically different from an Italian museum, except perhaps in the breadth of its collection which represents a range of European countries, so it is hardly a representative of a narrow Anglo-Saxon or French outlook.

The days when the multicultural policy was widely accepted are thus over. Artists are fighting for public funding in a period of cutbacks. The great question that remains is what constitutes excellence today: the so-called "avant-garde works" of the official art world or the works which speak to the ethnic communities. It is not an easy question to answer. I have included as examples a few works from Eastern European nations that happen to be in my neighborhood, but I could have mentioned very different ones. One of the most spectacular events in Toronto is the annual Caribana festival organized by the Caribbean community, which includes a superb parade like those in Rio and Port O'Spain in Trinidad. This visual feast may offer more art than the conceptual works in galleries, which few people enter. Multiculturalism is entering a new phase in Ontario, but what has been done offers food for thought.

Images from a Society in Transition
A brief survey of present day art in South Africa

by Esmé Berman
(South Africa)

Little known to the outside world, which shunned the indefensible apartheid program, and thus denied the country's artists international exposure, South African art of recent years has been both a medium of anguished protest and an incubator of cultural cross-pollination.

Particularly after the Soweto events of 1976, and the Biko incident of 1977, South African art was vitalized by a unique emotional energy and sense of common purpose. Visual art had but recently become a consequential occupation among the urban black communities; but white artists were no less determined to demonstrate their resistance to the prevailing political and social evils.

There will always be artists who remain detached from the realities around them. But formal exercises and stylistic innovation are robbed of meaning in a society in trauma, haunted by the questions: Who am I? Where am I? What time is it? And much of the work exhibited was distinguished from prevailing international trends by the evidence that these artists had something urgent to say and that their message was more important than were experiments with style.

Of course, those endeavors coincided with postmodernist rehabilitation of figurative idioms and thematic content. They also coincided with an international wave of new respect for ethnic artifacts and the unsophisticated output of folk artists: the United States celebrated the latter in a huge exhibition at the Corcoran in 1981. Perhaps a *fin-de-siècle* search for lost innocence was sweeping the world.

But there were more fundamental motives underlying South African attention to those neglected areas of art. The struggle for black self-determination was intensifying, and with it the need to regain pride in black cultural heritage. Art historians became aware of an unexplored dimension of South African expression; and gallery directors discovered a receptive market for the untutored works of black rural artists.

The innocent sincerity of such items was eminently appealing and the effect on urban professionals was unforeseen. Before long, "transitionalism" was a dominant artistic movement. The former drive among both black and white artists to keep abreast of North Atlantic trends gave way, in large part, to the urge to identify with an emergent local, multicultural ethos.

South African art, even at its most eclectic, has always mirrored the environment from which it stemmed. Today, it offers a more challenging reflection — an image of the complex spirit and the painful gestation of a new society.

(The above was the only text prepared for the AICA Congress. What follows is a summary of the visual information in, and associated commentary about, the 60 slides projected. The names in parentheses refer to artists represented by those slides).

Because South African art has been isolated for so long, an extended chapter —if not its entire history — has evaded international critical attention. Any attempt to unplug the vacuum within the limits of a 15-minute paper cannot but result in misleading generalization and simplistic analysis of the complexities entailed. It is preferable to substitute a range of relevant images and, as far as possible, allow them to speak for themselves.

The images are thus the text of this paper. They have not been selected for their aesthetic import (and many major figures are, regrettably, ignored). They are presented, not as masterpieces, but as messages, with multiple inherent meanings. And they fall into several categories:

Social Comment

South Africa was colonized by Europe in 1652. During the ensuing centuries, the country has been home to two disparate cultures, indeed two Worlds: a First World and a Third World, epitomized here in the early 20th-century painting of a typical white, urbanized, Victorian woman (George Winkles) and the bronze sculpture of a black rural tribesman, playing a traditional musical instrument (Anton van Wouw).

No attention was paid by white urban society to any evidence of an indigenous black artistic tradition. The ritual and functional art produced in rural tribal communities was, nevertheless, far less sophisticated and far less prolific than the now-familiar art of West and Central Africa.

With the passage of time, various white artists (such as Alexis Preller) became immersed in the mystique of Africa and explored the African theme in much of their expressive output. Conversely, however, the few black artists who made an impact on the urban exhibition scene (such as Gerard Sekoto), tended to adopt Western conventions and to depict conventional urban scenes, which differed from prevailing Western genre studies only in the dissimilarity of black "township" surroundings and experience.

That pattern continued (accompanied in the 1960s by important conceptual innovations, referred to below). But during the 1970s, a period of intense political upheaval and distress, the social consciousness of artists, black and white, was raised dramatically. Though few artists — especially blacks — dared to exhibit blatantly confrontational imagery, the growing mood of protest was manifested in various oblique references and/or metaphorical images exhibited by both race groups, e.g. Malcolm Payne's screenprinted ID card, *Color Test*; Mslaba Dumile's *Fear*; Paul Stopforth's *Cowl*.

In July 1979, prominent members of the South African arts community organized a conference at the University of Cape Town at which issues of artistic responsibility were aired. (Nadine Gordimer was a participant.) At that conference a resolution was taken "to work as diligently as possible to effect change toward a post-apartheid society."

Thereafter, the incidence of protest art became increasingly widespread. And, as tensions rose within the severely troubled society, so the images grew more aggressive and the anguish more painfully pronounced.

Even the works of previously abstract or primarily formalist artists (such as sculptor Edoardo Villa) assumed a confrontational character. And images of township riots, police brutality, interrogation horrors, human suffering and dispossession began to dominate the major exhibitions. (*Inter alia*: Michael Goldberg's installation, *Untitled* [The Family Bath]; David Brown's sculptures, *One Man and his Dog* and *Procession* [War Machines]; Berenice Michelow's *Promenade* [Police Dog]; Norman Catherine's *Apocalypse 1985*; William Kentridge's *The Conservationists' Ball* and his anguished *Heads*; Sybille Nagel's *My Houses are Burning*).

The list goes on; the content shifts between political and social suffering (Peggy Delport's District Six mural; Neville Hoad's appropriation of a "work wanted" poster). But the unbearable intensity of protest art could not be sustained indefinitely; there was already evidence of tendencies toward cliché and hollow propaganda.

Propitiously, other potentially therapeutic developments were occurring: on the one hand, a continuation of an earlier cross-cultural stylistic trend; on the other, the "discovery" of a neglected tradition; both engendering a new phase of Afrocentric "transitionalism."

Cross-Pollination

A central figure in a movement that began during the 1960s and was described then as "Africanism," the white artist Cecil Skotnes, sought, in his unique engraved wood panels, to exemplify the dual heritage of Africa and Europe, to which he, as a South African, was heir. His stylistic influence is reflected in the works of some of his students (e.g. Lucky Sibiya), and his Africanism was shared by fellow members of the Amadlozi Group. (Amadlozi means "Spirit of our Ancestors.")

A related trend toward blending of traditional African (Negro) and Western conventions has been perpetuated in the works of various younger artists; among them are Leonard Matsoso and, marginally, Helen Sebidi.

But a new direction was initiated in the mid-'80s. It was stimulated primarily by a bench-mark exhibition, sponsored by BMW and assembled by a single curator, Ricky Burnett, who included all the significant urban artists, black and white. But — more auspiciously — he also went out into the field and gathered works from previously ignored rural sources. The resulting show drew critical attention, for the first time ever, to a vital black ethnic art tradition. Originating from artists who served their communities by sculpting objects for initiation and other ritual functions and who were virtually unaware of, and certainly untutored in, Western conventions, these works arrived on the urban scene like a breath of fresh air (works by, among others, Johannes Maswanganyi, Nelson Makhuba, Phatuma Seoka, Noria Mabaso, Jackson Hlungwane, Owen and Goldwyn Ndou).

Inevitably, voracious adoption of those ethnic artists by commercial galleries invoked the latent threat of commercialization and debasement of the original integrity. "Transitionalism" became a buzz-word. But it also brought about a re-examination of South African art; and it led, in 1988, to a large exhibition at the Johannesburg Art Gallery, entitled "The Neglected Tradition."

David Brown, war machine from *Procession*, 1985.

Norman Catherine,
Red Rubber Man,
1990.

Today

As South Africa emerges from its Eurocentric, colonialist, and oppressive ethos, a new society is being forged, and it is seeking its identity. The several streams of cultural convention and expression flow alongside and across each other. There are black and white artists working along abstract formalist paths (Tony Nkotsi, Jenny Stadler). There are black "naives" attracting growing attention (Tommy Motswai, Clifford Mpai, Alfred Thoba, Phillip Rikhotso). There are those, black and white, who blend elements of the urban and the rural streams (Billy Makubela, Norman Catherine, Willie Bester, Andries Botha).

And, even where the formal elements retain an essentially mainstream Eurocentric character, there is nonetheless a profound revision of the text of serious South African art. Perceived reality has undergone a sea-change. Traditional Western genres, such as still-life, landscape, portraiture, and history painting, are being revisited, recorded, and invested with altered metaphorical allusions (Keith Dietrich, Marion Arnold, Karel Nel, Robert Hodgins, Clive van den Berg, Penelope Siopis). Furthermore, particularly in the work of Siopis, traditional images are being deconstructed, as she reviews the influence of stereotypical perceptions from the past on the race and gender prejudices that prevail in South Africa, and elsewhere, today.

Despite the dilemmas posed by the diversity of cultural conventions and the derailment of former critical canons — dilemmas by no means unique to this particular society — South African artists are engaging in what may be one of the more successful of the international exercises in multiculturalism. It is worthy of respectful examination.

Contemporary Creativity in West Africa: The Case of Senegal

by Amadou Gueye Ngom
(Senegal)

In contemporary African sanctuaries, as well as in everyday life, the Bible and the Koran have taken the place of the Word of God from those who breathe the spirit of our original divine patrons. These gods, first burned in the name of Islam by Arab conquerors in the 10th century, then transplanted by colonial regimes and missionaries, were later dissected by Braque and Picasso, who saw nothing but the fire that consumed their restless curiosity for an answer, however partial, to the academies of Cézanne.

If I were ethnocentric, I would applaud and gloat with pride contemplating Picasso's *Demoiselles d'Avignon*. In truth, however, I reproach these Cubists for having committed such sacrilege against my Gods in reducing them to mere *objets d'art*, static and numb — albeit saved from termites — in the climatized galleries of European and American museums.

Only criticism ignores these mistakes and misunderstandings, persisting in speaking of our ancient tribal fetishes as "primitive" negro art. And the worst is that our own artists participate in this ruse, not only accepting the term a "primitive" (why not seen as an insult in comparison with "first" or "original?") but the sterile polemic that marginalizes the subject, as well.

Henceforth, to which gods will the African continent subscribe? With the decrees of independence that showered Africa in the '60s, we should have the right to claim new gods bearing names such as *Republic, International Monetary Fund, World Bank*, the national anthem and the national flag. Such inane gods present themselves in Latin or Anglo-Saxon tongues to a people who have been forced to abandon their own languages, forced by the exigencies of the economic market to follow the voice of internationalism or commit *hara-kiri*.

It is in such circumstances that sub-Saharan Africa, particularly West Africa, takes to the task of making art. I mean to speak of art as an isolated act. To this end, the first and fatal stage is accomplished. In Senegal, for example, the creation of all sculpture in a school of art exactly replicates according to its pedagogical values that which has been done in France or Italy since the 19th century: copy this Greco-Roman plaster cast, study drapery before attempting to work from live models.

The first International Festival of Negro Arts organized by Senegal in 1966 revealed to critics the limits of such an education.

Returning to the case in question is the arrival of Pierre Lod, a libertarian of the arts, founder of l'Ecole de Poto Poto of the Congo, and whose instruction begins as follows:

> You, as black Africans, have nothing to learn from any formal academicism, nor any foreign model. Here is paint and here are brushes. Express yourselves!

The subsequent result, without naming it specifically, was a sort of surrealism "made in Africa." This proved prodigious: some of both the best and the worst, and inclusively hermetic (totally immune) to Western criticism that does nothing but make references to masks, myths, tales, and legends of Africa. A terrible discourse that is, in sum, naive and anecdotal, and, moreover, merely imitates without inspiration or talent Picasso and his School of Paris fans: Hartung, Manessier, Hajdu, Viera da Silva, Zao Wu K., Soulages. Even we, as critics, trained in the school of Western thought and the theories of Bergson, rely on such an interpretation in examining the work of our compatriots.

Due to the lack of traditional references to concepts considered albo-European, the black African artist finds himself faced with a terrible alternative: whether or not to sink into the rules and methods of international art without having the means to play the game of originality, that is to say, an ethnic signature, which is, ironically, precisely what Western criticism reproaches him for when it does not embrace folklore or ethnology.

However, no serious criticism would even dream of expounding on the Catalan temperament in Picasso's work, or the tortured Slavic soul and pessimism of Soutine. But the maxim of Max-Paul Fouchet says justly that art criticism (alas) is still based on literature, not on the examination of plastic quality.

Our artists today, tired of being sent back to the masks of their ancestors, primarily adopt, albeit unconsciously, the iconoclastic idiom of a Kandinsky for whom art was, according to Edward Lucie Smith, "a way of expressing one's identity or intimate necessity."

Yet the greatest challenge to our artists is to have to justify themselves: first, in relation to the West (Euramerica); second, in relation to themselves and their own audience; and finally, in the face of the imperious necessity of inventing new media and pigments.

We have already established the Eurocentric indifference of Euramerica to all that is not albo-European. As far as the African public is concerned, they identify only with naive figuration or realist representations of *les petits metiers* — hairdressers in the street, rotisseries of meat — or in *la peinture cruelle*, the foundations of colonialism that lack nothing in comparison with the collaborators of the Vichy regime.

It is thus that today our artists invent new materials: tree bark, jute, new pigments, mineral or vegetable, like Cola juice — created by the artist Youssouph Bath, a painter of the Ivory Coast who rejects systematic oil painting because he does not find it either noble or intense enough for his lyrical expression.

After 30 years of independence, albeit nominal, contemporary art in West Africa always sells badly, to say the least. Our artists in effect have not always had the means for their own freedom of expression: paper, canvas, film are expensive imports. Consider that a meter's length of canvas, two or three brushes, and the fundamental palette take up one third of the monthly salary of a West African office worker; that is to say one tenth of the monthly income of a French worker.

But who will buy the work? Only the tourist, the predator of modern times. The work will be like a hunting trophy, mounted in some living room merely to attest to its owner's trip to Africa. And this degenerates further into "Airport Art." Like a lottery, it doesn't cost the tourist much and yields much for the artist.

We will no longer accept this type of expedience. From now on we want an art inscribed by criteria of universal value, that reflects us all as powerfully joined to one another, and to all humanity.

Translated from the French by Lara Ferb

Changing Cultural Identities
Report from the tolerant Netherlands

by Tineke Reijnders
(The Netherlands)

Rembrandt was an exception. He stayed in Amsterdam all his life once he had left his hometown, Leiden. His contemporaries blamed him for not having undertaken the Grand Tour: he would surely remain an illiterate. Traveling and even migrating seem the rule for artists throughout the ages. Born under Saturn, born to explore the freedom of the mind, shouldn't the artist be fundamentally skeptical towards geographical frontiers? The Dutch-American painter Karel Appel formulated it this way at the opening of his 70th birthday retrospective in the Hague in 1991: "I had to leave Holland and break off everything I had built up so far in order to force myself to a new freedom." We all know dozens of artists with a *caesura* of countries in their curriculum vitae: Picasso, Duchamp, de Kooning, Kounellis, to name a few.

The free choice of settling and working is the positive side of the story. At the same time there is another side: artists whose immigrations are the result of forced circumstances. The reasons are manifold and range from political or economical refuge to former colonial relationship and to the search for a tolerant or modernist climate. In the Netherlands the free and the forced settlers live and work without obvious distinction. They live and work there in great numbers because the Dutch society seems to offer an attractive milieu for artists. Among artists, multiculturism is far more extensive than in our already strongly mixed society. Talking of the complex occurrence of different cultural identities in the arts has general social implications as well as specific art aspects. The reason why I want to consider the situation more closely is an actual one.

Alongside the general attention to the recent accessibility of Eastern Europe, which has in our country resulted in conferences, congresses, exhibitions, and exchange programs, an awareness arose of the divergent backgrounds of the artists living in the Netherlands. Never before had this been a topic. Our society is rather harmonious and as we have no racial conflicts there is nothing to fight for. Compared to America and England,

Holland is in a special position. But without conflicts we still have to deal with the question. Cultural differences became the subject of an event called *Het Klimaat*, or "The Climate," which took place from May to August of 1991. With the museum De Lakenhal of Leiden as the central location, a rich profusion of exhibitions occupied galleries and art spaces throughout the country. The qualification for selection was, apart from artistic quality, the place of birth, which had to be from abroad. So among the participants of the central exhibition were a sculptor and former Vietnamese boat refugee; a sculptor who spent her first nine years in Turkey; a conceptual artist who left the Hungarian university because of the lack of perspective of that time; an Australian painter of Russian-Polish Jewish origin; a painter born in the Moluccas, part of the former Dutch colony Indonesia; a Yugoslavian (actually Croatian) artist; and an English sculptress. Three of the seven stayed after a post-academic training, two are children of immigrants, and one was by chance selected from a refugee camp.

Most of them are young and eager to participate in a museum show. But some were skeptical, as were some critics. Believing in cultural identities is a romantic idea, said the artists, and presenting them in a context of strangers is dressing a mental ghetto, said the critics. Undeniably, without this initiative of the provincial authorities of Zuid-Holland, these young artists would not have shown in a museum at this stage of their career. Does this mean that the benevolence of the province is bigger than the talents or have they been overlooked until now because they are not Dutch by birth? It was the last factor that gave rise to this special event. It was organized by the active Dutch Gate Foundation (whose main purpose is to arouse Western interest for Eastern artists). Positive, apart from the broad participation, was the complete renunciation of any theoretical or programmatic approach. The presentation side-by-side in 30 shows of artists originating from all parts of the world — America, Western Europe, Eastern Europe, Africa, Asia, Australia — was of course an important statement. But exactly the fact that everything was open and unpoliticized kept this first attempt to mention certain things far from unfavorable polemics.

Why should the question be handled with care? First because of social reasons. A kind of national embarrassment exists towards certain groups of immigrants. We feel ashamed of the colonial past; we did not do enough to protect the Jews in World War II; we cannot handle, at least in an emotional sense, the countless Turkish and Moroccan families that joined their working fathers in the '70s. As everybody panics for fear of being suspected of discrimination, we rely on the political solution to this embarrassment, which is money: money for mosques, for sports clubs, for education, and for integration. Integration is the official goal. So multiculturism is controlled in a clean, distant way, directed toward the disappearance of the differentiation.

Het Klimaat invited quite the opposite. All the differences were named, enumerated, and the personal shades of cultural identities exhibited instead of concealed. This open-minded attention to both the phenomenon and the artists occurred obviously at the right moment. Soon after *Het Klimaat*, a leading newspaper started a series in which Holland-based artists were portrayed. Other shows were prepared. The Netherlands Office for Visual Arts organized an exhibition (*Rhizôme*) in the Haags Gemeentemuseum with the participation of Anish Kapoor and the Israeli-Dutch Joseph Semah, among others.

Except for the ongoing discussions about the best conditions for a multicultural cohabitation, the question for some people is how the disappearance of the Western European borders will affect national identity, as against the resurrection of so many national identities in Eastern Europe.

Did the art works shown in *Het Klimaat* tell us something about the way an artist deals with his or her roots? Not at all apparently. The artists are focused on the Western, international tradition. They consider, perhaps due to their Dutch art education, any emphasis on their different roots as a distraction from what they want to say. They communicate within the province of *l'art pour l'art*. The Turkish-Dutch sculptor Hulya Vilmaz was furious when a delegation tried to buy one of her pieces with the money designated for a policy of preference for minorities.

Nevertheless critics scrutinized the *oeuvres* for exotic impulses, while the context of the event consisted in the incongruity of Western and non-Western codes, because even without a theoretical base, the catalogue, with articles by Jean-Hubert Martin (*Magiciens de la Terre*) and Rasjeed Araeen (chief editor of *Third Text*) left no doubt about it, nor did the numerous conferences and debates.

You see how confusing the situation is. And yet a leap ahead is made.

First, because the topic of multiculturism has entered the art discourse, so that the question can be translated from politics and groups to the private experience of the individual. Secondly, this approach has resulted in more

Joseph Semah, *Vleeshal II*, wooden frame, glass and ram's horn, 1991, Collection De Vleeshal, Middleburg.

Joseph Semah, *Vleeshal II (Beli Bassar)*, iron and sheepskulls, 1991.

professional attention for artists unnoticed before. Thirdly, because the focus on Western standards will soon fatigue them and call for more differentiated approaches (as has already been shown by older self-confident artists such as Moroccan painter Nour-Eddine Jarram, in whose paintings Islamic decoration is becoming dominant). A general problem however is the struggle with the chimera of contemporary art, which invites a slowed-down, abstract formal language and more emotional distance than music, film, or literature. A talent of Rembrandt's caliber is yet to be found in another discipline: that of sports. When the admirable Surinam-Dutch sportsman Ruud Gullit dedicated his "world's best soccer player" trophy to Nelson Mandela, at the time still a prisoner, he really affected public sensibility.

At this moment visual artists often experience the modern aesthetic bounds as subcutaneous stumbling blocks. Only when artists operating in Western Europe succeed in developing a personal response towards these assumed demands, can they freely imply their own background. Joseph Semah is one of the few. He relates all creative activity to his cultural roots. As a descendant of the Babylonian Jews, who, far from the temple had to rely on the texts, Hebrew characters are an important starting point for him. He rejects modernism, considers contemporary art suffocating, and bridges the gap with centuries-old ideas. Life, in his view, is the small margin that death leaves us. When Semah was invited to make a site-specific work in the gothic Meathall in Middleburg, it came as no surprise that he took this butchers' hall for an altar. He transferred the surface of the floor (the content of this medieval market-place), reduced to one tenth, to the small backyard, exposing it to the changing influences of the weather. Besides installing sheep skulls, he divided the floor sculpture into pieces, each representing a letter which constituted the Hebrew word for Meathall.

Is the rejection of modernism the answer for the realization of differentiated cultural expressions? This remains a question. We are only at the beginning, at the point of realizing how impossible it is to speak in general terms. For artists, it is a private affair.

A common denominator could be the fact that abrupt changes and extreme comments elsewhere make us prudent. If Dutch art lacks the harassing features that attract international interest, it is because The Netherlands is a good refuge, with freedom, democracy, and a relatively small gap between rich and poor. However, as far as the state of art is concerned, things are in motion and new viewpoints cannot be stopped.

Multiculturalism and the Search for the Authentic Self

by Ann-Sargent Wooster
(United States)

When video art began as an art discipline in the 1960s, it combined art with politics and was dedicated to being an alternative voice and vision to mainstream media. Not all work was political, but the decision to use the tools of broadcast television as a new art medium was a radical one that led directly to what we now call multiculturalism. One of the goals of the earliest practitioners was to right the wrongs of mainstream television and enfranchise the previously disenfranchised, giving voices and faces to causes and people who were not included in mainstream media. To some extent this meant putting video equipment in the hands of grass roots organizations here and abroad. More often video artists, a marginal class existing poorly in all the old meanings of the word, from Grotowski's toward a poor theater (which could be rephrased as simplicity) to the personal poverty of bank balances reading in the red, became transcribers of "outsider" culture. Often this was because their political beliefs or sympathies lay with their subjects or because they themselves came from those backgrounds.

One of the earliest sources for what is currently called multiculturalism is the feminist practice of examining art and media and analyzing its forms of representation. An early feminist criticism of television and other forms of media was that it did not reflect women as they really were. Part of the art resulting from feminist analysis lay in taking the tools of representation from male hands and representing themselves. By asserting their right to a place in front of the mirror, women expanded the populations mirrored in video art. The feminist assertion that the personal is political has also had an impact on the subject matter of avant-garde film and video focusing on personal issues. Over time, women's issues expanded and included other alternative cultural perspectives.

Early on, video art divided into fine and applied art, with the documentary being an expression of the latter. Over time, video documentaries have come to resemble the classic non-fiction documentary film style set down in the 1920s by John Grierson. Although that style has established a no-nonsense format that seems to standardize causes, there have been innovations in the documentary technique. However, they rarely make it into museums unless they reflect a highly subjective meditation on an issue. The exceptions are usually presented in the form of personal inquiry or a highly personal interpretation of a subject that has autobiographical, idiosyncratic or diary-like sections, all of which challenge the veneer of objectivity that has marked the documentary style. Tapes like Juan Downey's "Hard Times and Culture, Part I," an imagistic analysis of fin-de-siècle Vienna, and Steve Fagin's "The Machine That Killed Bad People," an unusual look at Marcos's Philippines, offer alternative perspectives. Indeed the need to rewrite or analyze the real world in new ways was so great in 1991 that approximately half the film and videoworks in the Whitney Biennial could be regarded as variations on the documentary.

The significance of Jennie Livingston's popular documentary film *Paris is Burning*, with its voyeuristic look at an underground culture of transvestite balls, can not be underestimated. It has escaped the consignment of documentaries on the sidelines and has been shown in both movie theaters and museums because its intimate look at the new transvestite balls dovetails with the current emphasis on expanding cultural perspectives generally. Livingston shows us the evolving face of that world. Instead of the fake breasts, ball gowns, bouffant hair-dos and heavy make-up of older "Queens," the current phenomenon of "voguing" is to pass for "normal." Late at night, after most of New York is sleeping, the contestants compete in the categories of young executive, school girl, preppie, military officer, et cetera. The idea of seeing outer appearance as a mask that covers a hollow or hidden self is not new. The idea of gender roles as an artificial construct imposed by society has long been a staple of feminist criticism and art. The success of some of these men as women, going so far as to have careers as high fashion models, revitalizes and expands the ongoing postmodern discourse on gender.

As ethnic diversity and multiculturalism challenged the white, male, Eurocentric version of history and became the staple of social studies curriculums, so too has video art expanded to include African Americans, Asian Americans and Native Americans, as well as gender preference and age. Early video theory postulated the video screen as a mirror. Today the face in the mirror is as often Black, Red, Yellow, Brown, Old, Gay, or female as White and male. Indeed, in the film and video program at the 1991 Whitney Biennial, artists are often at a disadvantage if they are not a "significant other" to the dominant culture. I might add that there is a deliberate element of irony in suggesting current film and video has a multicultural basis. The proliferation of low-cost consumer equipment, which in theory might have opened the field to a greater group of people, has had limited impact on the upper echelons of film and video art, where high production values with the concomitant big-ticket budgets have been the mark of excellence since the early '80s. The members of this small group of successful film and video artists are predominantly white and male, although there are significant Asian and female inroads to this club.

Black has never been one of the dominant colors of the avant-garde, but the 1991 Whitney program addressed issues of race from inside and outside. Tony Coke and Donald Trammel, Marlon Riggs and Lawrence Andrews all deal with issues of what it means to be a black man in white society. In the video "Fade to Black," Coke and Trammel layer three overlapping and conflicting kinds of information that point to the inability of blacks to find a positive mirror of themselves in mainstream media. Soundtracks, sound effects and speeches by black leaders are heard while printed captions on the screen, such as, "There is nothing for me to see. . . . Why am I analyzing this film where I am silent? . . ." dissect the unseen commentator's feelings as a black man and a black filmmaker about being typecast and excluded from a world that is as white as snow. This "face-less" presentation clearly reinforces the makers' feelings of facelessness in white media.

No one deals more powerfully and completely with the issues of being black, gay, and living under the threat of AIDS than Marlon Riggs in "Tongues Untied." Riggs combines poetry with performance art and por-traiture to tell his own (and by extension others') story of the development of racial and sexual awareness. In early video theory, the TV screen was postulated as a mirror, but if you are black and gay your face was not reflected in the television mirror. Unlike other work dealing with ethnic origins, Riggs forces the audience and most importantly himself to con-front the black face he and society have tried to will to invisibility. His use of poetry by Essex Hemphill, himself, and others provides a lyrical yet angry depiction of the emotional landscape of growing up black and gay in America, a landscape where "it was easier to be angry than to be hurt" and the body "contains as much anger as water." At times Riggs's rhyth-mic, repetitious use of vernacular language becomes a waterfall of words. He follows his own and others' lives as they moved from isolated boy-hoods to gay liberation and an openly gay lifestyle. He shows how the *danse macabre* of AIDS colors being gay today, including a black and white montage of newspaper obituaries of friends and people involved in the tape. Riggs's most powerful tool is his use of the television monitor as an acute portrait space, collapsing the distance between the idea of black gay life and the reality, as we see the faces and close-up mouths (as close to us as our faces in a mirror, or a lover's lips moving in for a kiss) using radical and sexual epithets and words of love and fear.

Watching Riggs's tape in the cool, dark cube of the Whitney's film and video gallery, it is easy to forget how daring the showing of this kind of explicit yet natural depiction of gay life and homoeroticism still is. Just as Mapplethorpe's photographs continue to be at the center of censorship issues in the arts, Riggs's tape "Tongues Untied" has also been subject to the backlash of censorship. For its recent screening on PBS's P.O.V. (Point of View) documentary series, many stations either refused to show the tape or insisted it be shown at a later hour than its already- late 10 P.M. The good news is that Cincinnati, Ohio, the center of the recent controversy over Mapplethorpe's photographs, showed the tape on prime time. Jack Dominic, the program director, said, "It's not the kind of show I'd sit down and watch myself. But that's why people have on and off buttons. Choosing what people should watch — that's not the business we're in."

In different ways, Lawrence Andrews and Victor Masayesva address the conflict between mainstream concepts of knowledge and equally compelling alternative views that are usually marginalized and dismissed as "less than." Both tapes demonstrate the validity of "the other." In "Strategies for the development of/Redefining the purpose served/Art in the age of . . . aka the making of the towering inferno," Andrews alternates between a sculpture workshop where people are making ceramic heads of popular culture heroes like Michael Jackson and Diana Ross and interviews with art historians and scholars. He contrasts ordinary people's ways of relating to celebrities with scholarly readings of art, to emphasize the essential lifelessness and alienation of this kind of intellectualism. In "Place of Chasms" Masayesva contrasts scientific and aesthetic interpretations of American Indian pottery with traditional American Indian Culture. A group of young Hopi women taking part in a Smithsonian project using the latest scientific apparatus are contrasted with scenes of another young Indian woman who, made to stay home by her grandmother, learns how to dig clay and make pots using tribal techniques. In Masayesva's equation the importance of the living American Indian tradition with its enduring craft skills and spiritual beliefs is shown to have the same or greater significance than the dominant culture's scientific methods of analyzing culture.

Asian Americans Janice Tanaka and Rea Tajiri look back at their parents' experience in America, filling in spaces that have been left out of both their personal and cultural history. Tajiri's "History and Memory" examines her family's experiences in the World War II Japanese Internment camps in America saying, "I had never been there but I had a memory of it." In "Memories from the Department of Amnesia," Tanaka uses image processing, special effects, dream sequences and family photographs to peel away the layers of her mother's life. Tanaka creates a powerful and largely new portrait of what it meant to be a Japanese-American woman in the '40s, '50s, and '60s.

For film and video, the issue of multiculturalism goes beyond the issues of ethnic representation that are staples of the intellectual industry. As we deepen our understanding of social dynamics and expand our vision of society to acknowledge the realities of rape, battered women and child abuse, avant-garde techniques are used to create art out of these previously hidden cultures. As artists encounter Dante's dark wood mid-way in their life's journey, childhood has emerged as a major theme. Some artists, such as Mike Kelley and Ericka Beckmann in "Blind Country," make a fetish out of acting childishly. In the light of new knowledge about the vulnerabilities of children to all forms of abuse, several videomakers analyze this landscape of remembered pain. In "Belladonna," Beth B and her mother Ida Applebroog create a powerful and haunting evocation of psychic distress and childhood abuse that is very real, although based on an abstract tapestry of words. Alternating head shots of various male and female adults reading fragments of texts by Sigmund Freud, Joseph Mengele, Joel Steinberg and others create a growing crescendo of claustrophobic horror as the tales of the "witnesses" unfold against the velvety blackness of the darkened movie theater. The lasting horror of their stories is thrown into larger relief by the repeated chorus of the innocent victim, a young boy. Looking straight at the audience he repeats the damaged child's lullaby, "I'm not a bad person."

Two decades of feminism have focused on the issues of the young and middle-aged, topics such as the meaning of the erotic gaze, rape, childcare, pornography, and equality of employment. As our population ages, new subcultures are created. In a society that prizes the beauty of the young, the menopausal women is invisible or, worse, is seen as mad or disposable. Weaving together tangents and asides commenting on multiple and

Jennie Livingston, still from *Paris Is Burning*, videotape, 1990.

fragmentary narrative threads, Yvonne Rainer's films have dealt with the difference between real women's lives and the fictions society invents about gender and politics. In her latest film, *Privilege,* she gives speech to the basically unspeakable: menopause. Rainer's film is daring in speaking about this taboo, but her viewpoint is a subjective interpretation of menopause. Her film points to one of the problems of borrowing the term multiculturalism from the areas of textbook and curriculum reform and applying it to avant-garde structures. The language of avant-garde is personal and hermetic. It often partakes of the luxury of developing inner visions and private syntax. As a more diverse group of artists begin to make work that reflects their racial and social experiences we will have a more varied body of work, but not one that substantially alters the modernist idiom. The dominant visual language of avant-garde film and video presents all experience through a glass darkly. The essential abstraction of avant-garde film and video homogenizes the experiences of Black, Latino, Asian, Gay, Female, young, old, and/or disabled artists and presents the diversity of experience through a kinetic kaleidoscope. Yet there is room for growth and change. As chaos theory tells us, when an object or experience is examined closely its wholeness vanishes and is replaced by multiplying shapes that have never been seen before.

Art, Politics, and Ethnicity

by Elaine A. King
(United States)

> *"If art matters at all, it will shed light on*
> *something more than itself . . . ."*
> — Roger Lipsey

In my role as a respondent I wear the hat of Devil's Advocate — reading the arguments and issues presented in the foregoing essays yet always thinking, "but on the other hand." During an uncertain time of massive social, political, and cultural upheaval, it is imperative to ask numerous serious questions and to proceed with caution.

As we analyze the present state of culture and the impact of postmodernist theory on the art of today, a re-examination of the modernist paradigm is also essential. It is always easier and simpler to reject and discard than to find new solutions. Let us not forget the lessons of history concerning extreme and precipitous reactions.

I resist the postmodern canon which supports the "anything and everything goes" position about art: to label something art for the sake of "window" opening is merely a lame act. While postmodernist revisionism has afforded artists often associated with the "other" a new identity and has helped to clarify and expand the narrow definitions of art (cutting across history, class, and race), it has also contributed to volumes of excessive theoretical rationalization. All too frequently impressive statements are written about questionable and even third-rate works of art: mediocrity is justified because powerful critics use the works of weak artists as a means to support particular agendas and theories. In resolved works of art, a productive tension prevails throughout the formal structure, the content, and the intent of the artist.

Currently, we are living through an era which can be compared with the state of young, euphoric love. However, can one imagine living today with that 14-year old one idealized and adored as a teenager? Walls and barriers have crumbled in Eastern Europe, windows for opportunity are now open. This is the beginning of a long process and hope has become a key word of the '90s. But, hope is so powerful an emotion that it can blind and easily lead one to a false perception of reality. In his book *The Use and Misuse of Art,* Jacques Barzun cautions the reader about the dual nature of art, pointing out that if it has the potential to redeem, it also has the potential to destroy. We must keep in mind that the counter side to hope is despair. Frequently the latter surfaces more quickly then expected. After the tidal wave of global multicultural activity begins to subside, what will the larger issues be? How will critical discourse affect the new definitions of an international culture?

One cannot deny that the emergence of multiculturalism needs to be reckoned with as a force both in the art world and in the larger, ever-changing global society. During this critical time of complex international shifts, evolutions, and developments, citizens of the United States particularly need to become more aware of the history, customs, values, traditions, myths, and fears of many nations we have long ignored. There is no denying that a white,Western-European educational system has shaped and influenced our social, economic, and political consciousness. And there is no denying that for nearly 50 years this Western system has dominated the production of art and its surrounding critical discourse by manipulating and controlling the canons defining aesthetic judgment. Only by becoming open to a broader spectrum of information can we begin to enhance our perceptions and participate intelligently in a complex international dialogue.

On the other hand, people from other countries, including Western and Eastern Europe, need to transcend their fiction-derived, narrow view of the United States. Reducing our culture to simplistic clichés and characterizing our society as notable for fast food, bad manners, shoddy production, and the trendy art of Andy Warhol, Jeff Koons, Michael Jackson, and Madonna is to be guilty of just another form of micro-ignorance. There is no denying that such characteristics do pertain to some segments of our culture; but an onion has many layers and to stop at the top layer is to shortchange what one is looking at and oneself. Yet, many curators and critics from other countries continue to harbor such narrow generalizations about the United States. They develop exhibitions and statements that focus mainly on the world of Pop Art, pop culture, and a throwaway society.

Acknowledging multiculturalism cannot become a substitute for substance, or an excuse for the absence of quality. Intention, words, and rhetorical rationalization are not sufficient when one elects to communicate through or about a visual language. To settle for heavy-handed ideology is to blatantly supplant visual statement. Ultimately as in the childhood game, "The Farmer in the Dell," a finished work of art is like the cheese — it must stand alone!

The exotic, the unfamiliar, the new are always seductive and tempting. But once the patina of time has weathered them, what is left and what is of importance? The way we proceed now will determine the future canons of culture. To move too quickly can cause one to stumble and blunder. The time at hand poses many interesting challenges, but let us not be overwhelmed and blinded by our very enthusiasm for multicultural art, for political relevance, and the celebration of ethnicity. We cannot with one move immediately rectify years of isolation and limitation. The process of learning about others has to be a long one. It cannot be rushed without a loss of perspective.

Part II:
The Politicization of Art and Criticism

Antagonizing Modernism:
Art Criticism's Hegemonic Postmodernism

by Amelia Jones
(United States)

In 1980, Clement Greenberg defined postmodern art as "art . . . that [is] no longer self-critical," and postmodernists as "a more dangerous threat to high art than old-time philistines ever were." Greenberg is clear about the sources for this depravation of culture: "The yearning for relaxation [in modernist standards] became outspoken in presumedly avant-garde circles for the first time with Duchamp and Dada and then in certain aspects of Surrealism. [And] it was with Pop Art that it became a fully confident expression."[1]

In 1982, Hal Foster situated postmodern appropriation art as "aligned with the critique of the institution of art based on the presentational strategies of the Duchampian readymade." Of course Foster, unlike Greenberg, *values* this type of postmodernism for its radical deconstruction of the tenets of modernism. For Foster, representative of New York-based hegemonic critical formulation of postmodernism, Duchamp acts as originator of a set of practices that work precisely to undermine modernism, particularly in its Greenbergian guise.[2]

The strong parallel between Greenberg's and Foster's configurations of post-Abstract Expressionist practices begs the question of whether postmodernism as currently understood in art discourse is as free from Greenbergian ideologies as it is determined to be by Foster and other younger generation writers featured in the New York-based journals *October* and *Artforum*. This paper attempts to address the question of postmodernism in art discourse, arguing that, in fact, currently accepted theoretical models of postmodernism in the visual arts are in many ways ideologically continuous with aspects of the Greenbergian modernism they claim to supersede. I propose here that these theories of postmodernism perpetuate a binary logic that is eminently Greenbergian, maintaining oppositional categories to argue for progressive, "good" practices by opposing them to devalued, "regressive" ones. This logic is typified again by Foster, who writes, "in American cultural politics today there are at least two positions on postmodernism now in place. . . . Neoconservative postmodernism advocates a return to representation. . . . Poststructuralist postmodernism. . . [clearly for Foster a progressive mode] rests on a critique of representation."[3] These theories are also insufficiently suspicious of the identifiably modernist and masculinist notions of authorship and value they claim to reject. Paradoxically — just as Greenberg does — they frequently identify Marcel Duchamp as *paternal* source for the ostensibly anti-masculinist discourses and practices of postmodernism.

This relatively new hegemonic discourse privileges postmodern art practices for their alleged refutation or subversion of three interdependent aspects of Greenbergian modernism: Greenberg's opposition of high art to a devalued mass culture, his construction of a genealogy of progressively pure modernist objects, and his reliance on inflexible standards of mediumistic integrity to determine aesthetic "quality." Crucially to their situating of postmodernism in opposition to Greenbergian modernism, these critiques draw from the confluence of feminist and poststructuralist theories and practices to implicate Greenbergian modernism in gendered terms. Greenberg's valuation of the "virile elegance" and purity of modernist practices and his heroization of the Abstract Expressionist are now criticized as patriarchally invested and exclusionary. His *dismissal* of postmodernism as "wiping out . . . social distinctions between the more or the less cultivated" such that cultural standards are lowered for now "usually" female audiences,[4] is rejected and postmodernism is *celebrated* for this destruction of elitist and masculinist hierarchies of aesthetic quality.

In his later career, Greenberg wrote three articles in particular that attempt to make sense of postmodernism: "Counter-Avant-Garde" of 1971, "Seminar Six" of 1976, and the 1980 essay, "Modern and Post-Modern." In these articles Greenberg explicitly defines the absolute threat to his notion of high modernism posed by the strategies of Duchamp and his postmodern followers. Even as early as 1939 -1940, in his articles "Avant-Garde and Kitsch" and "Toward a Newer Laocoon," Greenberg had established his now familiar binary model staging high art in opposition to its degraded other, kitsch, and posing the heroic and pure modernism of the Cubists against the corrupted, debased, "literary" painting of the Surrealists. These oppositions set the terms for Greenberg's later conceptualization of American postmodern practices as successors to the debased impurities of Dada and Surrealist art. In the 1980 article, "Modern and Post-Modern," for example, Greenberg confirms the categories that devalue the *post*modern in contrast to its high modernist antipode, arguing that "what singles

Modernism out and gives it its place and identity more than anything else is its response to a heightened sense of threats to aesthetic value," while *post*modernism simply revels in "bad taste," as but another "rationalization for the lowering of standards."[5]

Greenberg's standards of value have been maintained more or less intact by some writers on post -Abstract Expressionist American art. Michael Fried's notorious attack on Minimalism in the 1967 article *Art and Objecthood*, for instance, is another attempt to define post -1960 American art as the debased other of high modernism. Fried draws on notions of quality that are not only strictly Greenbergian, but that mimic the gendered terms by which Nietzsche excoriated Wagnerian theater almost one hundred years earlier with the infamous statement, "in the theater one becomes people, herd, female, pharisee, voting cattle, patron, idiot — *Wagnerian.*"[6] Fried devalues Minimalist sculpture as the *impure, theatrical,* and *non* self-sufficient antipode of what he calls the "wholly manifest" modernist painting — presumably "full" within itself.

While Greenberg, Fried, and other modernists have worked to devalue postmodernism by associating it with the failed "avant-gard*ism*" of a Duchampian tradition, the younger generation of "pro-postmodernists" argue that the feminization of so-called high culture is politically progressive. For these writers and scholars, by critiquing the art institution via readymade-type strategies and by questioning the process of signification itself, postmodern practices disallow the oppressive regimes of patriarchal power that Greenbergian modernism reproduces and reinforces. As New York art critic and scholar Craig Owens has argued, "the postmodernist work . . . actively seeks to undermine all . . . claims [to authority]; hence its generally deconstructive thrust [toward the modernist] subject of representation as absolutely centered, unitary, masculine."[7]

The problem I see with these pro-postmodernist arguments is that they refuse to recognize their complicity in certain very Greenbergian strategies. They perform an inversion of Greenberg's categories to reclaim the postmodern, but tend to maintain the existence of the categories themselves. They critique Greenbergian modernism for its exclusionary logic but sustain his binary model of aesthetic value. They reject his dependence on heroic authors as individual and autonomous from the social, and yet — just as Greenberg himself anticipated — draw on Duchamp as the source for postmodernism. Perhaps art criticism demands these oppositional discriminations and authorial labels, but while we employ them we cannot claim to be completely *beyond* modernist notions of authority and value.

Since the 1970s, the predominantly New York based discourses on contemporary art have progressively narrowed the term postmodernism toward its present common usage as a rubric to categorize appropriation art
and other critical, anti-modernist art practices. Thus, as artist Robert Morris
describes it, postmodern art falls in "Duchampian territory," working out
of the reproductive strategy of the readymade gesture towards the disrup-
tion of modernism, the "rejection of the Western myth of wholeness," and
the "love of otherness."[8]

For many contemporary theorists of the postmodern, the role of Duchamp
as the father of postmodern practices of appropriation is now taken for
granted as "true." One *Artforum* writer, Daniel Soutif, states, "Conventional wisdom tells us that the father of 'object art' was Marcel Duchamp."[9]
Soutif continues, "almost a direct line runs through Jasper Johns's *Painted
Bronze (Ale cans)*, 1960, and Andy Warhol's *Brillo Boxes*, 1964, to a contemporary generation of artists such as Haim Steinbach. These latter figures,
of course, are all post-Duchampian." I could cite innumerable other examples of this use of modernist genealogical frameworks to define
postmodernism, but for now Soutif's text gives the role of Duchamp an
implicit, if sometimes repressed function, an origin of Greenbergian proportions, subtending postmodernism's claims for progressivity. Duchamp's
"radicality" is seen to inseminate the specifically anti-institutional and
anti-masculinist American postmodernism, investing it with an immanent, genetically ensured criticality vis-à-vis patriarchal modernism.

I would like to suggest that perhaps we can question these reinstalled
Greenbergian hegemonic notions of postmodern practice — notions that
tend to result in narrow, fixed, hierarchies of practice in categories of
"good" or "bad" postmodernism — by rearticulating the relationship of
postmodernism to modernism through a pointedly politicized model: that
of *hegemony*. In Gramscian terms, as elaborated by political theorists Chantal
Mouffe and Ernesto Laclau, hegemony is a contingent operation formed
itself out of conflict such that it allows for, even produces, a variety of
subject positions in antagonism to it.[10] As Greenbergian modernism's
"antagonism," then, postmodernism is not a fully oppositional discourse
as would be commonly, and reductively, understood. An antagonism
results when the presence of the "Other" disrupts a discourse so thoroughly as to prevent it from being itself. Greenberg himself anticipated
this obtrusive "Other" in his earliest writings (the corruptive Duchampian
function) and worked to eliminate the presence of this unwelcome element — which he recognized *as a part of modernism itself*, always threatening to destabilize it from within. The model of hegemony allows us to

conceptualize how postmodernism retains Greenbergian assumptions, but also — precisely because stimulated by the crises and overdeterminations that rupture Greenberg's own texts — serves to modify earlier limits, reinscribing or disrupting what Mouffe and Laclau call "concentrations of power" immanent in Greenbergian ideology.

While I question the insufficiently self-critical notion of postmodernism currently prevalent in art discourse, I do not mean to deny the powerful success of specific interventions in modernism by particular postmodern criticisms and art practices. The very acceptance and celebration of kinds of art practice previously excluded from art discourse is proof enough of certain radical and welcome changes that have occurred through the critical articulation of a postmodern resistance to modernist values. And the very fact of this articulation of postmodernism testifies to our desire, whether successful or not, to rework our relationship to exclusivist modernist models of determining aesthetic significance. But to avoid reifying critical practice in simply another configuration of oppositions, we would best be served by recognizing our relationship to modernist theories and practices, *not* as one of simple, and definitive patricide, but as one of self-aware antagonism — seeing that the specific forms our rebellion has taken are drawn from this very model we want to move beyond.

NOTES:

[1] Greenberg, Clement, "Modern and Post-Modern," *Arts* 54 (February 1980), p.66.

[2] Foster, Hal, "Subversive Signs," *Recodings: Art, Spectacle, Cultural Politics*; Seattle: Bay Press, 1985, p.99.

[3] Foster, Hal, "(Post)Modern Polemics," *Recodings*, pp.121,128-129.

[4] Both Greenberg citations are from "Present Prospects in American Painting," *Clement Greenberg: The Collected Essays and Criticism, v. 2, Arrogant Purpose, 1945-1949*, ed. John O'Brian; Chicago and London: University of Chicago Press, 1986, pp.167, 162.

[5] Greenberg, "Modern and Post-Modern," p.66.

[6] "Nietzsche contra Wagner," *The Portable Nietzsche*, ed. and tr. Walter Kaufmann, NY: Random House, 1967, p. 161.

[7] Owens, Craig, "The Discourse of Others: Feminists and Postmodernism," *The Anti-Aesthetic: Essays on Postmodern Culture*, ed. Hal Foster; Seattle: Bay Press, 1983, p.58.

[8] Morris, "Three Folds in the Fabric and Four Autobiographical Asides as Allegories (Or Interpretations)," *Art in America* 77, November 1989, pp.148-49.

[9] Soutif, Daniel, "Found and Lost: On the Object in Art," tr. Hanna Hannah, *Artforum* 28, October 1989, pp.155, 157.

[10] Mouffe, Chantal and Laclau, Ernesto, *Hegemony and Socialist Strategy: Towards a Radical Democratic Politics*, tr. Winston Moore and Paul Cammack, London: Verso, 1985.

The Hegemocentric Conclusions of Criticism in a Changing World

by Silvano Lora
(Dominican Republic)

From the very outset, the debate on art and politics provokes the old quarrel over the definition of territories, and the suspicion of intentionality surfaces when art has engaged itself with a circumscribed conception of it own parameters.

If we conceive of art as a category that encompasses various branches of knowledge and is linked to categories of reason — in the entire range of critical and creative thought, nothing is more opportune than to engage in discussion illuminated by the spark left by expectations of the collapse of established systems, the certitudes or exclusivities concerning the grand goals of historical vanguards — then the debate today about modernism and postmodernism is appropriate.

The debate on modernism and postmodernism, with reference to contemporary art and criticism, brings us to a revision of concepts as historical categories and their relationship to philosophical and political thought. Does modernism have validity, and why are differences over the fundamentals of modernism being dug up or exaggerated? It would be necessary to mark the boundaries of the opposing sides: those on the one side who would bury modernity and those on the other who deny the decline and end of the principles of humanism as the basis for modernity.

Better to reformulate it as a debate than as a crisis of modernity or of avant-garde ideology, based on the ideology of the permanently new confronting the resistance and structure of the industrial system that perpetuates and increases benefits. We raise the question of the emergence of forms after the end of colonialism and totalitarianism.

The concept of post-colonialism carries with it an affirmation of the end of colonialism, just as the postmodernist position carries an affirmation of the end of modernism. In order to arrive at these conclusions, it would be necessary to demonstrate that the basis of the doctrines which propelled the currents of thought and the practices resulting from the implementation of those ideas either reached maturity, met their demise, or were defeated.

We will attempt to establish such concepts: modernism and colonialism to be treated as models that, from our perspective, respond to values, aspirations, and concepts whose credo is determined within the frame of necessity. The determining factors may be the historical forms of the manifestation expressed in philosophical concepts or the fundamentals may be the individual and societal goals upon which the movement is based. In this respect, it would be worth the effort to observe whether or not the specific elements of the colonial condition (the merging of aspirations and interests) have disappeared and given way to another system and a new body of doctrines that permit us to confirm the end of a historical period, the disappearance of paradigm such as modernism, or the end of forms of oppression characteristic of totalitarianism. What kind of totalitarianism? Bossism (*caudillista*), monarchical dictatorship, despotism, class dictatorship? We would have to study the contents.

We accept the challenge of postmodernity in conceptual and ideological terms, but the formal and systematic appearance of its manifestations is yet to be demonstrated. At least the emergence of modernism is put back toward the end of the 19th century with romanticism, liberalism, and, in the visual arts, Impressionism.

Contemplating the end of colonialism and, in a hypothetical sense, the end of totalitarianism, we might possibly aspire to the hope, in this same sense, of postmodernism. It originates from the moment that modernism incarnated a corpus of philosophical, ethical, and social ideals that have liberty at their core.

But to be precise colonialism is a form of domination that in our day dons a new guise. We are far from the dawn of the end of plutocracy and totalitarianism framed within the manifold forms of manipulation of the ideals of democracy that modernism embodies. Of what end or what "post" can we speak?

Criticism is in such a hurry to label tendencies, periods, and inflections in the expression of semantic-epistemological thought that, already unsatisfied with the liquidation of modernism, it proposes the leap from postmodernity to the void of techno-culture. It is not about the illusion of an all-encompassing cultural revolution with the dissemination of technological diversions facilitated by electronic gadgets in the United States. For already the electronic and cybernetic instruments have made their appearance in the Amazonian jungle; in any store (*bodega*) a native makes use of a computerized calculator because, before learning the multiplication tables, they turn to electronics. In the free-trade zones of Japanese and European industry, primitive labor by hand is employed, converted into the prosthesis of technology.

It is frustrating and lamentable, conjectural, and simplistic in the extreme, that the end of modernity was established and the beginning of postmodernism proclaimed dated according to the day of the destruction of an architectural complex with a style that characterized the modern, or according to the camouflaging of facades, or within the framework of a museum-like vision of ruins. Risk is now expressed in the disappearance of the aesthetic of art, the quotidian quality of the aesthetic, or the aestheticization of reality.

The failure of culture in the face of the avalanche of the industrial image provokes reflections about an exit to a refuge in elitist solitude: a step toward the past, maintaining positions, and not a step leading to optimism.

Translated from the Spanish by Felix Cortéz and Lanny Powers

The Exploitation of the Dead

by Branka Stipančić
(Yugoslavia)

Artists in former Socialist countries, as well as in Yugoslavia, which is currently experiencing the agony of the breakdown of communist power in the most drastic way, are particularly sensitive to the complex relationship between politics and art.

In this paper I have chosen to concentrate on one artist: Mladen Stilinović. His work since 1974 has utilized various media such as film, photography, text, book as art, collage, and installation. His oeuvre covers a wide variety of themes from the language of art, the language of ideology, and their interrelation. The cycle *The Exploitation of the Dead* was exhibited in 1984, first in Zagreb, and then was elaborated and shown in Vienna, Tübingen, Köln, Melbourne, Sydney, and elsewhere; most recently on a smaller scale it was included in *The Interrupted Life* at The New Museum of Contemporary Art in New York.

The installation begins with a photograph of Malevich on his deathbed and ends with empty slates with mourning bands. The space in between is densely filled with paintings which are copies or interpretations of Suprematism, Constructivism, Socialist Realism, and '50s geometric abstraction; collages of photographs of political meetings, work brigades, sports gatherings, and cemeteries. Endlessly repeated squares, triangles, stars, crosses, factories, and flags alternate with painted suits, ties, loaves of bread, and boards with inscriptions: "Exploitation of the Dead," "Dead Optimism," "Onward Cakes." Thus the saturated space resonates with red, black and pink, and evokes both death and the exploitation of the dead, as suggested by the installation title.

Whence the title? What does it mean to the author? In an interview conducted by Darko Simicic (published in the exhibition catalogue), Stilinović explains this in detail, revealing a number of possible approaches to his work. Assuming the role of an exploiter, he utilizes the poetics of the Russian avant-garde, Socialist Realism and geometric abstraction, which he claims are dead. He exploits signs which are dead because they no longer transmit meaning; he uses the signs of death or signs to which he ascribes the meaning of death, while his treatment is a demonstration of the exploitation so frequent in ideology, religion, and art. Aware of the brutality of this act, Stilinović opens a "discussion" on language (of art and ideology) and on power, a narrative that has dissolved in dis-order, with a series of contradictory stories about death.

Despite various materials and means of presentation, including theatrical set design, misleading references, unexpected connections, and metaphorical speech, several themes are immediately discernible. One is Russian avant-garde art: Malevich's "paintings," Mayakovsky's "caricatures," Rodchenko's photographs. Yet, what has remained of them? Nothing but shells of the Russian avant-garde, signs that have already acted out their historical role and no longer denote the utopias, ideas and ideologies of their time. Devoid of their meaning, they are but patterns, recognizable and manipulated by the author. Rather than formal structures, it is the process of adoption of a language and its "unscrupulous" translation into another — its exploitation — that intrigues the artist. Shifted into a new semantic center, the signs become more blatantly empty and further removed from their historical source. Paradoxically the Russian avant-garde, associated with the myth of freedom, progress and artistic prosperity, in this context signifies the manipulation and debunking of art.

Linked to the Russian avant-garde theme is that of Socialist Realism and the art of the early '50s. A number of symbols and signs characteristic of Socialist Realism and the period of rebuilding are combined with elements of this historical avant-garde movement. Calisthenics and work brigades, flags and factories, stars and suns are designed in the Russian avant-garde fashion. Why equal treatment of different historical sources? Is the author's choice of certain models also his value judgement? Is it also his apology for them? Since Stilinović's earlier works are characteristically subversive, apology seems to be out of the question. Opting for a position far from any ideology, yet aware that art is by no means a virgin territory free from its influence, the artist develops his theme about the language of painting, its use and death. Socialist Realism is therefore placed alongside the Russian avant-garde because it appropriated many of the signs and elements of the Russian avant-garde idiom which fitted in with the new ideology, divesting them of meaning and pushing them into "death." The relation between the two poetics is used by the author as the genuine historical example of ideology interfering with and manipulating art. Encounters of figuration and abstraction in paintings paraphrasing Yugoslav art of the early '50s bring this theme closer to our own time and space.

Stilinović's works with photographs introduce another area of manipulation of signs. Photographs of "collective rituals" (political meetings, sports meets, funerals) shift the emphasis from the language of art to the social context of this discussion. Analysing both social and artistic models, Stilinović uses the structure of both. Singly and as an interrelated whole, the works appear to be an attack on social practice. They insult, they touch on taboos which the artist exploits: the taboo of death, the taboo of collective unity, the taboo of socialist and religious signs, the taboo of the original in art (many of his works provocatively copy or paraphrase other artworks) the taboo of connotative colors — especially red in socialist countries. And finally, they touch on emotions.

To what extent, then, is the subversive note relevant to the interpretation of the whole? Obviously it is only one thread in the dense weave of parallel meanings that exude from the nearly four hundred works exhibited. It is in his attitude to society that the subversive element is emphasized, making this "discussion" suggestive, live, and painful for us. However, the installation is full of inversions. It contains irony in relation to art as well as in relation to society. Irony turns into self-irony. Producing art, the artist emulates a social practice: the practice of manipulating signs, so typical in political discourse. Nor is art itself innocent; it is also a field for the manifestation of power. Drawing from the writings of Bahktin, Barthes, Rosi-Landi and Foucault, Stilinović has evolved his own methods where the language of art, the language of ideology, and everyday language are his material. His montages and simulacra neither attack nor advocate (changed relations in society); rather, they reveal structures of power concentrated in those languages.

There are also elements of humor. A cream cake has been thrown into the face of the painting (recorded on video tape), the cakes stand on pedestals, a small pornographic painting is hidden behind a curtain, a flag is painted on a suit, or a zero on a tie, which is then framed as a masterpiece. A number of subtle puns enhance the multi-layered meaning of larger themes. Various meanings can be deciphered gradually and endlessly. Small-size monochrome paintings can be treated as conjunctions if we do not delve deeper into their differences and the stories they tell. The elements of humor are accompanied by elements of extreme pathos — especially in the group of works dealing with the ritual of death, with photographs of graves that were then painted on or burned. A tension is forged between the serious and the tragic, the banal and the humorous — a certain contradictory and elusive quality. When we think we have got the essence, the

Mladen Stilinović, from the cycle *The Exploitation of the Dead*, installation, 1984-90.

details mislead us; the complex texture of the context draws each rational thought back into the dense mass of paintings and objects for re-examination.

The author speaks directly, and indirectly, with pathos and wit. What then is his position in the "composition of meaning?" Employing various 20th-century styles as "commonplaces" he embarks upon a critical interpretation of the present. By simulation and montage he creates new structures of meaning which are interesting today.

The author claims that he only indifferently repeats the well-known practice of manipulation he calls "exploitation of the dead." Only a person who is not involved, who is aloof, can be indifferent. "Simulation, a new rule of the game," characteristic of the art of the '80s, is also non-participation. In the Western art scene, his distancing work would probably be considered an intelligent analysis of the interaction between the language of art and the language of ideology. In the Yugoslav context, however, from the viewpoint of those entangled in a series of traumatic social situations from the past and the present, Stilinovic's work causes anxiety, pain, and pessimism. The impudence and power of manipulation — the theme of the installation — are received through emotions which the author also manipulates.

The Slaying of the Shaman: Romanian Artists and Critics in a Transitional World

by Calin Dan
(Romania)

The Discovery of Politics

Romanian culture is now paying the bill for almost 60 years of complicity with Power. Dictatorship has been commonplace in the modern political life of the country: it began with King Carol II (early 1930s), continued with Marshal Antonescu, and then with the Communists, climaxing in the '80s when Ceausescu efficiently synthesized local and international methods in the art of destroying a nation by all manner of direct and/or refined humiliations. Compared to other countries of the region between the world wars, Romania lacked two important ingredients: an influential avant-garde and a democratic, pro-communist local intelligentsia. Usually, those two realities were combined and promoted by the same groups (persons) in Central Eastern Europe. Considering that the Russian empire (communist or not) was the oldest, most powerful and most cruel enemy of Romania in the recent centuries, one can understand the failure of leftist ideas in Romania at a moment when progressives elsewhere on the continent sympathized with Marx. Nevertheless, such an unanimity among Romanian intellectuals proves a fundamental disdain for polemical attitudes, for all the discomfort connected with fighting the mainstreams of history. When Soviet communists took power in Romania, they had only a few partners to deal with. This allowed them to impose their own rules more easily than anywhere else. At the same time, they were warned that the genuine anti-communist feelings of the Romanian people called for energetic measures: the terror established in the country after 1944 was comparable only to the worst periods of the Stalinist era. Hundreds of thousands of people died; and all structures of resistance were crushed. Moral and physical intimidation/destruction worked quickly. Romanian artists were assimilated by the socialist realism system of propaganda without any noticeable opposition. Even the old masters were in the peculiar position of having to adapt their images to the commitments of a secretly disdained political conception of art. Non-involvement was no longer possible and the time of compromise had come.

The brief opening of the system (between 1965-1975) was beneficial to the visual arts. But in that lapse of time, efforts were made to restore the old apolitical structures, to re-establish a reasonable distance between the State and the Artist. Considering that the communist system looked stronger than ever, the only solution was to adopt what seemed to be a complete isolation of visual arts from everything else except the formal problems of avant-garde. The echoes of 1968 had no significant impact in Romania, where artists remained skeptical of any connection with social-political problems — even toward a polemical one.

The Failure of Avant-garde

An avant-garde is, let's say, unavoidable in any modern society. Romanian society is still a mixture of pre-modern and modern, which leads to non-typical postmodern-tolerant neighborhoods. But this tolerance is mostly superficial, considering the tensions produced by the permanent contact between a rather new modernity and a still very strong archaic tradition. One of communism's main goals was the massification of society: the upper classes were destroyed in camps or by deportation; the villages, with their economic stability were destroyed by collectivization, and peasants moved to town for hard work in unproductive factories. This internal emigration created new social structures with no roots, subjected to ever greater pressure in the '80s. The cruelty of political movements in Romania, beginning with December '89, finds one explanation in the hermeneutics of that situation. Romanian society developed amorphous tribal tensions and no catharsis succeeded in lowering the pressure during the last decades. Speaking in tribal terms, no Shaman was allowed to assume the disease of the collective soul, and therefore the crisis spread violently.

That accuses, indirectly, the visual artists too. And with this, we return to the problem of avant-garde, and to the '80s. The previous decade settled the limits of modernity in Romanian visual arts: painting and graphics explored conceptualism; sculpture oscillated between a post-Brancusi monumentalism and minimal-conceptual tensions; new media were disapproved of and were strictly banned by officials. Despite the ideological and economic problems, the art of the '70s was witty, ironical, self-confident, and, most of all, proper, neat, and beautiful. The development of ceramics and tapestry in new forms, connected with *"les arts majeurs,"* is a highly significant feature of that optimistic atmosphere. In the '80s the art terrain didn't change radically, but a new stream appeared in connection with the extension of New Expressionism. It worked alike in painting, sculpture, photography, installations, and Happenings. The lessons of Bad Painting, Arte Povera and Pop Art were assimilated because they were adequate to a populistic situation. This New Expression, which changed the positive values of the '70s into negative ones (promoting cynicism, despair, ugliness), raised the arts field to a new consciousness in relation to the social and political reality. But that tendency was strictly limited to a few artists of the younger generation. The "Shamanization" of Romanian culture failed in the visual arts too. There was no gain for the public from the stylistic changes of the last decade. There was only an illusion of tolerance among artists more and more oppressed by a totalitarian regime at its climax. This was highlighted by the "Alternatives exhibition" (1987), organized as evidence of postmodern tolerance between abstraction and figuration, expressionism and classic nostalgia, intermedia and traditional communication. But free acceptance was unacceptable for the officials, and the show was abusively closed after a week by activists of the Communist Party.

Censorship — A War of Ambiguity

Every system has its own censorship criteria, whether political, economic or of group interest. In Romania, the cultural censorship was a subtle combination of all three, with an emphasis on the political. After the '50s and early '60s, when the only rule was obedience to the aesthetics of Socialist Realism, a period came when no more rules were available. Every moment and every particular situation had its own specificity; censorship became equal to Fate, and the censor to an anonymous, multi-faceted and ubiquitous God.

Sex, religion, and politics were absolutely forbidden; a tenacious hunt began for phalluses, crosses, stars, subversive colors (reminiscent of the Hungarian banner, or the Romanian fascists' uniform). Artists who in the '50s were on the edge of ruining their careers for perpetrating abstraction became highly favored in the last few decades, while figurative painting was suspected of secret dissidence.

The New Expressionism was detestable because of its stylistic violence. But there were many priorities in that banishment: first came the painters reflecting in a Post-Pop ironical way the misery and fear of day-to-day life; then members of the "Prolog" group, who were restoring an old religious feeling by painting landscapes with churches or flowers. And then the allusive, the oneiric-symbolistic-punk, which was detested because it was not easily classifiable. The most persecuted were the avant-garde artists who used alternative mediums. That type of expression was attacked from all sides: by censors, by officials of the Artists' Union, and by artists of all generations.

Returning to the hermeneutics of tribal psychology, I suppose it was (and, alas, still is) a problem of unconscious rejection of a shamanistic situation. These nontraditional mediums exalt the self, putting the energy of the artist and the energies of the viewers more directly in contact with each other. The Romanian public (and most Romanian artists) reject this participation, along with the "lack of decency" and the exorcism of hidden ugliness and violence. Those tensions remain unresolved. The rootless archaic society I have sketched rejects — as all archaic societies do — Otherness and Difference. Finally, in the last 30 years, there were few official arts in Romania. The ones that existed included, first, art that perpetrated the Socialist Realistic ideology (portraits of the Dictator, compositions with Workers or official visits); then, a type of pleasant, rather decorative painting and sculpture connected vaguely to the problems of the "Ecole de Paris" in the '30s; and, last and most odd, the New Expression proposing allusive statements on religion. And this proves the perversity of a declared atheistic regime, which secretly exalted a kind of art connected to national values (traditional 19th-century-like conceptions of painting) in order to create diversions and conflicts.

The Crisis of Art Critics

What is the heritage of the '80s? A new official art, issued from the "soft" avant-garde, from the formalism acknowledged by officials, and most of all, from the religious underground; a weakened New Expressionism, translated more and more from the figurative to the informal. An exhausted multimedia avant-garde, diminished by shortage of money, by political persecutions and, not least, by lack of efficiency.

An avant-garde is subversive, but it has to keep contacts with the big army of the public, or else its activity becomes schizophrenic. Typical of the Romanian concept of avant-garde is a workshop organized in Sibiu (1986). The money was taken from the Communist Youth organizations. The "happenings" (of a violence recalling the "actionists" of Vienna) took place in a cellar and only the initiated few were allowed to assist. On the very last day, at the end of the last event, the secret services (Securitate) showed up. All the participants were blacklisted, with no chance to repeat the experience. Most artists and critics agreed this was a natural consequence of outrageous, useless, non-artistic acts. The public echo of that secret dissidence was nil. The mutual ignorance between artists and public and between artists and critics is the worst heritage of those years. Both artists and critics ignored the proper solutions: a better ideological involvement, a practical engagement in reality beyond the limits allowed by the officials. No theoretical program resulted that could unify this rich and diverse living material; and no documentation remained of these many ephemeral actions or shows which were abruptly interrupted. In a way, this period has no history, and the new generation, dangerously amnesiacal, will discover things already consumed.

In the '80s, art critics and artists acted as if the communist power would last forever. No alternative structures were installed in Romanian cultural life. And now, when the whole society is structureless, the critics fail by their silence, or by a kind of post-revolutionary activism. Today, some critics are trying to work as performers or installation artists, directly sharing the practical problems of the avant-garde. Meanwhile, others are curating retrospective exhibitions in a nostalgia for the '80s, considered as a successful period despite evidence to the contrary. This pessimistic attitude has to be changed by a more realistic concept of relationships between the political power, the power of money and the media.

Western Art Criticism and Art in the Former German Democratic Republic

by Bernhard Schulz
(Germany)

The opening of the Berlin Wall initiated the definitive and unstoppable collapse of the German Democratic Republic. Preceding this momentous event, however, was a long-term creeping erosion of the dominant Communist ideology. Art and artists, it was said soon after, had long been cooperating in this demolition of ideology. Indeed, according to this line of thought, they had been the motor of this demolition in the midst of an apparently functional ideological machine and were the true pioneers of the *Wende*, the "turn," as the ruin of the GDR was called for a couple of months. Whether artists had been critics or supporters, underminers or stabilizers of the system, however, they had not been dissidents. Whoever became suspect of being a dissident in the GDR, after all, was forced immediately to emigrate to the West.

The existence of a Western Germany, that is, part of the same nation but belonging to the opposing ideological group — a condition pertaining to no other European country — resulted in the fact that at least part of the theoretical and ideological debates over culture in the GDR actually took place in the Bundesrepublik. Among these debates art criticism was — and still is — assigned a special role. As opposed to, for example, literature or theater, where links between the two Germanys existed, the prevailing ideologies and practices in visual art were opposed. What in West Germany is now summed up as "Westkunst" was clearly posited against the "Socialist Realism" (whatever may be covered by this loose-fitting label) in the East.

Art criticism in the West was never able to think of art in the GDR as anything other than part of a specific "GDR-culture," a particular kind of art clearly and obviously distinguished from Western concepts. Consequently, such an art had to be criticized according to different standards. Regardless of all changes that Western art criticism underwent in its estimation of GDR art, one thing remained constant: the assumption that this art was fundamentally different and followed its own rules.

My point is that art criticism in the Bundesrepublik, as regards art in the GDR, has followed and to a considerable extent continues to follow the dominant political paradigm. By emphasizing the autonomy of GDR art, art criticism has followed the changing Western evaluation of the GDR itself: from Cold War to Détente Policy to a morally inspired conservative criticism under the influence of Soviet *perestroika*, and now, after unification, towards a critical view of the impediments to this unification which can be summed up as problems in finding a new identity. This acceptance — unintended and, for that matter, unconscious — of the dominant political paradigm brought about a regard for art in the GDR from more a sociopolitical than aesthetic point of view.

Towards the end of the '50s, when the cultural politics of the GDR was still completely enmeshed in Stalinist doctrine, the SED — Communist Party of the German Democratic Republic — defined "Socialist Realism" as a method of serving "all artists as a means of overcoming the remainders of bourgeois decadence and formalism as well as the tendency towards sentimental kitsch." It was on the occasion of the highly official "German Art Exhibition" in 1958 that the then-leader of the GDR, the autocratic Walter Ulbricht, added to this definition the implicit demand that "the artists have learned more than before to view our lives through the eyes of life-affirming, progressive individuals of our time, the successful builders of Socialism."

The distance from the abstract art which predominated in the West at this time could not have been more profound. Western art criticism was not able to see GDR art as anything other than flat-out propaganda — which in that respect was not far removed from actual East German art doctrine. That changed when, in 1971, Erich Honecker succeeded Ulbricht. Also in that year a new aspect opened up for the arts in the GDR. *Weite und Vielfalt* ("wideness and variety") was the catch-phrase which guaranteed, more or less until the end of the GDR, a certain ideological flexibility. Honecker indeed emphasized the "affirmative shaping of the Great and Beautiful of our time" — which could easily be read as confession to the GDR's "real existing Socialism," as the official phrase went. Later Honecker added that, as long as art simply started from the "stable platform of Socialism," there could be no taboos. As should soon become obvious, the SED opened herewith a wide range of possibilities for interpretation without questioning the primacy of content. By agreeing that the future of the country had to be a socialist one, the state could feel safe with its artists. Debates on artistic freedom were confined by this consent.

All in all, West German art criticism implicitly accepted this premise. It did not even recognize the premise as a fundament, let alone criticize it. Between 1969 and 1972 a basic change in West German foreign policy took place, from Cold War policy to Détente. The policy of "rollback," which had become obsolete long ago and had obviously been terminated by U.S. acceptance of the Berlin Wall after 1961, changed into the doctrine of *Wandel durch Annäherung* ("change through rapprochement"). The GDR's existence was no longer subject to doubt. Now singular improvement, especially concerning travel and visit regulations, contact and exchange in general, were on the agenda. It was then that the GDR's culture came into sight as an autonomous and promising achievement. Western criticism no longer proposed to advance the Western model. The "special conditions of creation" for GDR art were accepted in the West as the basis of any judgment. What was accepted, in other words, was the embedding of GDR art in the Communist party system and its ideology, just as demanded by Honecker's doctrine.

Since the 1977 Documenta, the number of exhibitions of GDR art in West Germany has risen steadily. The art shown was primarily work by the four painters of the so-called Leipzig School: Willi Sitte, Bernhard Heisig, Wolfgang Mattheuer and Werner Tübke, all of them protagonists of the Honecker era. This art was granted a kind of "GDR bonus." To criticize it would have meant to criticize socialism as a utopian dream, and making such criticism would have seemed a flashback to the despised Cold War mentality. Actual conditions in the GDR were generously ignored or at best recognized only insofar as they were represented in the works of art. The exhibition *Zeitvergleich* ("Time Check") in 1982, co-organized by the magazine *Art* and given enormous publicity, cemented this affirmative view of GDR art. In the words of *Art*'s editor-in-chief, "Socialist Realism is overcome, artists no longer accept a prefabricated world view decreed by the state." Thus, the Western ideal of the autonomous artist could be applied to artists in the East and the contents — the meaning and the message — remained unexamined.

Interestingly enough, it was actually the aforementioned protagonists of the Leipzig School who pursued the long-dogmatized adoption of the German historic legacy with an unanticipated force. West German criticism, which, stimulated by the 1968 student movement, had diagnosed the lack of awareness especially of the Nazi past in West Germany, advocated the historical legitimization of the GDR. A strange though unanticipated paradox could be observed: qualities were praised in the art of the GDR that at the same time were condemned in Western art as historically obsolete.

"Fine art in the GDR was caused by traumata," wrote Eberhard Roters, long-time West Berlin museum director who was born in Saxony. "This is its peculiarity, which is evident in the paintings of the Leipzig School. There aren't only heroes and victims in any black-and-white sense. Especially in our efforts to act morally, we are all culprits and all victims, cowards, and heroes at the same time." Culprits and victims at the same time: this is indeed the ambiguity of art in the late years of the GDR. To the extent that the "winners of history" ideology gave way to the pragmatism of "actually existing socialism" — which means no longer in need of historic justification — art in a way crossed ideological boundaries to become a moral conscience for East and West alike.

A common attitude in the West considered the GDR the "better" Germany, conceding that its realization was until then insufficient but regarding this fault as a minor defect. This attitude could be substantiated with the paintings of Bernhard Heisig and Wolfgang Mattheuer. Heisig's retrospective, which (contrary to the rules then still valid in the GDR) started its West German tour in West Berlin only months before the collapse of the GDR power structure, was viewed as proof of the existence of an all-German historic awareness. Dealing with the final stages of the Third Reich took the place of the social present, which Heisig's work did not address. It became awkward when those same artists — Heisig among others — turned to contemporary historic events after the *Wende* and produced, as if nothing had actually happened, paintings of the Wall's opening and of popular uprising which had not even been dreamed of before. Or had they? It is remarkable to note how many paintings of the GDR's last decade depict the metaphors of dreams which could easily be read as "exceeding utopia" (in the East) or as concealed criticism (in the West).

The SED state ultimately lost control of the arts as tools of ideology. This was exemplified by the history of the making of *History of the Early Bourgeois Revolution*, the gigantic panorama painting the government ordered from Werner Tübke. Tübke, renowned for his programmatic painting *Working Class and Intelligentsia* at Leipzig University, was commissioned to paint a 122-meter-long picture — a new world's record and as such the immediate object of propagandistic efforts. Tübke accepted no directives concerning the content. The result was his emphatic imitation of German 16th-century painting — a disturbing testimony. Western critics

Werner Tübke, detail of the panoramic painting *Early Revolution in Germany*, Bad Frankenhausen (detail shows Ship of Craftsmen), 1979-87.

Bernhard Heisig, *Studio Visit (Portrait Helmut Schmidt)*, 1987, Ludwig Institute for Art in
the GDR, Oberhausen.

did not hesitate to applaud Tübke's ten-year effort. They overlooked, however, the inauguration of the panorama, attended by the heads of party and state. Thereafter, Western criticism praised Tübke's artistic refinement and ignored its content.

With the *Wende*, the collapse of the Communist system in late 1989, the well-drawn distinctions were abandoned — though in favor of an aesthetic rather than a moral critique. Now it was the artist himself to whom attention was directed. The term "state artist" was heavily used, and this time it was noticed how much artists were tied into the party system and what privileges they enjoyed, from villas and visas for the successful ones to economic security even for the average artist.

However, the outraged criticism emerging after the collapse of the SED was more or less an attempt to ease the critics' own conscience. Had we not made all kinds of occasions to praise GDR art as an autonomous achievement? This writer himself, on the occasion of officially-acclaimed Bernhard Heisig's retrospective in West Berlin, masked his own critique of the artist's rather arbitrary anti-fascist theme paintings behind an overall approval of the intra-German cultural exchange. That was a fitting excuse for all such events, that any exchange conceded by GDR government was to be regarded as an improvement in itself, notwithstanding the ideological implications nor the exchanges that did *not* take place.

That is what the fundamental critique expressed by ex-GDR artists exiled to the West aimed at. Georg Baselitz, who had moved to West Germany by 1964 and who subsequently rose to stardom, rather bluntly called all GDR artists "assholes." The more gifted artists, in his opinion, always moved to the West. Baselitz's rude label was remembered. The many artists who had to leave the country (especially after the eviction of poet-singer Wolf Biermann in late 1976) — not all of whom, like A.R. Penck, had already made their reputations in the West — came to be recognized as the victims of intra-German détente, whereas the so-called state artists had been celebrated as the heralds of long-awaited cultural exchange.

The moralistic phase of Western critique, however, was to pass as quickly as the GDR itself faded. As the possibility of a fundamental moral renewal of the GDR — put forward by the writers' proclamation "for our land" in early November 1989 — decayed into the completely run-down substance of the GDR itself, the moral critique transformed itself into the historical question: "Who had sinned and to what extent?" That, in turn, made room for a purely immanent critique which still prevails. Soon, all official GDR artists felt free to portray themselves as victims of the political system; the well-known pattern of *Vergangenheitsbewältigung* — meaning coming to terms with the past — was soon applied to the GDR leftovers in general. Every artist now had his stories of difficulties with small-minded functionaries and inflexible institutions. The danger, though, is that all the differences are leveled. As in all systems relying on censorship, no truly consistent cultural policy actually existed in the GDR. That which was banned yesterday could be allowed today and vice versa. Some artists fared well and some did not.

Now that the GDR is gone, it is time to adopt unbiased standards. West German criticism faces some difficulties in doing so. The notion of a more or less linear artistic development has to be abandoned. The content-oriented art of the former GDR forces us to acknowledge contextual conditions that have not been taken into account with regard to Western art. The appraisal of Werner Tübke as an almost postmodern simulationist clearly denotes a tendency to avoid the necessary revision of history. Sheer artistic brilliance becomes the yardstick. Thus Western criticism has arrived at what it has long been criticized for: the appreciation of formal brilliance regardless of meaning, perfectly in tune with the art market. The reformulation of our critical standards with regard to contemporary Western art lies ahead of us.

From Production to Deconstruction: Finnish Paradoxes

by Kimmo Sarje
(Finland)

Now that the Soviet Union has effectively ceased to exist in its old form, glasnost has finally reached Finland and the terms "Brezhnevism," "Finlandization," and "self-censorship" are being examined in a new light. Previously, the mere mention of these words provoked anger and anxiety in Finns, who found it easy to write them off as Western propaganda.

The decade of Brezhnevism, the complex, introverted 1970s, has increasingly become a focus of interest for research. The *Retro* exhibition of 1970s Finnish Social Realism[1] shown in Helsinki in the spring of 1991 can be seen as part of this climate of self-inspection. In Finland, there has been a tendency to dispute the existence of the whole 1970s Social Realist movement.[2] It has been seen as a bothersome taboo, and has been swept under the carpet.

Compared with the rest of Finnish political and cultural history, the 1970s were peculiar, to say the least; and even in international terms the developments in Finland during that period were an anomaly. The country's political culture at that time was authoritarian and oriented eastwards. Through the convergence of various chance events, young radicals too vigorously supported the same general aspirations. The leftist wave reached its peak in the youth and student movements of the 1970s, which was also the time of its ossification. Free, spontaneous leftism was marshalled into rigid ranks, and ideologically shackled. The concrete fight for social justice was the hallmark of its political strategies.

In terms of the "Beyond Walls and Wars: Art, Politics, and Multiculturalism" theme, Finnish social art of the 1970s is a remarkable example of how official socialist institutions, primarily from the USSR and East Germany, took root in the politically radical aesthetic of young artists in capitalist Finland, and of how official Soviet ideology became an integral part of the youth counterculture or subculture. At the same time, it is an example of how Western Photorealism and Neo-Realism acquired Socialist Realist and Finnish national themes in our art.

It is paradoxical that in the 1970s Finnish artists and cultural workers adopted the already moribund Soviet cultural organizations as their ideal — without irony. In 1972 a Marxist-Leninist Union of Cultural Workers was founded in Finland. This organization attracted the most active young artists. Students and researchers also formed into Marxist-Leninist unions, and thus a considerable section of the young intelligentsia — myself included — became intoxicated by Brezhnevism. It was a shock to our parents, the generation of war heroes, but in time the joke rebounded on the rebels themselves. Pekka Haapakoski, one of the few independent leftist intellectuals in Finland, captured the situation well in an article entitled "Brezhnevism in Finland" published in the *New Left Review* in 1974:

> The SKP minority (the orthodox faction of the Finnish Communist Party) absorbed most of the radicalized authors, actors and artists, by appealing to their *ouvrier*-ism. Many of these intellectuals originally held views close to those of the Russian Proletcult of the '20s. The "fighting art" produced in these circles generated an influential subculture, which often became a substitute for political action among students. Gradually, however, these artists too were domesticated into the framework of the "democratic culture" and "peace culture" advocated by the SKP minority. They became enthusiastic admirers of Socialist Realism in the USSR, accepted the arch-conservative moral precepts of this school, and eagerly calumniated oppositional Soviet artists and authors in tones reminiscent of Gorky in the '30s. . . . *(New Left Review,* Number 86, July-August 1974, p 29.)

In the Finland and USSR of the 1970s official and unofficial culture were, of course, two quite different matters. The official movement in Soviet art was Socialist Realism, while Finland, being a Nordic social democratic welfare state, a land of "good taste" and "design," wanted to project an official image that verged on Constructivism. The mainstream in Finland was based on Western models, and Social Realism was only one trend, albeit a pronounced one. It was often aligned against Modernism and abstract art. It was astounding, yet ideologically consistent, that political radicalism should wear the artistic guise of conservatism and dogmatism. Young radicals' attempts to be more conventional than the conventionalists certainly irritated the mainstream culture with its canonized values. Surprisingly, young, radical artists also acquired allies among right-wing arch-conservative critics, who cherished the idea of a return to traditional folk art and to Realism. There arose a populist alliance between the left and right wing which defended national, folk art against Modernist high culture.

The situation in Finland in the 1970s followed the logic of the modern: the dominant culture and popular cultures were fiercely opposed. The Realists' discourse on "representational art," "national tradition," and "painting as a traditional medium" nevertheless planted the seeds for the neo-Romanticism and *transavanguardia* of the 1980s. Social art, in turn, confirmed the myth of Finland as a crossroads between East and West. In Finland in the '70s major shows were mounted of both Western contemporary art and the art of the Socialist countries. Brezhnevism gave a whole generation of Finns direct experience of Soviet culture and "cultural Stalinism" — but from a safe distance.

What then was the Finnish Social Realism of the 1970s like? Inari Krohn was one of the major proponents of the movement. As an artist she had no encumbering group loyalties, but she was sympathetic to the international solidarity and labor movements of the 1960s and '70s. Krohn's artistic stance could be called Socialist Naivism. In her paintings she captured the collective spirit of a happy family of nations that "smashed tyranny and racial oppression." Leftism, from the hippy movement to Maoism, provided ideological inspiration for her paintings. Krohn's naivist stylized idiom depicts human figures as blatant symbols, which arouse feelings of either love or hate. The uniformed figures foreshadowed the dogmatism and intolerance of the decade.

Jarmo Mäkilä's masculine paintings combined Finnish tradition and socialist iconography. The models for his sturdy worker figures mostly came from East German art, but his palette and composition were rooted in Finnish Modernism. Mäkilä's factoryscapes and images of workers stressed the values of work and production. The bold rhetoric of his paintings accurately captures the faith in progress and the worker romanticism of the socialist movement of the '70s.

Realism was the mainstream art of the '70s in both the West and East. In the work of the Finnish artist Sven-Olof Westerlund, American Photorealism was fused with local values. Westerlund's output consisted of large pencil drawings based on photographs, yet their view of the world and iconography were close to traditional Finnish Realism and Socialist Realism. Ordinary people, such as construction workers and cleaning women, were his heroes. Nevertheless, for Westerlund, Photorealism remained more of an external tool than a specific source of content or method.

George Segal's art provided plentiful models for the sculptor Rauni Liukko's sociological art. Different social groups, such as children or migrant work-

Inari Krohn, *Bread and Flowers*, 1972, City Art Museum of Helsinki.

Järmo Mäkilä, *Iron Foundry Worker*, 1975, City Art Museum of Helsinki.

ers, interested her. Liukko cast her figures in fiberglass, and used them in assemblages together with real objects. Liukko's art was piercingly objective and devoid of idealistic rhetoric. It was Realism almost in the Positivist sense, although marked by a concern for the plight of the weak and oppressed.

Finnish political art evaporated surprisingly quickly at the end of the 1970s, and few mourned its passing or longed for its return. The Constructivist values of the artistic establishment had stood up well to this anti-modernist attack. If anything, they were actually strengthened by it, and attracted new worshippers from among former supporters of Social Realism. In the mid-1980s politics again began to appear in artistic discourse, but in a negative form, as deconstruction.

The Rodchenko Society, a group of young artists from Tampere, poked fun at political slogans and the Constructivist idiom. Their art subjected lofty utopian ideals to good-humored ridicule, by combining exhortations to study and take up the class struggle with playful taunting of the bourgeoisie in an amalgam of absurd graphic schemes and advertising avant-gardism.

Alvar Gullichsen's art deconstructed the language of advertising and marketing. His works parody the yuppie culture and business-mania of the 1980s. Gullichsen developed a fictional company, Bonk Business, which produced and marketed absurd, useless machines. They met all the requirements of "trademark" and "design," but were no more than delightfully useless. The Bonk Business corporate identity also included an art collection, made up of Gullichsen's own paintings. These are a combination of cartoons, Mad humor and Modernism. His art represents a concise critique of the instrumental reason of the Enlightenment. But even combined with the irony of the Rodchenko Society, it seemed unable to shake the faith of the Finnish establishment in the basic values of Modernism.

Translated from Finnish by Michael Garner

NOTES

[1] The show was financed by the art collector Matti Harkonmäki, and most of it was put together by the artist Jarmo Makila and myself. The City Art Museum of Helsinki acquired the Harkonmäki Collection in autumn 1991.

[2] Sarje, Kimmo, *Realism and Utopias — Social Realism in 1970s Finnish Art*, Harkonmäki Collection, Helsinki 1991.

Beautiful Perverted Flowers:
Some Effects of the Sovietization
of Estonian Art

by Mart Kalm
(Estonia)

Before World War II, art in Estonia, as in any other small European country, had a normal life. There were art societies and higher art education, with regular exhibitions and corresponding critical attention in the media. The art was, for the most part, Paris-oriented. After the war, the Soviet occupation imposed a Stalinistic model of art. Most of the artists joined the Artists' Union; those who refused were sent to Siberia or died of hunger. Collaborating artists, i.e., those artists who wanted to survive, achieved a privileged position within society. In the beginning of the '50s they painted pioneers and tractors in an Impressionist-Realist manner. At the end of the '50s, the ideological control over art weakened, and Estonian art was once again influenced by modern art; the School of Paris tradition of colorism was still very evident. At the end of the '60s, avant-garde style broke through to Estonian art with the groups ANK and Soup '69. These groups rejected the traditional values of art (unlike Latvian art which has continued its traditions to the present), and proclaimed the artist's uniqueness as the highest value. Performance art, Happenings, Land Art and conceptual art were also born at this time in Estonia.

The first shock to hit the artists was the change of attitudes in art criticism. Since the end of the '50s the main purpose of criticism had been to protect and justify the artists in front of the authorities. There were no longer any taboos in art, except political. By the beginning of the '80s, criticism began to be more independent: its sole function was no longer to be an advocate of artists.

Under the new ideological pressure of the '70s, the avant-garde artists in Estonia faced a dilemma: should they continue their work underground or compromise and maintain their position as officially recognized artists? The second possibility, which was chosen by the majority of avant-gardists, guaranteed a relatively large income and the opportunity to travel abroad, as well as the acquisition of apartments and cars. This is not funny; it is a sad fact. But the compromise was not as humiliating as it might have been because of the relatively liberal atmosphere here. There hadn't existed any official court art in Estonia since the beginning of the '50s. Therefore when *perestroika* brought Russian art out from the underground, the Estonians did not have an unofficial underground art to come out. Still, dramatic changes began to take place in Estonian art.

In Estonia, with its population of one million, the art world was like the court of any 18th-century German principality. Before *perestroika* the artists belonged to the elite of the society. They felt comfortable and protected because they were well-paid by the state, and they were well-known and admired. In the cafés people gossiped about artists and writers because they had no politicians and businessmen to discuss. In the mid-'80s, an Estonian political scene emerged and so artists were pushed from the center of the stage. This was the second shock for them. However, thanks to the rise of national consciousness, artists could temporarily maintain their position because they interpreted national mythology in a postmodern way.

Now the system of values in Estonian society has begun to resemble a typical Western mentality. Culture has lost its extremely high position in society. Although the previous order was in a way perverted by a delay of 50 years, this delay enabled the Baltics to maintain some cultural attitudes of pre-World War II Europe. To lose these now when they have an established historical value is sad, but it is impossible to keep them as they were if we mean to be an open society. The best example of the new mentality is the situation of the Estonian National Gallery. It lost its building and the government is unable to support it. The National Gallery was located in a fine Baroque palace but its technical equipment broke down; since then they have not been able to find a place to install the collection. Moreover, exhibition rooms at other museums are now closed because the National Gallery's collections are stored in them.

During the last decades Estonians have considered their art to be more closely connected to International art than Soviet art. Even our closest neighbors, Latvians and Lithuanians, have accused us of being too trendy: they maintain their national schools. It is now becoming clear just how closed the system of Estonian art has been. The inner hierarchy of values does not respond to that of the world. Some of the art which was considered to be high art is not actually so, but rather a specific kind of kitsch. However, there isn't much appreciation for common kitsch thanks to the traditionally Finland-oriented cool taste. An art market began to form in the mid-'80s. Thanks to the naive Lithuanian archetype, the artists were quite surprised that in the market the art generally considered bad was proven better than the real avant-garde. Also as a result of the previous system, there are many artists who are used to thinking in terms of technique or material but not in terms of art. They don't realize that ceramics is not a kind of art but a means for the artist to make art. Therefore the present art situation in Estonia is confusing; the changing values of our society are dramatically painful not only for many artists but for the critics as well.

The Shaping of Utopia, A Time-Slice Attempt: Bulgarian Art Today

by Philip Zidarov
(Bulgaria)

I prepared this paper, or rather, these notes, not with the intention of describing contemporary Bulgarian art, but rather to look for an explanation as to why this art remains virtually unknown abroad.

If one is to look for typical characteristics of Bulgarian art today, they should be the same as for the Bulgarian art of yesterday, and only peripherally in relation to the movements and ideas of 20th-century European art. A quintessentially Bulgarian "delay-syndrome" can be observed in the arts as well. This creates a phenomenon that may be the best way to illustrate the situation in which we in Bulgaria find ourselves now.

Manifesting Stalinist virtues, the severe socialist regime of the '50s threw most of the artists possessing individuality out of artistic circulation for at least a decade, and forced the rest to obey the commandments of its teachings. In the '60s and '70s there followed a somewhat softer version of this doctrine, labeled in Bulgaria the April-Line of the party (named after a Communist Party Congress in April, 1956, that simply replaced the Stalinist old-guard with new hypocrites). The new government skillfully tied together a demagogic loosening of the grips of ideological taboos by tolerating a wider spectrum of artistic interests, unless, of course, they manifested themselves as a hidden form of political dissent. With total economic dependence on the totalitarian communist state, such cases were unlikely. In that way, the entirety of Bulgarian art became, in effect, official art, controlled and guided by ideology. Thus, an artist who was not recognized as an artist by the regime was deprived of any means of being an artist. Censorship was unnecessary and irrelevant, considering the auto-censorship that ensued as a price for professional survival.

The result of all this was to create a total lack of any underground or alternative aesthetic forms. The absence of an alternative culture deprived the art scene of new ideas. But since unofficial artistic presences in other Eastern Bloc countries usually resulted in political dissent, this would be the last thing a stable communist regime such as that in Bulgaria would tolerate. In the totalitarian state, an artist was seen only as an instrument for producing such art whose aesthetic values served the glorification of the new life under Soviet-style socialism.

During the '80s, the absence of underground art, which had a long history elsewhere in Eastern Europe, was filled by a movement oriented towards an artificial synthesis of a so-called local avant-garde. This mild form of resistance against the dominant image of an ever-optimistic, metaphorical social realism could be detected among some of Bulgaria's official, younger artists. Against the silent disapproval of the establishment, consisting of an all-mighty union of artists and its high party members, this resistance took the form of works and exhibitions marked by conceptual, Arte Povera, and assemblage styles that were later combined with land and performance art. These rather isolated "new" artistic acts of individualistic younger artists or of small groups sharing similar aesthetic ideas were nothing other than an example of the Bulgarian delay-syndrome. At that time these acts were only creating a potential situation for the emergence of a new generation in art, with a different concept of what it is to be an artist. But the threshold of an age of quiet evolution is not to be crossed in such a way.

The quite unexpected collapse of the communist order terminated the "delay-syndrome" solution, and left artists in an uncomfortable no-man's-land between the disappearance of the *ancien regime's* artistic establishment and the absence of an alternative culture ready to fill the vacuum. An easy and almost carefree existence among friendly communist patrons had fostered a weak and inactive Bulgarian intelligentsia. Overnight the intelligentsia found itself helpless and useless in an unfamiliar and hostile environment of intellectual freedom, political instability, economic destruction, and desperate struggle for survival. That was the reason that not a single Bulgarian exhibition had been torn down by bulldozers as was the case in the Ismeilovo Park in Moscow, not a single artist had been killed or imprisoned for his stand, not one barricade had been built or mounted by art or artists in Bulgaria.

So the "delay-syndrome," and the apathetic state of artistic non-conformism left at least two generations of Bulgarian artists without support or self-confidence, and without any conviction of the social indispensability of art itself. In a time of political change, in which they took no part, artists lacked any conviction of being able to make a living with dignity. The absence of an alternative culture leaves us with a disintegrated art market:

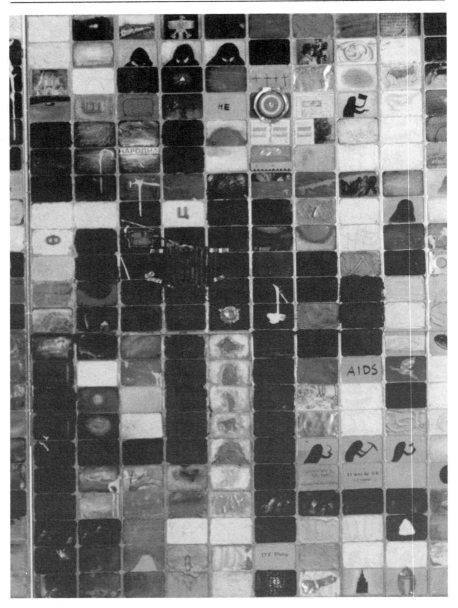

Nedfko Sokolov, *Untitled*, 1989.

state galleries lack money and interest to buy art, new patronage is precluded by a lack of education and knowledge about art investment, and contacts with foreign markets are closed due to Western ignorance of Bulgarian art. The rapid decay of the entire art scene in Bulgaria has forced considerable numbers of young and talented Bulgarian artists, with no secure prospects at home, to try to incorporate themselves into the Western European or American art scenes. This leaves the danger that mediocre substitutes and total commercialization will shape everything done in art in Bulgaria in the coming years.

This present time-slice situation can be seen as the beginning of a blank page. Everything that was until yesterday has already passed. Everything else has yet to happen. There is no present tense in Bulgarian art today. We are in a time of transition. And about the future? There is nothing more and nothing better than great expectations.

The Art of Argument —
Where Are the Limits of Rhetoric in
Criticism?

by Altti Kuusamo
(Finland)

Nowadays, when it is possible to see almost anything from the point of view of rhetoric, criteria for discerning easily adopted opinions from competent arguments seem to be more than difficult in art criticism. The old distinction between opinion and knowledge has also disappeared and has been transformed into options.

What is the role of argument in a situation where the possibilities for expanding the scale of styles in criticism seem to be the only alternative left? The challenge to broaden the scope of criticism was made unintentionally by conceptual art some time ago. A common habit then (and now) was to use emblematic critical slogans in works of art.

Apparently the first necessity in the rhetoric of criticism is to distinguish arguments from strategies. But how can we prove that interesting arguments are closer to innovative critical writing than are good strategies? Of course, we are entitled to ask whether there is any place for strategies in rhetoric at all. If strategies can be defined as modes for arousing social attention, or types of practical interest in order to take up positions, they must be in the margins of criticism just as gestures of the speaker (the rhetorician) are when trying to acquire public approval. It will be more difficult to define the role of argument in critical discourse.

According to Aristotle, "rhetorical arguments . . . are the substance of rhetorical persuasion." But what exactly is the state of this substance today? It seems that we have a hierarchy of concepts according to which artistic "facts," works of art, are represented in critical discourse. "Facts" have to be represented with style and in style — and style is in fact persuasion. So, what we have is: *artistic objects represented* in discourse through *arguments, opinions,* and *strategies*. In composing critical arguments one needs *judgement* as well. Nowadays the term judgment is quite unpopular — as if it has ceased to exist, as if it were too archaic to be mentioned.

But we need judgment, and judgment needs the art of memory and the art of forgetting: namely the *politics of selecting facts and values.*

That seems to be the core of the mystery of artwriting. But it is only the beginning. Good style is closely connected to interesting arguments (ruled by judgments). As David Carrier has said: "Each interesting new style of argumentation in artwriting . . . is linked to a discovery of new ways to narrate." When the language of criticism is changing drastically, the ways of arguing change too. At least we hope so. The truth is usually quite the contrary within the politics of rhetoric: the language of criticism does not change as quickly as objects, the targets of the critic, seem to change.

If we have to make a rough distinction between *argumentative* and *strategic* criticism, how can we prove that argumentative criticism is more rhetorical than strategic criticism? For that we need good arguments and good style.

Argumentation and the desire to narrate are closely linked to each other: more closely than objects of art and objects represented in narration. This explains the difficulty of making a distinction between argumentative and strategic criticism in the first place. Only the length of elaboration of arguments seems to work as a criterion.

Recently there have been efforts to widen the cultural scope of criticism: criticism is taken as one genre of art. It can be a performance, or anything else. Any attempt to expand the range of criticism in the direction of art commentary, which more precisely includes every commentary on art *as art,* seems to threaten the argumentative aspects of written criticism. We have experienced the pathology of self-referential art. Should we now go into the pathology of self-referential criticism? When being self-referential, criticism is hardly argumentative.

When writing a critique we usually choose a way between the extremes of *ars combinatoria* and *ars argumentativa.* No doubt the art of interesting critical persuasion is also an art of good argument. The better the argument, the better the possibilities of making breakthroughs in written discourse.

But strategic criticism is challenging us all the time: in practical criticism, or in newspaper reviews, there is little room for argumentative procedures, but there are many genres of strategic criticism.

Is criticism doomed to be only the serious praxis caused by the play of art? (The idea of criticism as a kind of praxis contrary to art has been proposed by François Lyotard.) Or could it also be a play? If criticism is a part of the artworld, could it also be a part of the big play called art? Haven't we been told that walls no longer exist between the play of art and the grave praxis of criticism?

If we devote ourselves to impractical and playful criticism, what then would be the fate of argumentative criticism? In fact the interest leading to playful criticism entails a paradox. Let us illustrate this paradox in the following way:

To begin with, we know that the task of strategic criticism is to be practical — for it wants to gain maximal social approval. It seeks conformity with the latest radical and most widely spread opinion. It adopts superficially the latest fashionable intellectual ideas — and uses them for strategic needs. Argumentative criticism, in turn, tries to find new ways of describing and evaluating art objects. If we accept this, we can't help thinking that the argumentative criticism has the best competence and best chances to become impractical and playful criticism. But who then is going to maintain the criticism which will take into account rational standards? How will we distinguish play from arguments? When argumentative criticism wants to play and has to play, what is the fate of the so-called good judgment on which the argumentative criticism is based?

Part III:
Post-Colonial and/or Post-Totalitarian Art:
Is It Postmodern?

Post-Colonial Art

by Beral Madra
(Turkey)

At the end of this century we are participating in conferences to discuss the modern art system with retrospective thoughts and futuristic calculations. Historical and futuristic consciousness based on 20th-century myths and end-of-the-century multiculturalism is the keynote of recent discussions. The focus upon art, politics, ethnicity, multiculturalism, politicization of art criticism, censorship in art and post-colonial and/or post-totalitarian art in this conference leads us to the crucial realization that the myths of universality, individuality, freedom, and pluralism in modern and postmodern art are still far from reality. They may be our "end-of-century illusions" — in which we are all consciously or unconsciously involved.

The presence of art critics and curators from developing nations in recent conferences is a feature of today's art situation, a necessity observed by the art system in late-capitalistic countries. This feature is clearly underlined by Kim Levin, in her book, *Beyond Modernism*: "The future has become a question of survival for everybody" and, "Identity and behavior is important for every human being." I take these as the basis of my opinion, and I say that any kind of discrimination, political subversion, depersonalization, or dislocation of the artist according to his or her racial, national, or regional background is an act of the utmost vanity, stupidity, or ruthlessness. This is not the critic's task. Our task is to eliminate the mediocre art which invades our art scenes. The ideas of Janet Abu-Lughod in her "On the Remaking of History: How to Reinvent the Past," suggest that the current reevaluation of the art system may have resulted from the emergence of the Fourth World in world geopolitics, shifting the axis to the Pacific. Abu-Lughod's ideas guided me to review this subject in Turkey.

Abu-Lughod further said: "It was the unpreparedness of the East, even more than the strength of the West, that was responsible for the ultimate outcome, 'the rise of the West.'" However, Westernization is a long story in Turkey which started with the so-called "Rise of the West" in the 16th century; but this is not our subject here. Art, in the sense of 20th-century Western art, has existed and developed since the middle of the 19th century and was first evaluated as one of the sanctions of colonialism (or Westernization) and then, in the second half of the 20th century, was accepted and assimilated as a "must" of capitalism. It should be noted that Turkey has not been a victim of colonialism in the full sense, but was able to manipulate the colonialist ambitions of the West, first, into the so-called Westernization movements and then, into the Revolution of Independence with Ataturk. Based on Western or Westernized art's 150 years of existence in Turkey, to say that it is a phenomenon against the Islamic religion is a superficial and mischievous view.

The relationship of art and religion in Turkey is different. I cannot say that the mythical content and aura of 20th-century art affects the public as much as might be expected. Since the beginning of the century, modern art has formed a world of myths about the existence of the artist, creativity and the phenomenon of art against all other phenomena. Today, this world of myths has caused art to acquire the status of religion, the artist being its prophet and the art critic its priest. Thus, contemporary art museums have replaced cathedrals in late-capitalist countries. In today's art, transformations are inevitable; they are the essence of avant-gardism.

These transformations require strong actions and reactions in order to destroy a myth and replace it with a new one. This so-called postmodernism is a phenomenon which should be experienced not only by the artist but also by society. When we evaluate the state of the avant-garde in our country, where capitalism is still developing, the religious aspect cannot yet be attributed to art. Moreover, Islamic religion is still too strong to be replaced by an alternative phenomenon. Art cannot compete with religion in Turkey as much as it does elsewhere.

Although the mythical effect of art on the masses is partly absent, the complexity of inherited cultural elements together with foreign influences, and media and information explosions, are mirrored in the art of the last three decades. If the principal character of culture now is the common faith in something, the masses have faith in consumption, media, and triviality. They discover their identity through this "faith." This all happens in Turkey in the midst of the rich historical background and tradition. In Turkey, as elsewhere, the intellectual minorities have faith in contemporary art, science, and technology. And, as elsewhere, when contemporary art approaches the faith of the masses, it integrates consumption, media, and trivialization and acquires the strength of religion.

The problem of the artist in Turkey is to live through this dilemma. Not being able to communicate with his public, nor being able to go beyond

Turkey itself, he has to live through the various stages and experiences of postmodernism, or maybe I should now call this post-Westernization. As I have doubts about postmodernism in Turkey, I also have doubts about "real" postmodernism in Europe and the United States. Postmodernism, because of its dissipation and the way it spread, can be considered an inflated myth of the "business art" system. In order to determine the "real" postmodernism, one can only rely on outcome and meticulous evaluations. Otherwise, it is not surprising to encounter counterfeit and superficiality when art without real myths is disguised as inflated postmodernism.

However, postmodernism (post-westernization) regarded from another aspect seems to fit the *Zeitgeist* in our country. Like India or Japan, Turkey has a postmodern culture without truly having lived through a modern one. The term "westernization" is a much more honest term to use for the modern period in Turkey. The art heritage of our country contains contradiction, conflict, various myths and layers of different literary, philosophical, religious and artistic cultural elements. In addition to these, it has different regional identities, being an East European, West Asian, and Mediterranean country. The cultural identity of Turkey has been deconstructed and reconstructed for 200 years, which has resulted in an identity crisis. If postmodernism is a process of reorganization and the seeking of a new world language, then we are experienced in practising this reorganization and research.

Here in Turkey, until recently, when we examined "art" we asked ourselves, is it original? is it derivative? is its similarity to Western art (noticed very often, in the last ten years, in international exhibitions here and abroad) conscious or unconscious? More often, we judged the Western artist as original, and the similarity as a matter of relativity or of re-interpretation. We thought the Eastern artist could not choose elements from art history. But, now we are more sophisticated and we know that one production is not more worthwhile than another, when one artwork is a production of "business art" and one of "art for art." Artists all over the world have the same general art context, even if they have not the same economic, political and social background. This universal art context, traveling from west to east, from east to west, from north to south and from south to north with the same speed and density, has the influence and power to determine art production.

Now, we discuss influences as evident adaptations, and we know they open up new directions for new languages. This is called intercultural

Ayse Erkmen, *Ceremony to the Past*, 1989.

Serhat Kiraz, *God of Religions — Religions of God*, installation, 1989.

transaction, and it creates a general reorganization. At the same time, we must admit that the source of this intercultural transaction has been colonialism and post-colonialism.

This fact bears a more detailed inspection. Western art concepts influencing Eastern art concepts, and vice versa, do not lead to the same expression or language. There are differences among the results of both influences: differences in time, context and process. These differences must be understood, known and discussed before anything else. I propose that Western art critics and curators investigate art in the "other" countries with objectivity and rigorous art historical methodology from now on. The Western artist of the past built up a language through "superiority," i.e., through colonialism or imperialism. It imposed Renaissance and modern art concepts, which in fact hold assimilated borrowings from the East, onto the world, while pretending not to see that, at the same time, the East is also borrowing, lending, and allowing itself to be influenced.

The assertion of the West holds some truth, considering its early development of this new language. But when considering the development of Eastern art, it is evident that the formation of its new language will take time. If modernism, which was influenced by the East, is the final development of the Renaissance, then the final outcome of Eastern abstraction and aniconism, with its borrowings from the West, has to be awaited. Proclaiming, in this period of transformation, that "this has been done before" has lost all validity. Postmodernism itself is but a vast array of intercultural transactions — to which the Western artist turns as a source for new ways.

Post-Modernism in "Totalitaria"

by Brandon Taylor
(England)

I should like to try in a few short paragraphs to raise some issues concerning one dominant interpretation of major cultural alignments in the 20th century, particularly those that relate to terms like "totalitarian," "liberal," "anti-modern," "postmodern," and "modern." To show conclusively that the interpretation I am calling dominant is indeed dominant, one would need to look minutely at standard textbooks, works of criticism, exhibition arrangements, curatorial practices and the like, and that is something that in the nature of the exercise cannot be done here. Suffice it to say that most cultural practices make classificatory assumptions which are at the same time evaluations of a particular tendency or direction in art, and that much of our talk about art is suffused with the terminology that I now want to question.

The assumption that I want to examine says "modern" culture has consistently stood above and against, contradicted and undermined (and has been undermined by) something else we call "totalitarian" culture, the culture of the dictatorships in the 1930s and 1940s.

The so-called anti-modernist aesthetic positions introduced in Nazi Germany and the Soviet Union were the very antithesis of all which is youthful and progressive in 20th-century culture. These oppositions can be easily extended: "traditional" versus "contemporary," "backward-looking" versus "forward-looking," "unoriginal" versus "original," "popular" versus "elite," "national" versus "international," "accessible" versus "specialized," "univalent" versus "polyvalent," "conventional" versus "experimental media," "mass" versus "minority" consumption, and many more; above all, "anti-modern" versus "modern." Indeed, it is now quite normal to say that because this sort of art was integrally fused with reactionary political regimes, it is worthy only of being vilified and ignored. In aesthetic terms, this same association often implies that so-called "totalitarian art" is so bad as not to be art at all.

The trouble is that the reasoning behind this verdict has recently begun to look increasingly odd. Is it really credible that the 20th century contained only two artistic ideologies, both of them sharply polarized from each other — rather than five or seventeen? Isn't it also symptomatic that the epithets hurled by each side of this debate at the other are in many ways equal and opposite? Thus the "conservatives" accuse the "modernists" of ignoring content and elevating form, of experimenting and losing touch with the masses, of having lost touch with craft and skill; the "modernists" accuse the "conservatives" of ignoring form and elevating content, of conformism and appealing to the lowest denominator in taste, of relying upon outdated practices and techniques. What is really at stake in this careful construction of opposites, in this elaborate definition by exclusion of the "other?"

The first intriguing fact is that the attack upon "modernism" was initially developed by those whose cultural judgments we otherwise distrust. Certainly the terms of the attack far exceeded the language of aesthetics. The National Socialists in Germany lambasted "modern" art as Jewish, incompetent, culturally decadent, the product of criminal and lunatic minds; here was a policy designed to bolster racial stereotypes and affirm a "popular," managed culture — no doubt a contradiction in terms. The Soviet Party bosses attacked "modernism" because it was internationalist, formally experimental, and of supposedly "bourgeois" origins — hence inconsistent with "socialist construction." The inverse construction, that the art of the dictatorships was "traditional," "unprogressive," and "backward" was largely the result of Cold-War rhetoric which required the starkest division to be drawn between two opposed ideological camps.

If "modern" and "anti-modern" excluded each other mainly in the minds of those with political or social programs to promote, then it seems to me a clear possibility that as hindsight increases we shall begin to discern a wider meaning of "modernity" in which both parts of this symbiosis belong. In fact, I want to suggest that within the pervasive rhetoric of both parties there lies a scarcely concealed regard for the other camp.

A very few examples will have to suffice. In Germany, the best cases by far are those from the design fields: they include the Bauhaus-inspired classicism of Troost and Speer, the efficiency and functionalism of automobiles, roads, and bridges, the modernizing attitudes towards health, safety, personnel management, and corporate identity of the *Schönheit der Arbeit* movement, and the classical lines and ergonomic functional styling of interior design fittings, furniture, and the domestic space.

Even in painting and sculpture, forms are either classically smooth and polished, as in *Neue Sachlichkeit*, or else crude and expressionistic, as in

Brücke art. In terms of exhibition display, the National Socialists were highly modernistic, using space and architecture in surprisingly advanced ways. The notorious "Entarte Kunst" exhibition of 1937 — recently reconstructed in Los Angeles — used the techniques of Dada disorientation and confusion brilliantly against itself, as well as against Jewish examples of Cubism and Expressionism. One is inclined to say that "tradition" here comes in quotation-marks: it is in reality a highly subtle blend of militarized modernized ideology dressed up in inauthentic 19th-century dress.

In the Soviet Union's retrenchment of the 1930s and 1940s, aspects of the other "modernism" were also subtly accommodated and deployed. The aesthetic positions negotiated in the later 1920s by OSt, Four Arts, NOZh, Bytie and Makovets had already explored compromises with Cézanne, Matisse and Impressionism. The 1932 *perestroika* which closed down these organizations ruled many of these compromises out. But in the large-scale official history painting that followed, what was reinstated was not (as the rhetoric claimed) 19th-century *peredvizhnichestvo*, but an original artistic language that used many of the distortions of perspective, color, and scale that had been and were being explored in modernism further West. In the 1970s, the so-called "severe style" comes out as a highly modernized comic-book imagery of action and achievement. In architecture particularly — as is already well recognized — the classicism of the 1930s ran parallel to the modernizing classicism of Europe and the United States.

The point can be made by talking about "tradition." If "tradition" is defined as "that which is handed down: a statement, belief or practice transmitted from generation to generation," or else as a "long established and generally accepted custom or method of procedure, having almost the force of law . . . the experiences and usages of any branch of art or literature, handed down by predecessors and generally followed," then German culture in the Third Reich was not traditional. Here, artistic creeds from the past were taken rather than received; imposed by fiat rather than "long established and generally accepted."

It should be borne in mind of course that these politically reactionary cultures were powered by an uncompromising desire for industrial superiority: in Germany's case linked to military ambition, and in the Soviet Union's linked to a fixation with ideological transcendence and eventually with "burying the West."

That makes an enormous difference to how our aesthetic categories have evolved, but not to whether they have finally settled down. The conse-

Adolf Wissel, *Young Farming Women*, 1937.

quences of this look at definitions are worth spelling out. First, the argument requires us to see all dynamic cultural forms as part of the century's quest for utopia, its rush for the future, in the course of which many different aesthetic credos were invoked. Technologies of striving and improvement, of industry, production and transport, of communications, education and awareness — these took many forms. If some of these forms proved poorly adapted, even unworkable, then this surely offers no proof either for or against the modernity of their impulses.

Secondly and finally, there is an argument to be made about "postmodernism." In common with the so-called "anti-modern" manifestoes of the 1930s and 1940s, postmodernist polemics of the 1970s and 1980s also looked selectively back at a narrow range of early modernist experiments — the preoccupation with style, author, and so on — and moved to discard them. A host of stylistic reversals, the recuperation and recombination of previously discarded imagery (including, sometimes, the imagery of fascism itself), a strenuous rhetoric of the "anti-modern" combined with an extraordinary impulse to renovate and to console: these tendencies could be used to situate "postmodernism" as a further form of modernism, the latest in a long series of economically-led experiments to lead the non-post-modernizing world. Thus equally, the virulent "anti-modernism" of half a century ago can now be seen as a form of "postmodernism" *avant la lettre*; politically reactionary to be sure, but ultimately no less modernizing for all that.

SOURCES:

Igor Golomstock, *Totalitarian Art*, London, 1990.

Brandon Taylor and Wilfried van der Will, *The Nazification of Art: Art, Design, Music, Architecture and Film in the Third Reich*, Winchester, 1990.

Applied Arts
Between Function and Disfunction

by Bohumila Milena Lamarová
(Czechoslovakia)

To speak about applied arts in Czechoslovakia, it is necessary to make a brief historical introduction to describe its characteristic features in the totalitarian period and possible development in the post-totalitarian times.

Between the two wars, Czechoslovakia belonged to the ten most developed countries of Europe both economically and culturally. Its economy was based on a highly developed industrial production. Its culture was marked by long periods of national revival and searches for national identity in art and literature, and also by several generations of internationally-oriented modern avant-garde artists.

The search for national identity in the fine arts was closely followed by arts and crafts. The decorative arts, especially glass and textiles, flourished, thanks to a long tradition of craft schools, which were founded in the 19th century. The strong background of arts and crafts enabled the great success of Czechoslovakia at the International exhibition of Decorative Arts in Paris in 1925, where it was second only to France in the number of gold medal awards.

This tradition continued well into the '30s, using a completely new vocabulary of modernism as well as being influenced by the avant-garde of the late '20s. This was also the "golden age" of Czechoslovakian design, which began to take over in the field of industrial production. The function of applied arts before the Second World War was clearly defined by the structure of an advancing society. In connection with building activities, there were demands for works of monumental character; and the modernist movement introduced design to the struggle for new housing. Generally, the applied arts and design have been considered as media of cultural development and supported by a number of institutions, associations, and committees.

When the Communists took over in 1947 with the slogan that the arts must serve socialism and above all the needs of the working class, the values and meanings of applied arts began to disintegrate. The decorative and symbolic values were totally subordinated to propaganda aims, especially at big political events, meetings, and congresses. Naturalistic symbols of the sickle and the hammer, and completely false portraits of heroes and heroines of the "socialist struggle" were interpreted in a sort of vulgar romanticism. Monumental size was used to emphasize the irreconcilability of the class struggle. But it was also employed to make the symbols visible to the masses and to represent the gigantomania of communist ideology.

The credo was that art should be omnipresent, art should belong to everybody; but in fact this fake presumption created an alienated sense of proportions in the environment and in the perception of "beauty." Monumental political decoration became a functional illusion of beauty for daily life accessible to everybody, and at the same time to nobody. It was a puritan ideology, which fiercely opposed bourgeois hedonism — for both theoretical and practical reasons. The so-called socialist society soon faced abysmal pauperization, especially in product design. Not only did technologies stagnate, but quality was debased. Meticulously executed details in precious materials were obliterated. The elegant simplicity of the pre-war modernist design ended up as dull, primitive, unbalanced forms. Moreover, the hermetism of a society behind the Iron Curtain did not allow it contact with European trends, which had been, historically, a natural part of Czechoslovakian culture — a culture based on the exchange and transformation of European cultural forms.

In the late '50s, thanks to large international exhibitions, applied arts based on traditional arts and crafts became a surrogate for common cultural standards. Applied arts were patronized for the sake of propaganda and representative exhibitions, but at the same time they were frustrated in the development of design for individual use, or for the expression of individual creative visions.

This constant frustration of the applied arts — a constant feeling of alienation from the real artistic idea and its spiritual emanation — led to an interesting shift in the '60s: artists began to seek a refuge in abstract forms, moving slowly into the realm of fine arts, be it graphic art, painting or sculpture. The tendency to monumental forms and sizes however remained. But it was — as had been the tradition in Czech visual arts — a new reactivation of crafts' potency through the impact of fine arts. The '60s, in general, were marked by a strong opposition to so-called Socialist Realism. Late surrealism, abstractionism, and structural forms were followed by geometric abstraction and new imagination in the '70s. The field of product design was abandoned, since the material world was sinking deeper and deeper into poverty or falsely pretended Good Form. The applied arts served as the media of interpretation for developments in the fine arts.

This happened especially in the two most traditional fields of Czech applied arts: textile design and glass. In both, artists used the long-established traditions and skills to express their ideas, which by no means confirmed communist ideology. It was the attitude of escapism, rather than real criticism or irony; it was a time when artists still acknowledged their truthfulness towards the material, trying to use it in a highly professional and innovative manner in order to convey their visions.

To mention some important names of this period, Professor Antonin Kybal, a master of the language of textile, Bohdan Mrázek, Jindrich Vohánka and Jirí Tichy´ distorted the rectangular convention of tapestry and introduced a three-dimensional vision, suggesting that tapestry can be an object, not just another mural decoration. And Jirí and Jenny Hladík transformed their graphic experience into superb autonomous works, which predicted the era of postmodernism.

Czech glassmaking, with its historical tradition and continuity of skills, was able to oppose totalitarian demands in a powerful way. The doyen of Czech glass, Professor Stanislav Libensky, and his wife, Jaroslava Brychtová, developed monumental works in an independent manner. Above all, they were able to transfer the message to two generations of their pupils. This was also accomplished by professor Václav Kaplicky in a more subtle, but perhaps more philosophical way, directly linked to the pre-war avantgarde. An important person in this respect was, and still is, Václav Cigler. He introduced abstract architectural forms, eliminating any decoration. He has a great sense for constructivist purity and at the same time rediscovers the optical potentials of glass. His work has poetic vision; his later landscape and cosmological projects reach far beyond the decorative function.

The connection between postmodern and post-totalitarian seems to be clear. Yet, for Czech art, the most significant feature was that postmodern tendencies served as a means of criticism, both in the political and social sense. Since modernism was never part of an affluent consumer society in Czechoslovakia, the vocabulary of references lacks the type of symbolism that would invoke Pop Art. Rather, criticism has been directed at the fake and meaningless symbols of the totalitarian regime, at pretentious senti-

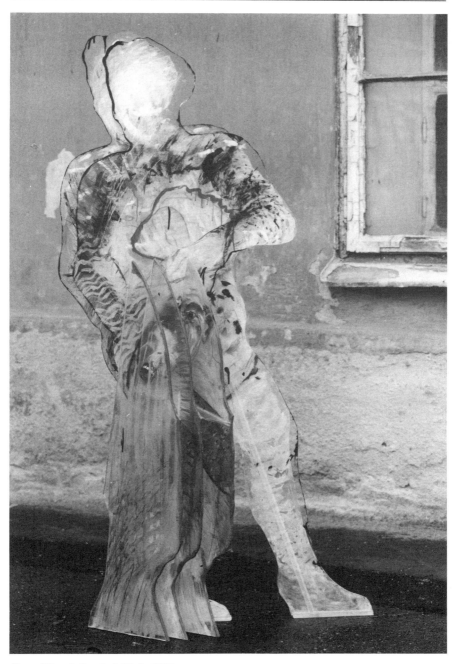

Dana Zámečníková, *A Walk*, 1991.

Jeřina Žertová, *The Hill*, 1991.

mental symbols of national romanticism, and at the schizophrenia of life under the totalitarian system. Mainly ironical quotations govern recent works, but sometimes there are also references to romanticism, poeticism or expressionism, which had been milestones in the development of Czech Art.

The freedom in mixing material and technological media is certainly one of the features of postmodernism, but it is also a natural sign of the development, which has brought integrity to the fine and applied arts, sculpture, and architecture. The previously strict functionality of applied arts has been vanishing. Today, the concept of applied arts as separate from the fine arts seems questionable. Yet, it may be the new ecological and architectural concepts which will determine the functions of the so-called applied arts.

From this point of view, Czech studio glass artists in recent years have been examining new forms of artistic and technological freedom with interesting results. Czech glass artists were not looking for a revival of old glassmaking technologies, but used them innovatively to forward their artistic visions. Glass has been used as a material for sculpture, or as a basis for painting. At the same time, the optical qualities of glass were exploited — either positively for its brilliance and transparence, or nega-tively as a mimicry hiding the real message under thick layers of color or paint. The technology of cast and painted glass has been a major source of new sculptural ideas.

Among the older generation, remarkable is the precision and unbound imagination of Václav Cigler, whose sculpture penetrates the landscape with monumental but subtle forms. His antipode is Vladimír Kopecký, whose work transforms glass with violent color and mixes it with other materials; proceeding from constructivism to sculptural environment. Jiřina Žertová seeks abstract forms which demonstrate the inner tensions of glass. Marian Karel works with flat glass to create architectural objects with hidden poetics. His wife Dana Zámečníková combines glass with painting. Her most recent three-dimensional objects, products of very sophisticated technology, are dominated by a narrative quality reminding us of the language of James Joyce.

Other important glass artists could be mentioned if there were space. However, this report has tried to show how the functions of art developed in a particular society, in which the artistic imagination had to surpass traditional categories.

The Case of Lionello Balestrieri in Samobor

by Želimir Koščević
(Croatia)

Once upon a time, when the postmodern aesthetic was still in nascent swaddlings, something important occurred at Samobor, a town near Zagreb. A color reproduction of the famous painting *Beethoven* made by Italian artist Lionello Balestrieri in 1900 was removed from the wall in the dining room of a well-to-do family house. The reproduction had decorated that room for a long period.

Who was the artist who made this painting and what is its significance? Let me briefly give you the facts: Lionello Balestrieri, Italian painter, born in Cetona, near Siena, on September 12, 1872, where he died on December 29, 1958. He was educated in Rome and Naples, where his teacher was Domenico Morelli (1826-1901), an artist known as the master of strong light effects. From 1893 to 1914, Balestrieri lived in Paris. His work belongs to the academic tradition, thematically concerned with bohemian life in Paris (e.g., *Awaiting the Glory, Mimi's Death*). At the World Exhibition in Paris in 1900 Balestrieri exhibited his famous painting *Beethoven*, and was awarded the Golden Medal. This painting is now in the collection of Museo Revoltela in Trieste. After his return to Italy, he was the director of the Art Museum in Naples, but by that time he was almost forgotten as an artist.

As you can see in the illustration, the reproduction is dirty, dusty, and in the center there are some scratches. But what can you expect, if you find it in a local junkyard as I did two years ago? Even before its end in the local junkyard, the reproduction probably had not been stored under good conditions. I did not hesitate to take home this reproduction of a formerly famous painting, and now — it happened two years ago — I use it as a teaching aid in my courses in Museology at Zagreb University, where I am a part-time professor.

Frankly, in 1966, I would not have given any attention either to a dirty reproduction, or to Balestrieri's originals. But in the meantime, the whole system of aesthetic values has undergone huge changes. I do not want to waste your time explaining the nature of these changes, because as art critics you know what I have in mind. So we shall not concern ourselves with the postmodern as a change of style, but with the postmodern as the change of attitude toward art and culture. With these changes the whole Eurocentric system was entirely destroyed. It was not only that Mannerism, Boullée and Schinkel appeared again, but — more importantly — the Euro-Asiatic axis, set up by Joseph Beuys as a metaphor for the "new, end of the century" sensibility, was definitely established. In this way, aesthetic legitimacy was finally given to artistic expression of South Africa, Estonia, Iceland, Slovenia, South Korea, and Scotland, as well as that of informal social groups such as Puerto Ricans, Aborigines, feminists or punkers.

"We cannot go back to the aesthetic practice which has been developed on the basis of dilemmas which are not ours any more," said Fredric Jameson in 1984, suggesting at the same time that "a new global cognitive cartography has to be made," which, of course, involves the aesthetic dimension also. On this fascinating map, whose configuration reminds us of the cartographic redesign of the globe done by Surrealists in 1929, the reproduction of Balestrieri's painting emerges from the local junkyard as a culturally and aesthetically interesting phenomenon, and as evidence of aesthetic relativism. And, by the way, we have not even moved geographically far from the local area of, for instance, the Alpe-Adria Community (where, in spite of simultaneous translation into German, Italian, Slovenian, Hungarian and Croatian, the conversational language at meetings is English!).

But not only the aesthetic values are in question; the find at the local junkyard has an extreme cultural and informational importance. The theme of a Balestrieri from Samobor gives us — *cum grano salis* — a lot of possibilities to depict art and culture in a certain space and time as the example of an ordinary commonplace 20th-century locus.

The reproduction was printed in Berlin, most probably shortly after the glorious success of the original at the 1900 World Exhibition in Paris. We don't know where the reproduction was acquired, but almost certainly not in Samobor; rather in nearby Zagreb, or abroad. So, can you imagine the proud owner who brings the reproduction of the famous painting back to his home! Framed, on the wall, the reproduction enriched the home atmosphere in a provincial town with the exciting scene from bohemian life and with Beethoven as the topic.

At this point we can eavesdrop on the cacophony of the 20th century; soon we shall be able to quote Walter Benjamin: "the technology of multiplication — so we can generalize — isolates a reproduction from the tradition." And this seems to me to be essential: the local and the regional have been gradually transformed into the folklore of the global village, and into the postmodern universe. Between Beethoven, Paris, Berlin, and Samobor there exists a secret connection and this connection crosses the boundaries and changes the definition of the local and regional. With all respect for the differences, here I am speaking precisely about a certain standard of the European Outskirt cultural structure, because there is no reason to presume equal diffusion of Balestrieri's reproduction all around the European rim. Therefore, the Samobor model can be applied in Finland as well as in Ireland and the Ukraine.

Like a ring, this "Outskirt" cultural structure encircles the European Center. The structure has its own characteristics, similarities, and specifics, thus creating a much bigger space, which we tenderly call local or regional.

The well-known art school of Anton Azbe in Munich at the turn of the 20th century is marginal for Munich; as a matter of fact this school is much more interesting in the case of its students: David Burlyuk, Harmos Karloy, Josip Racic, Wassily Kandinsky, which means, after the amalgamation with the Outskirt's cultural and traditional sedimentation. Twenty years later, the same happened with the School of Andre Lhote in Paris.

As we move through the interpretative paths of a new history of 20th-century art, the argument of the genuinely local loses its meaning in a serious critical judgment and becomes a support for local artistic substitutes. We shall continue to speak about this hidden European Ring, the Outskirt structure, which abounds in creative phenomena (personalities). Thanks to more serious consideration of cultural anthropology, the cultural map of Europe is changing; so, without going too far — even if I am deeply linked with the art of Frida Kahlo (1907-1954), and the paintings of Tyko K. Sallinen (1879-1955) are not strange to me — the local "Balestrieri Case" opens many questions on real and contemporary understanding of the local, regional, and national. The question is whether these notions are still valid. We know that Joseph Beuys is German, and that for understanding the work of Ed Kienholz it is necessary to see California, and for decoding Jan Dibbets we shall not go to Greece but to Holland. This is the propaedeutic of art criticism; management of these data leads us directly to folklore having nothing to do with the noble aura which adorns the core of Europe.

The power with which the center defends its conquered position is frightening indeed. It is true that some people from the center comprehend that the center's narcissism leads nowhere, and that even in the center the anxiety is rising. The idea of regionalization, which picturesquely fits the theory and practice of postmodernism, turned out to be useful only to regional politicians, but even they ride their "Toyotas." *Genius Loci* of the region where I am living with the delicate accent of Californian postmodern style may be the challenge to a curious intellectual, but architecture with such characteristics furnishes the local "Balestrieri Case" with the consequences which put in question the criteria of the local, regional, and national in our aesthetic judgment.

The subtle dialogue with this matter is not only the privilege of the center; there are so many "magicians" all around the world. When we free ourselves from the prejudice of European science about beauty (aesthetics, and when — as Picasso said in one of his dialogues with Malraux — we explain to the people that creation only exceptionally appears as beauty — then we shall be able to enjoy freely everything that has been created in human spirit.

The imaginative use of "Balestrieri's Case" gives us an opportunity to explain many specifics in art during its history. But in the 20th century, many cultural and aesthetic phenomena demonstrate irregularities and deviations from the manifested rules in the Outskirt structure. The picture clouds: it is not clear as in the innocent times of Rome and Byzantium.

It may be assumed that the distribution of the Balestrieri reproduction was more or less equal through the European outskirts; we are therefore not surprised with the creative exceptions such as Hilma af Klimt (1862-1944) in Sweden, Olexandar Bogomazov (1880-1930) in the Ukraine, Avgust Cernigoj (1898-1985) in Slovenia, or Mikolaius K. Ciurlionis (1875-1911) in Lithuania. In the last decade, their almost forgotten opuses have been internationally recognized and re-evaluated. In this way the facts about Paris, Berlin, London and Cologne become much more real.

The reproduction of Balestrieri's painting which circulated through the European rim we understand as a metaphor of European integration; that means creating a delicate network of odd harmony.

We can also presuppose that the reproduction of Balestrieri had simultaneously been removed and thrown to the junkyard around the European outskirts. Soviet troops and Coca-Cola entered this area at the same time, together with the local drummers. Balestrieri on the wall was replaced

Lionello Balestrieri, *Beethoven* (reproduction), 1900.

with the TV set in the corner. There are many indications that precisely at that time the Outskirt structure lost its alchemical ability of amalgamation, and that right there began the process of spiritual atrophy, transforming itself into the State of Urlo "the country of spiritual torment" (Cz. Milos). McLuhan only crosses the "t."

Willy-nilly, the world is expanding, changing, and intertwining. The subtle spiritual alchemy of the European Outskirt has been strongly modified by a more advanced chemistry. The structure is slowly losing identity, and anxiety is increasingly spreading through the Outskirt. The appeal for the local, regional, and national was a normal reaction at the time, but not the way to a dialogue.

Once we have tried to define the Outskirt structure as the entity between — at least — two cultural mega-structures, and such a definition could only work as long as so many irregularities appeared. There is no doubt that the global politics of superpowers desecrated the Ring of European Outskirt structure. But I'm not interested in this form of group-sex; I am much more curious about the life-tale of Balestrieri's reproduction, which had been found at the junkyard, and recycled into a tool in my courses in Museology at Zagreb University. Common history of all Balestrieris all around the European Ring ended nearly a hundred years later in the efforts to establish histories and qualities. This, it is true, corresponds to the postmodern image of the world, but — the question is — does this image correspond with ours?

Sometimes it seems to me that I am watching schizoid particles of an ex-Europe which was once decorated with the string of Balestrieris. His way of painting had style. A reproduction hung on the wall at home is the expression of an attitude. In other words — the style had an attitude. Andy Warhol could not boast of it. And, honestly, nor does Slovenia (Alto Adige, Burgenland, Bavaria) have it any more.

Disorganization as Cultural Pattern?

by Alexander Jakimovich
(USSR)

When the part of the globe which was called Communist stepped in to drastic changes in the '80s, the idea emerged that we have reached a post-totalitarian stage in cultural development, and that, furthermore, we are far enough along to compare the post-totalitarian to postmodernism. It seems that with the passing years we are getting a bit wiser, or, at least, disillusioned (which is necessary to become wiser).

Obviously, the priority of art criticism and cultural theory in the former USSR is to interpret the independent art and literature existing in the context of the late totalitarian society. We have not left the enchanted continent of totalitarianism, we only try to embark.

Some people say the world has entered Post-History, and its artistic potential is exhausted. Others prefer to apply the notion of postmodernism to the newest phase of development, and sometimes they cannot even explain what they mean by it. This is in a large part due to the theory of society, man and culture that goes back to Lyotard and was expanded by later contributions from Deleuze, Jameson, Baudrillard, Welsch, and others. They designed a picture of a new human condition. Pluralism and the "schizophrenic" disjunction of values, the disappearance of reality criteria, and the lack of what Lyotard called the general ontological foundation are but a few symptoms of the postmodernist adventure.

Artists create mammoth monuments with multiple, changing, vacillating meanings marked by ironical disillusion. Jonathan Borofsky constructs a huge puppet clown for the big "Metropolis" show in Berlin: man, woman, colossus and children's toy all at once. Anselm Kiefer builds up his *Population Census* — a house-size bookshelf filled with superhumanly big and heavy lead books with 60 million peas pressed into the pages. Is this political criticism, joke, credo, or what ? All efforts of art criticism and common sense fail to grasp any clear, stable and definitive meaning or message. The artist's aim is not a "meaning" but a vast field of possible readings. In a sense, these works are "schizophrenical." Or, as Gianni Vattimo has put it, fragmentation is the normal situation of man today.

At the time when Western artists created the works we see, and Western thinkers proposed the theses we quote, the cultural, artistic, and intellectual development in the Soviet Union took on new forms. Independent and underground thinkers like M. Mamardashvili, A. Zinoviev, A. Piatigorsky, and M. Epstein were on their way to describing the late totalitarian human condition and the mentality of human beings who come from the nether World of the disintegrating Soviet system. Alexander Zinoviev said once that man molded by Soviet reality is an extreme reactionary who runs ahead of progress. Merab Mamardashvili saw in the late totalitarian condition an undiscernible mess of contradictory values which lost its footing and arrived at absolute chaos. In fact, using methods of the so-called Social Conceptualism, as Kabakov, Bulatov, Orlov do, or holding to other means and methods, our independent art offers a chaos of values and meanings.

It is not difficult to see that the Western theoretical formulations (loss of ontological foundations, agonizing reality, "schizophrenical" fragmentation and a mess of values) are in a way applicable to the independent art in the Soviet Union. And, vice versa, what we know about Homo Soveticus, his blurred mentality and his strange reality of life, can serve as a commentary on Western developments. This is a parallelism which hardly makes us happy with man and culture, but which urges us to contemplate our unusual age. It is unusual because the late capitalist and late totalitarian conditions of existence have brought to life many results in minds and arts which have more in common than people ever suspected.

Until our age every cultural entity was a project of organizing reality. Every culture proposed an order of things, a model of the Universe. All of these historically known models from antiquity to classical modernism express the pretensions of human collectives to dominate nature, time, and history. Cultures serve to tame dangerously skewed reality.

But it seems that in the 20th century this basic principle of culture has been largely dismantled. I cannot describe here at length the stages and operative forces of this "deconstruction." But I can mention that only two ways to disintegrate the old idea of culture have been used in this century.

First was the Freudian mythology of subconsciousness which has triumphantly expanded in the West since the 1920s. In his late works Sigmund Freud gave way to his vision of an endless subconscious depth which goes beyond Eros and the "pleasure principle," and even beyond the exigencies of living substance as such. At the source of erotic drives, Freud claimed to find the spirit of Thanatos, the death god, and the drive to return to the lap of the Universe and to be dissolved in it.

This psychologizing mythology (or mythologizing psychology) was a true dismantling of the idea of culture as it previously existed. Freud saw in the basement of our psyche pre-human, pre-cultural, even pre-animal factors. Eros, who changes appearance and who is, in essence, none other than Thanatos, is anything but a stable force in the Universe. It cannot support human claims to dominate the world and to understand it.

The second symptom of a new state of mind was the Soviet communist ideology enthroned in Russia. This was concurrent with the success of Freudian psycho-philosophy in the West. What the people called Communists did in Russia was to radically eliminate the criteria of truth and moral conduct. Eternal or firmly established truths for everyone and always were also abolished. All that is true and good was defined and prescribed by the high ideological priests of the Communist Party according to specific and changing situations. "Interests of the working class" defined what was true and good, and Party leaders defined what the working class was interested in. What was true and good yesterday may not be so today.

This undermined the very principle of culture. A stable model of the universe, an organizing principle, and an order of reality were denied. On the basis of this approach, called "dialectical" by its partisans, Socialist Realism emerged in the '20s. Perhaps it was the first sketch of future postmodernism. Communism was proclaimed a kind of Utopian post-history, a happy forever. The body of official Stalinist architecture, design, painting and sculpture was formed by an almost "schizophrenic" plurality of styles and means, from ancient Egypt to Impressionism. Only modernism was rejected, as an ideological offensive of capitalism. In literature, expressive modes were no less lavishly extensive, from Oriental and Greek epics up to the subtle psychology of Chekhov and Stendhal.

Socialist Realism had no substructure of its own, no idea of any stable order of things. The officially proclaimed and forcefully imposed relativity of truths allowed and urged it to produce "Gothic" silhouettes of Moscow skyscrapers, "classicizing" sculptural monuments all over the former USSR, exuberant "Baroque" interior and exterior decoration, "Impressionist" visions of a sunlit Utopian world full of Communist happiness and monumental Art Nouveau stylizations. In the most pathetic way, Socialist Realism praised the fragmentation of the new man. His presence everywhere — from ancient Greece to modern France — in effect meant being nowhere, and having no sense of one's own localization in history. Socialist

Realism was the art of extreme reactionaries who ran ahead of progress.

And so, the great mutation of man and culture took place East and West. I have no moralistic schemes to denounce the mutant. My aim is rather a Weberian value-free statement of the fact that the principles of culture have undergone a dissociation.

The key figure in this process of dissociation was not any Soviet artist but one of the founding fathers of the avant-garde — Pablo Picasso. After he abandoned his Cubist system of representation, his artistic practice turned into a constant denial of any stable vision or any crystallized language. He introduced a plurality of languages comparable in multiplicity to the whole of Socialist Realism or to the whole of postmodernism. Parallel to Picasso, Marcel Duchamp destroyed the very idea of a definite border which could divide "art" from "non-art" or could separate a definite message from a diffuse and vacillating pulp of meanings.

Mutation went on throughout the century. Any stable identity of meanings evaporated from ideology, politics, philosophy, and the arts. The Western governments aligned themselves against Hitler at the side of Stalin. Fighting for freedom as Stalin's ally is a great historical paradox. To stop the extension of Communist powers, nuclear weapons were developed to shield the democratic order — but only at the price of mortal danger to man's existence in general. Defending oneself effectively became synonymous with mankind's radical self-destruction.

Our age has one dominant tendency: dissociation of firm meanings and clear propositions. Notions, actions, events are becoming more and more ambiguous and unreliable. The most graphic expression of the main historical trend of our age is a theory discussed in recent physics and philosophy which portrays the world order as a universal chaos. That is contrary to all previous models of science and culture. Previously, people tried to define the logic and the law of nature and history; now they stress the illogical and lawless aspects of these same subjects.

The artistic activity which is most appreciated by critics aims at creating unspecified invitations to deciphering, without providing any reliable keys. Susan Sontag and other thinkers affirm that evasion from any definite interpretation is what artists now want most of all. In fact, the overwhelming majority of current art complies with the principle of an elusive plurality of meanings.

Everyone is aware of the social factors, political developments, and everyday realities in the West which enable and enforce this state of art and mind. Consumer society, political pluralism, and mass communication enhance the late capitalist "schizophrenia." Jean Baudrillard claimed that differentiating fictions and realities is impossible in the epoch of "fabricating realities"; Jacques Derrida supposed that by special analysis of any philosophical or other proposition we may discover the opposite of what the author expressly meant. In essence, reality, truth, and sense are supposed to be questionable things. Western postmodernist thought is gaining influence in the East, too, and it is more than just a new intellectual fashion. It is felt to be relevant. Perhaps the time will come when Western and Eastern thinkers on man and culture will form a kind of community, and students will approach them as comparable ways of thinking.

The arts and the philosophical formulations in the East and West come to life in conditions which are extremely different. The Soviet Union currently has no consumerism, no real political pluralism (only hopes and tentative efforts to attain it), and no information glut. But, strange or not, our late totalitarian era houses art and literature which pose comparable problems to those in the West: anthropological crisis, blurred thought, loss of criteria, loss of reality. We have no artists to rank as high as Kiefer or Boltanski. Now, as before, we are more comfortable in the realm of the written and spoken word, that is, in literature and, maybe, in theater art. But in all of our arts, visual as well as non-visual, there is a multiplicity of languages and an irresistible longing to pose social, political, and psychological enigmas on a monumental scale.

This puzzling and delicate situation calls for prudence. We have to renounce broad intellectual gestures. Therefore, we have to withdraw the pathetic idea of the post-totalitarian stage, presumably parallel to postmodernism. We have to abstain from direct neophytic concentration on the Western theoretical arsenal when studying contemporary art in the former USSR. Our critics, and Western ones, are strongly prompted to bring the theories of postmodernism directly onto the late totalitarian soil. But the gap in historical, social, and political backgrounds makes this transfer worthless or deceptive. Our background is formed, not by the Western trio of Consumerism-Information-Pluralism, but by the legacy of the Soviet system and by the human response to this unusual experience.

Totalitarian ideology and politics destroy the foundation of any organized culture even more successfully than the Western factors. Man finds himself in a very strange world with floating coordinates. For instance, the "left" and the "right" orientations in politics make up a mixture, a puzzle of changing elements. On the one hand, we know well what is considered to be "left" and "right." On the other hand, as a result of our history, we in Russia now call "left" those who defend privatization, classic free market, and capitalist enterprise with no state control of the economy. The rest of the world calls this position "right." But the "rights" in the former Soviet Union are those who remain for socialism, collectivism, centralized State planning, and close control. Ideas which have been sculpted by political thought and practice over the centuries perform a break-dance.

This strange upside-down condition of political positions and notions goes back to Stalin's times, when conservative cultural politics were adopted by the revolutionary Socialist state. As a result, the tastes and outlooks of a Soviet Communist activist are often very close to the tastes and attitudes of an American conservative. Today, the disorganization of political foundations and notions takes on an almost totalitarian character. Communist forces, leaders, and institutions supervise the privatization. They do it for themselves, of course. The Party elite tries to be the first in the former USSR to enter the world market and have a monopoly on capitalist business in the Soviet Union. This is a full collapse of clear-cut foundations of any organized political order. The idea of the Communist Party becoming a union of Capitalist monopolists is as surreal a notion as that of the West joining a Communist dictator in the struggle against Fascism, or nuclear suicide as a means of salvation.

At the end of the century, neither East nor West produce any organized or logically consistent politics, art or culture. The support and enthusiasm given by the West to *perestroika* and Gorbachev are very indicative: his refined late totalitarian Soviet system has been greeted as an achievement of freedom and humanism. Political and cultural logic was different in the past. Even Karl Marx and Vladimir Lenin would have been surprised to see capitalist businessmen support Marxist-Leninist forces building up the Capitalist monopoly of the Communist nobles in the biggest country of the globe. In terms of logic, it is unthinkable and completely mad. But it is the inevitable result of historical development.

The arts of this age produce a "disorder of things," a deconstruction of meanings, and the merry apocalypse of a supermarket. In this sense politics and art of the East and West shake hands. This is not very reassuring, but it is a captivating spectacle for an outside observer. The final question that arises is whether this peculiar situation in politics and culture will last for long. But a cultural historian does not have the prerogative of a prophet.

The main preoccupation of postmodernist art is the questioning of the problematic identity of a consumerist, pluralistic, informative, and permissive civilization. Art in Russia questions the identity of a different civilization, with its serious confusion of basic meanings and values. In our culture, steps towards justice, as in 1917, led to the greatest crimes in history; gaining freedom from the enemy, as in 1945, was progress toward slavery. And so, being immensely rich we are abjectly poor; without any guilt, we are punished — no longer by repressive institutions but, perhaps even more ruthlessly, by everyday life itself. At this point in the historical fiasco of totalitarianism, artists analyze the epochal problem of a shaky and unreliable identity from a specific, non-Western viewpoint.

Alexander Roitburd, *The Whispering*, 1990.

Vitali Komar & Alexander Melamid, *We buy and sell souls*, performance, 1983.

Getting Off the Orbit

by Vasif Kortun
(Turkey)

In those countries like Turkey, which were in the orbit of a center, there was a controversy between the artists. Some were for the production of art work from what they claimed to be a universal perspective. The others supported a local and authenticist view, claiming that the only way of attaining universality would be through the indigenous.

Neither argument ever meant much of anything in itself. The argument between the local and the universal was more complicitous than oppositional. The first meant the production of art from within the hollowed-out forms of a hegemonic culture, in particular that of Paris and then New York. The second resorted to reworking its own traditional and local archaeology — within an archaeological framework in the name of authenticity. That was margin's modernism, willfully self-provincializing, locked in mere visuality and representation. Visit any modern art museum in Sao Paolo, Istanbul, or Warsaw; you will find similar-looking decorative and derivative work. And folks, some had fooled themselves to believe that was the real art.

The closed circuit of the local and the universal is in fact one of the oldest imports of the self and the other. They have lately been in vogue: center and periphery, first and third world, official culture and popular culture, high art and low art, and *et cetera*. The terms, however, have always been issued by the center, the first, the official, and the high.

The self used to chart out the cartography. Lately, he or she produces his or her self criticism through the body of an other. Meanwhile, the other, whose only reference is that cartography, becomes alien to his or her own neighborhood.

What authority could one assume in speaking about a site from which one is absent? And why do those who claim that site fall silent on their own ground? Silence finds a reformed and manipulated voice in another language, as I stand here and communicate with you in a tongue that is not my own, in a discursive practice which I have invested in, borrowed and broken away from, a discourse, laid out, proposed, and authored by Europe. The dilemma here is that there is no philosophy outside Western philosophy, despite the fact that it can no more claim a signature from within.

Although there are still those places and institutions that view artistic production in vertical, hierarchical, and geographical terms, it is no longer sufficient to posture behind a biological and cartographical given if the only issue at stake is initiation into the institution of art.

There is a difference between margin and marginality as well as a difference between center and centrality. Once cartographical terms, margin and center have now become ubiquitous. How marginal is, for example, an artist of middle-class origins in the margin? How marginal is a token representative of the margin in the center?

Marginal production in the margin is a key issue that has to be tackled. Cultural production in the margin in general still feels shut out from the mainstream, but has a right to self-representation. But as long as the sole operation will be within the framework of the institution, art will fail to communicate in a deep and meaningful way.

Trans-nationalization, inter-culturality, deterritorialization, have become household terms. We attempt to create new strategies and shift our positions in rigorous pursuit of equal time, facing a market which had killed ideology and laid out the equality of cultures as a free circulation of the commodity.

Together with this is the new internationalist discourse which is fueled by a "compulsory sincerity," a discourse laden with cultural reductionism that aims to represent the other in friendly terms.

There is no way of representing the other, and no way of representing the anomaly, or the exception.

There are sites without a witness or spokesperson, and a universe of cultural production that falls outside the destination, the course, and the continuity of the history of art. These are sites that can no more be put away as ethnographical material in museums.

Will the margin's increasing articulation in the center be another centennial shot of vitalization in the arm for the tired and heavy European civilization, or will everything turn upside down, towards the global culture? Global culture after the massacre of a million Iraqis? The mediatic and mediated global culture?

Selim Birsel, *5 Canonical Elements*, installation, 1991.

Canan Beykal, *51 Days Later*, 1992.

The incorporation of what was on the fringes of cultural activity, such as East and Central Europe, Turkey, and Latin America, merely follow the commercial internationalism or benefit from it. It is, thus, hard to legitimate the validity of institutional-representation in international exchange. If our genuine goals towards righteous representation are reduced to assimilation, this leaves much to be desired.

Kurds speak Russian, Romanians speak Turkish, while Iranians trade passports, and symbolic exchange finds a ground in the autonomous markets of Istanbul. Turkish youth adopt black inner-city paraphernalia as a style and fight gang wars with the skinheads and the neo-Nazis. Black and Latin American transvestite culture informs popular culture on all levels all the way to Madonna's "Justify My Love" video. Gender performances contribute to the collapse of a privileged and centered sexuality. On a mediatic level, I come from a country where we watch Mexican soaps, American cops, Japanese cartoons, Italian soft-porn, and a religious program all in the course of one day; Beethoven in the morning, rap and arabesque in the evening.

There is more to be discussed in the general cultural critique than there is in the exclusively narrow practice of art, at least in terms of legitimation and pertinency. This is ultimately the area of multiculturalism and post-coloniality.

Art problematizes life, poses questions, produces ruptures, and communicates. But the site of production, a mental site, gives a different reading at the gallery or the museum, which have a curious memory of their own and a tendency to level difference.

The media-critical work of the '80s, having experienced that there was no "outside" of the institution, resorted to the manipulation of graphic and other media as a critique of power. It was a dangerous game in that it involved a degree of complicity. The limits of the institutional presentation of art have to be recognized in the general perspective of its position as a branch of the cultural sector. From the non-societal, but artistically communal secret milieus of the "socialist" countries, to the imaginary publics elsewhere, art had little to do with its viewer, and we don't even know how to correct this, except for adopting our own micro-strategies.

Part IV:
Censorship and Art

Art and Censorship
Toward a wider understanding of the role of power in ART

by Gloria Inés Daza
(Colombia)

So many violent upheavals have occurred in Colombia, starting in the '70s, that there has been little time to do an in-depth study of the cultural implications of the change of values in our society. In fact, such changes have been ignored. In art, a greater fondness has arisen for those names consolidated in the already-remote '60s, so that access to a scenario of new values in plastic art is blocked. For example, the 1991 Sao Paulo Biennial Exhibition invited art masters for the nth time, without considering that a 30-year reign is sufficient, and that art, like life, must continue.

Maybe because of political and social stress, and the systematic intimidation and vulnerability felt by individuals in daily life, open debate and criticism, not to mention actual confrontation, have disappeared from the Colombian scene. A scenario has been created where individual thinking does not count.

Not only is the ability to think thus reduced, but if people do decide to express opposing ideas through communications media or the public tribune, they are not only judged and vetoed, they are also ostracized. The most qualified art critics have disappeared into professorships, research, or curatorships. Very few have access to editorial space to analyze artistic work, and those who do are often the less qualified. They lean towards a sensational pseudo-criticism that judges art by throwing personal darts without stopping to analyze the work. In other words, we move between two extremes: an absolute lack of concepts or an insolent sensationalism to feed the appetite of the public that attends the circus and asks for blood, guaranteeing the consumption of that edition or advertising space.

Censorship is not limited to totalitarian regimes. It is also exercised in many countries and societies that proclaim their freedom, through subtle and hidden means of domination. This censorship is imposed by power groups and, although it does not have an obvious official, political, economic, or social profile, it is generated and formed by these forces. In the late '70s, the power of the Catholic Church disappeared as a form of totalitarian power. Today, as we are sheltered by pluralism and religious freedom in Colombia, its inquisitorial role is extinguished, as are extremes of censorship and ex-communication of artists whose work was considered scandalous or damaging to good habits. In Medellin, for instance, the work of Expressionist artist, Debora Arango, was censored in the '50s; that of the master José Rodríguez Acevedo was removed from the National Museum during the '60s; and Leonel Góngora's installation of *La María* was vetoed during the second Coltejer Biennial Exhibition in Medellin in 1972 for being irreverent and pornographic.

Censorship is exercised not precisely for religious or moral attitudes which might affect the community, and even less for strictly plastic considerations. Censorship is based on extra-artistic motivations and exercised for the pure manipulation of power, a power distributed among stagnant departments, but conformed by the same four estates — official, political, economic, and social. The constant is a veto over whatever is free, the individual who is not slavish and yielding, and the one who does not identify with the ghetto. Thus the social codification is established in the same way that power is distributed in closed societies, similar to the way mafias operate in Colombia as an instrument of multinational drug companies. In art, the person who enters one of these associations or tiny groups is unable to leave without being thrown into outer darkness or subjected to refined forms of extreme cruelty and Machiavellianism. Thus there are a significant number of artists, ranging in age from their '30s to '50s, who despite a consistent record of creative work have no access to museums or art galleries, and even less to the communications media. Their modesty and total concentration on actual work, their concern for essential art problems, not worldly things or substitutes distant from artistic reality, leave them adrift.

Managers, dealers, and promoters from museums and galleries, even from state organizations, act through a frivolous viewfinder of maximum mundanity. Art, now part of a social-posture spectacle, moves more under the whim of fashion than eternal values. It has lost its ritual spirit and sacred nature, obeying strange rules in order to enter territories closed to mystery, magic, and poetry. Even though art could be sold at the supermarket, promoted on campuses to the masses, or, to the contrary, in exclusive salons, it will always respond to the need of interiorizing the phenomena of life and human beings in the end.

Martha Morales, *Untitled*, 1991.

A launching platform was recently raised for a rehash of the European transavangardia, which had among its outstanding figures Italians and Germans of more than a decade ago. This was set up with a group of "gray" artists living in Paris, as a panacea for Colombian art. However, as happens with contrived things, these artists did not respond powerfully, nor did their works show the value of the new circumstances, of something more than the purely apparent. Nor, from a technical point of view, could their work defend itself: it was big, strident, smeared, impastoed canvas, gratuitous, shameful copies of artists like the Italian painter Sandro Chia.

Today, this famous movement has broken down, although certain insular values remain that are not necessarily Neo-Expressionist or postmodernist. As always, the best artists respond to an interior process carried out with sincerity and decorum, transcending the artistic reality (the actual product) with honesty, force, poetry, and originality.

Art is almost a miracle. It requires great force and integrity to free oneself from a power that imposes rules and tendencies. False postures that weaken and prostitute art, turning it into a product, stuff the spaces of an ignorant and captive public that acquires not only the work, but also the artist, who becomes a vedette in the emerging temples of fashion and frivolity.

Still, tomorrow's art arises in a vital manner. New presences, new works reflecting intelligence, audacity, and originality, impose themselves in the middle of the roiling river. Because the Colombian phenomenon is so complex, negative and positive factors coexist at the same time: an honest and hard-working country which has not lost the faith lives side by side with a delinquent sector that would destroy the motherland, putting easy, lucrative interests and a fierce desire for power first.

Current conditions are based on social injustice. Colombians live in a state of war due to the phenomenon of drug-traffic mafias. Multinational corporations of organized crime manage the drug traffic, and through this traffic they detect the degree of social frustration in Colombia. They connect with a sector of the discontented: those who, having failed to locate their space in the social infrastructure, took the bait of easy money.

In this acute process of social decomposition, the ruling political class exercised a disproportionate degree of patronage. This in turn became a style, a way of life whose codes were based on "Everything has a price"; "The end justifies the means"; "Let's live less, but better" (young hired

Miguel Huestar, *Untitled*, 1990.

assassins from the Medellin Northeast community); "Nothing is bad, but badly done"; "Lord, save us both from good and feeble-minded people"; and "When I talk about rights, I talk about my own rights."

The Colombian middle class has paid a high price in its struggle to preserve ethical and moral values, in terms of lives, space, property, work, and justice — in sum, in opportunities for surviving. An underground economy contributing to excessive inflation has devalued the standard of living, imposing new values and new forms of power, even a new aesthetic. This is a major cause of the arbitrary and tasteless art that abounds. The uneducated emerging class takes us from absolute tastelessness to a craving for the consecrated art masters of the '60s. At that time, the Colombian artistic panorama held no more than 50 artists. Today we can still talk of 50 notable artists, among a jungle of thousands of minor artists in the national territory, but the empire of money buys signatures and does not want to take risks. Moreover, there is no one to educate them or present a real panorama of the ample and unprejudiced art being made today.

Can art be saved from the manipulation of power and recover its own space, dignity, and freedom? Is this a Colombian problem, a Latin American one, a problem of countries in development, or is it a worldwide problem? While we wait for the answer, let us remember the words of Kandinsky: "Thousands of artists create millions of works of art without enthusiasm, with a cold heart and a dormant soul" (On the Spiritual in Art). We must continue to await the day when, as Favre, the noted French entomologist, said, "Man directs his steps toward the triumph of justice over power."

Jesse Helms: Muse of the Nineties

by Rebecca Solnit
(United States)

First, a few words about walls and wars:

While it is true that around the world in the last decade many walls fell, in the U.S. dozens of low-profile wars raged and many walls were erected. The U.S. had its own perestroika, *its own economic restructuring: a wall went up between the classes, the rich became very much richer, the poor more desperately poor, and it became far more difficult to move out of poverty. Ten years ago the huge population of homeless people did not exist. Meanwhile many social programs, for health education (and arts education) were gutted. The Bill of Rights was whittled away.*

As this war against freedoms and against the poor was being waged, the U.S. government was spending about a million dollars a day to support right-wing death squads in El Salvador; creating and financing the Contras who harassed the Nicaraguan government and people throughout the '80s; and supporting dictatorships around the world, from Pinochet to Saddam Hussein. The war against the domestic environment escalated, as deregulation allowed greater levels of pollution and toxic dumping, and allowed the ancient forests of the Northwest and California to be destroyed for lumber. The nuclear arms race stepped up under Reagan, posing a threat to the whole world and creating terrible problems of radiation for the environment and human health, even if the weapons are never used.

These are the walls and wars against which the pageant of U.S. art in the '80s unfolded, although from most of the art and criticism of that decade, you would have never guessed it.

I think that all of us in the art world in the United States owe an enormous debt of gratitude to Jesse Helms. Helms has been a veritable muse for the American art world, the most eye-opening and inspiring thing to come its way in decades. This may be a surprising statement to some of you, and I want to make it clear that I say this not as a closet right-wing sympathizer, but as a longtime left-wing political activist, historian, and individual who fears and loathes the larger scope of Helms's activities. (By Jesse Helms, I hereafter mean Helms and all his henchmen among fundamentalist and far-right circles; by the art world, I mean not every individual involved in making art, but the consensual mainstream of opinion at a given time, the *Zeitgeist* of it.)

Before Jesse Helms, the art world was a very placid zone in American culture. Politics was not central to its comfortably elevated discourses, and most people seemed to regard a sense of political urgency and involvement as naively alarmist and a little vulgar.

Then Jesse Helms decided art was dangerous. This was the most flattering thing anyone had thought about American art in decades, and I'm not sure it was true, within or without Helms's terms. But art responded by trying to live up to its reputation as dangerous, and thanks to Helms we had what, in honor of the Prague Spring, I think we can call the Penis Spring: a season or a year or so in which explicitly sexual imagery flourished, both in the work of artists and in the exhibitions and publications that celebrated this work. Not only did the work of Andres Serrano, Robert Mapplethorpe, and Karen Finley, among others, become far more visible, but the ruckus inspired many new works of art dealing with sexuality and brought to prominence many other artists. Sexuality became heroic rather than dirty. In the long run, the people and issues most threatened by Helms's agenda have come in from the margins of the art world because of him.

Jesse Helms's intentions and his effects have been very different, and I want to make it clear that I am here to laud only his effects. First of all, we have him to thank for all those explicit anti-censorship images that blossomed everywhere. Secondly, we must thank him for stirring the art world from its long stupor. Artists were not the first to be censored, but very nearly the last: Ronald Reagan had gone right to work in 1981 defanging the First Amendment. It signifies how little danger art posed to the rest of the right wing that it loitered untouched while journalists, federal employees, gays, political activists, and others had their freedoms pruned back — until Helms, practically the only politician who thought art was important and influential. (Somehow the position of the art world in the rise of the Reagan Right reminds me of that anecdote about the Protestant minister in the Third Reich, who did nothing while they came for the Jews, the Gypsies, the Communists, the Catholics, and then they came for him.) So the Right came for artists, and they experienced oppression. And theirs was a dignified oppression: they were being denied funding not because they were an unimportant budget item but because they were an important threat.

The artists secretly loved their threatened status. The hardest thing to find in America is a sense of driving purpose. And Helms backfired so beautifully that hordes became far more political, far more willing to stand up and to stand out from the mainstream. Or did Helms backfire?

I don't think he achieved what he wanted, but I do think he plugged into what I might as well call the post-Hegelian dialectic of (art) history, or the No News Is Bad News principle. At the beginning of the '80s, Julian Schnabel rose to fame on a wave of bad reviews; at the end of the '80s Serrano rose to fame on a wave of censoriousness. By opposing certain kinds of art, Jesse Helms gave them a kind of prominence they lacked before; by opposing them as threatening, he gave them power. Helms has taught me to think in terms of engaged and disengaged, rather than for or against. He is obsessed with homoerotic imagery, and he has inspired a heightened level of attention to homoerotic imagery. Helms is engaged with repression and sexual freedom, and now so are the rest of us. In that sense, we're all engaged equally, in terms of subject matter. That Helms is opposed to it is a detail, and in opposing it he generated a kind of Passion Play in which he stars as the villain, providing us all the rare opportunity to be heroes of freedom. Helms has not only supplied us with a theme, but with a narrative, a plot line, with which to engage it. If artists had been as radical in 1988 as they have become since, Helms would have come as no surprise, and he would have generated little response: a narrative that has been couched in terms of epic opposition has in fact been a romance of developing consciousness.

The prominent Eastern European journalist Timothy Garton Ash writes of the changes there after 1989, "Everyone finds it difficult to come to terms with the loss of the common enemy." Everyone in the U.S. art world, on the other hand, found it exhilarating to come to terms with the discovery of a common enemy. How well I recall all those meetings, those flyers, buttons, demonstrations, faxes, exhibitions, articles. Strangely, the drama has unfolded against the background of recent changes in Eastern Europe and the USSR, in which the hostile relationship between artists and government has been pivotal, and an often-vocalized concern has been that art will lose its potency when it comes in from the shadows and margins. But while the artists of the East are beginning to meet the vertigo of freedom, U.S. artists have been discovering the merits of oppression. When you direct water into a narrower channel, its force increases. U.S. artists are acquiring that sense of themselves as dangerous, marginal, as guerrillas in the battle to determine who will create the culture. Or maybe the oyster is

Robert Mapplethorpe, *Thomas (in circle)*, 1987.

a better metaphor, with Helms as the irritant around which a pearl is being shaped.

So far I have patronized the art world a little, because it discovered the right wing so late and played its part in the censorship drama so zestfully and so blindly to its dialectics. But this is a genuinely important shift for art in this country. The U.S. art world seems to be getting better as the context is getting uglier: it is energized by opposition. Oh Hegel, where are you now?

It's better to be censored by someone else than by yourself. It's better to have something to say and obstacles to saying it than to have nothing to say. And this is the shift I'm trying to trace in the art world. It has something to say now. It realizes it has a stake in the direction of the larger culture. It has woken up from its shackles of self-censorship. Jesse Helms has taken it upon himself to embody the ugliest role in the dialectics of culture: he is not only the trumpeter stirring the sleepers, but the scape-goat embodying all they cast out. (And if they hadn't been asleep, that trumpet would have been nothing more than an annoying noise.) Now it is Helms and his ilk who say that art should be utterly apolitical, an opinion I used to hear from artists themselves. The censorship of American art has largely been self-censorship, and only Helms's lively polemics awakened artists to their responsibilities and vulnerabilities as part of the body politic. He demonstrated that freedom is vital to art, and perhaps even that art is vital to freedom.

Now I only hope that we can continue to be as dangerous as Helms thinks we are and, rather than letting him call our tunes, draw up agendas of our own.

The Arts and Art Criticism
in an Overpoliticized Society

by Alexandre Morozov
(USSR)

It is common knowledge that the authorities brought tremendous pressure to bear on the arts and art criticism in the USSR for many a decade. Ruinous effects resulted less from the overt reprisals launched against some artists than from the omnipresent machine of ideological coercion that sought to put the arts exclusively in the service of propaganda.

Attempts at setting oneself free from that pressure, one way or the other, started as early as the 1930s, when the suppression of artistic freedom was institutionalized. At the same time, one ought not to overlook the fact that official policies in the arts were pursued, allegedly in the name of the generous revolutionary idea and revolutionary society, to usher in a bright future for every workingman. Belief that a paradise on earth was just around the corner was inherent in the thinking of numerous generations of Soviet Russia's artists until recently. Even today the communist idea is not as dead as some believe it is, as we witness the downfall of the political organism it props up, hence the characteristically ambivalent situation in which the Soviet intellectual or artist finds him or herself. Of course, there were and still are some fortune hunters who are as ardently committed to anti-communism today as they were bent on keeping intact the purity of communist concepts yesterday. But nonetheless quite a few members of the artistic community were tortured by this vexing question: what is it that I object to when I object to the dogmas of official ideology and official doctrine in the arts?

Numerous tacks were tried to identify an alternative to totalitarian officialism in the Soviet arts. These efforts led but were not confined to overt dissidence in the arts. However, it should be pointed out that in the post-Stalin period the artistic community's rekindled interest in the experience of the original Russian avant-gardists and in the creative experiments that paralleled latter-day modernism in the Western arts were not at all tinged with anti-Sovietism or anti-socialism. Rather the opposite was the case. For example, the kineticists from the Dvinshie (Movement) group were involved in producing festive decorations for Soviet national holidays at the turn of the 1970s. In his studio Eliy Belyutin developed his own technique similar to Abstract Expressionism and sought to share it with the Soviet artistic community and art lovers at large. Dissident art with modernist leanings was provoked mostly by an ideological reaction following Khrushchev's "thaw" but it was not alone in its opposition to officialism in the Soviet arts and art criticism.

Up until the late 1980s the Soviet press, especially periodicals that were closely involved with the party bureaucracy, never tired of denouncing dissidence in the arts, spotting its manifestations far beyond the modernist movements. And it came as no surprise that numerous artists and art critics, who enjoyed their official member status with the USSR Union of Artists and were employed by various cultural and educational institutions, fell prey to ideological harassment. A never-ending war was waged on people who appeared politically loyal but were "professionally," by their mentality, heretical. They called that harassment "ideological struggle on the cultural front." To explain the need for that struggle, Stalin's famous concept was invoked: "as we move closer to socialism, the class struggle grows more intense." They would have us believe that in the era of détente the peaceful coexistence of the two systems could not mean ideological disarmament for socialism either. On the contrary, it called for intensified ideological confrontation in no ambiguous terms. A special structure was set up to provide a liaison between the top political leadership and the artistic community. The liaison function was assigned first of all to the USSR Academy of Arts. The Academy was exactly what produced instructions as to what the artists should or should not do in the arts "from the Marxist-Leninist standpoint." Academy officials imposed their views on government bodies charged with directing cultural policies and member organizations of the USSR Union of Artists. Those official theoreticians were bent on ostracizing not only, shall we say, abstract painting, but also artists' attempts at practicing primitivism, invoking the tradition of medieval art, and any experimentation with new forms of realism, such as hyper-realism and photorealism.

Since our foreign counterparts are not always aware of that, I would like to drive this idea home over and over again: the trends imposed on the Soviet arts from on high were hostile not only to the modern consciousness. They also led to a virtual rejection of traditional art and culture and to a vulgar profanation of their values. Hence followed a peculiar conflict of interests that was perhaps not typical of Western art. Even fascism pales in comparison to bolshevik totalitarianism in terms of the immensely devastating effects the latter has had on mankind's pantheon of culture and on its intellectual and artistic patrimony. The regime was busy murdering the culture of its own country (and perhaps elsewhere too?) for a longer period of time, more ferociously, and on a larger scale than it did in any other country of the world that was afflicted by an epidemic of totalitarianism in the 20th century. At the same time, Soviet society witnesses a bitter conflict between culture and pseudoculture. Therefore, bringing the cultural heritage and artistic gains of diverse epochs and nations, including popular classical traditions (largely "a lesson long since learned" by Western consciousness) within the close reach of the Soviet artist was like a breath of fresh air. The need to make a breakthrough toward the space of culture is as crucial to us as is a breakthrough toward the space of free modernist experimentation. This is what imparted originality to numerous manifestations of artistic traditionalism in the Soviet arts. In terms of the country's artistic life in general, this stream of unique traditionalism would constitute a sort of mainstream that is identical neither to modernist alternative art nor to officialism.

This broad trend (and I believe that its creative quality often compares favorably to the commercial figurative products the West's "mass culture" turns out) has been embraced by large numbers of artists and art critics who were, in fact, intent on dismantling the dogmas of Socialist Realism. Such was the role played, for instance, by the "youth art exhibitions" movement active in the '70s and '80s. But it ought to be made clear that the best art they produced was foreign to political bias. Instead, the most talented artists of the movement used to pick "extratemporal" or "perennial" topics of a philosophical and moral nature. Obviously they derived their inspiration from the Bible and ancient myths. In leafing through the history of culture, the young artists of the '70s appeared to demonstrate that their art entitled them to start a dialogue with masters and thinkers of bygone times and in so doing they were opposed to the patently time-serving and faked "traditionalism" practised by the academic maîtres of official art.

Back in those days youth art exhibitions were held in the exhibition rooms owned by the USSR Union of Artists. But they often triggered conflicts. The authorities tried to close and ban those shows or at least to have the key works on display removed from the walls. Liberal segments of the artistic community, especially art critics, took pains to protect them against harassment. As a result, those officially authorized youth art exhibitions proved to be as active a driving force in the political and ideological confrontations of those times as were the actions of the modernist underground, even though their creative objectives were essentially at variance with one another. That youth art exhibitions won their place in our country's artistic life despite the Academy's and the USSR Union of Artists' obscurantist opposition was a politically significant phenomenon, but I would like to reiterate once again that political bias was not typical of the younger generation's intentions back in the '70s.

Incidentally, I would argue that the political bias of our modernist underground is often overrated. Rather, it was only partly fact and partly legend in more recent times, closer to the Gorbachev era, when the young Soviet "avant-garde" rushed to invade art exhibitions *en masse*. There were few, if any, underground artists of the '60s and '70s whose influence on our society was comparable to that of *samizdat* literature, let alone to Solzhenitsyn's. It was only natural that major personalities in Soviet unofficial modernism were rather introverts.

And here unfolds the paradoxical evolution of the postwar underground: the more eagerly it rushes to fight on the barricades of social confrontations, the more vulnerable its organic creative, social, and moral attitudes appear to be. This is very typical of what we call "sotsart." Its nonconformism is highly suspect. Firstly, the rise of "sotsart" happens on the sidelines of actual social confrontations. It happens either outside the USSR among the emigré communities where the founding fathers of the movement operate, or in the context of Soviet *perestroika* at a time when anything that derided the clichés of totalitarian consciousness was doomed to public success, even to some official recognition, not to mention commercial success. Secondly, "sotsart" draws upon the same clichés of low-grade Soviet ideology and it does so consciously and ambiguously. Its masters' creative ambitions very seldom venture outside the tired banalities of the Soviet agitprop. In short, that art is just one big compromise. Some of the art critics try to vaunt "sotsart" as the first original movement that emerged from the Soviet artistic domain to occupy its fitting place on the world's art scene in the '70s and '80s, when latter-day modernism gave way to postmodernism. I do not believe that the attempts of some of our art critics to attribute genuine historical significance to "sotsart" were made for reasons more fundamental than the time-serving commercial success won by the little pictures about the downfall of the "red bear" among a public that grew sick and tired of the Soviet missile scare.

Russia has been given a tremendous overdose of politics in the 20th century. It may be argued that Russia is a country sick with politics. As I see it, now that we operate in such a specific environment, any amount of politicized art with the artist plunging himself into politics, whether good or bad, leftist or rightist, will inescapably lead to a crisis and self-discredit. And feeling the heartbeat of Russian artistic life today, I see the prevalent trend: more talented artists are rejecting politics. This at least is what is happening in the plastic arts. Given our experience, this, perhaps, should come as no surprise to us. But fresh problems arise. For example, does there exist some sort of no man's land separating the artist and broad-based democratic movements? You could see artists and art critics among defenders of the August barricades around Russia's White House. But there is no denying that the new structures of democratic power lack, for instance, a new art policy concept. Members of the artistic community today have a vexing feeling of frustration, for they do not know what they should offer to a society undergoing democratization and what that society would accept. The situation calls for some serious thinking. But I do not believe that resolution of such problems lies in a new political euphoria. I do not think that yet another massive political baptism of our artists would help further the cause of art.

Whether our art today needs some ideological incentives is another matter. It appears that, given Russian cataclysms, such a need is more pressing for us than it is for the West. I would not expect anything good from even the most progressive politicization or ideologization of our art, should that happen all of a sudden. What appears to bear fruit is a dialogue that must be intensified and expanded between persons sharing artistic and philosophical awareness. An important subject of this dialogue is the problem of values, supreme values and human values. I mean, for instance, that aspect of thinking, which was personified in Russia and in Paris in the early parts of this century by Nicolaj Berdiajev and in New York in the last decade by Vittorio Hosle. As I see it, the art critic in my country should contribute to such a dialogue today too.

Censorship L.A. Style

by Merle Schipper
(United States)

In recent decades, Los Angeles seems to have overcome an earlier puritanical disposition reflected in the censoring of art. Indeed, if the brouhaha aroused by Senator Helms in 1989 over the grant awarded and later reversed by the NEA for the Robert Mapplethorpe exhibition at Washington's Corcoran Gallery propelled other cities to a near-psychotic state of paranoia, L.A. was relatively untouched. A show of David Wojnarowicz's paintings, including some images that could be considered explicitly sexual, opened at the Santa Monica Museum of Art without effective complaint. Only a handful of souls representing the "Traditional Values Coalition" in Orange County showed up to picket a talk by the artist. Their leader, the Reverend Lou Sheldon, tried to persuade Santa Monica church leaders to join his protest but found almost no cooperation.

Concurrently, that 1990 summer, Blum-Helman Gallery hung an Andres Serrano show featuring the allegedly blasphemous *Piss Christ*, which had added a layer to the Helms/NEA flap, but here it raised neither ire nor eyebrow. Previously shown at the Los Angeles County Museum of Art without fuss, its later notoriety failed to provoke any protest.

This situation suggests that insofar as sexual attitudes go, L.A. has achieved a level of maturity that puts it way ahead of much of the country, but there was a time when vigilantes swarmed over La Cienega Boulevard, known as Gallery Row in the 1960s, armed with magnifying glasses. Groups such as the "League of Decency" and "Sanity in Art" made sure that nothing improper in their view was going to infect the eyes of innocent beholders.

Back in the city's earliest years, it was illegal to exhibit paintings of nudes, a taboo that continued well beyond the turn of the century. Nevertheless, some tried to break down the forbidding wall. As early as 1914, Italian-born Felix Peano defied the status quo with a naked Eve on the bronze *Door of Life* commissioned by Inglewood, California's Episcopal Church of the Holy Faith, but the work was rejected on presentation.[1] Although the figure is hardly sensuous, that she is reaching for the apple may have endowed Eve with wicked intentions!

Local attitude very probably persuaded the remarkable Henrietta Shore, Southern California's then most radical modernist — who came here from Toronto in 1914 — to move to New York in 1920. Her undated *Nude*, considered to have been painted before 1920, is unabashedly erotic. Certainly it was an unlikely presence in any gallery of the day, especially considering that the model was known to be a fellow artist, Helena Dunlap.

The puritanical wave continued well past mid-century, when raids on so-called obscene art occurred with some regularity. Yet, you would have thought that when it came to the alleged "lewd and lascivious" Wallace Berman show at the Ferus Gallery in 1957, the Los Angeles Police Department would have known a dirty picture when they saw one. In its haste the vice squad ignored a sexually explicit photograph that brought about a citizen's protest and confiscated an innocuous drawing by Cameron, a local artist and friend of Berman, whose work was included in his shrine-like assemblage, *Temple*.

Berman's show was closed and the artist briefly jailed, then released on payment of a $150 fine. There were other incidents, the most newsworthy involving Edward Kienholz. When his *Back Seat Dodge — '38* (1964), was shown at his 1966 exhibition at LACMA, the show was shut down. The plaster and chicken-wire figures of a young couple were rather less than anatomical and hardly explicit, but viewers could identify the legs protruding through the truncated car's open door. To County Supervisor Warren Dorn (thereafter known as Porn), the work was offensive. The exhibition was allowed to re-open with *Back Seat Dodge's* door closed to minors. A museum docent opened it on I.D. clearance, to viewers willing to wait in the very long line that publicity conferred on the work.

Art dealers prudently kept their racier stuff in back rooms most of the time, but at least one took the bull by the horns and displayed it out in front, to brave the charges and legal problems that were sure to follow. That was David Stuart, who waited until 1969 to present a show of erotic art at his La Cienega gallery. His exhibition included works by Picasso and other modern masters, most notably, a 1922 piece by George Grosz, portraying a German general being pleasured by a woman. With the general's cap adorned by a swastika, the sexual reference served as an ironic metaphor.

Works by several contemporary Southern Californians such as Kenneth Price and John Altoon were among those seized by the vice squad, their safety assured by being stored in the station locker room! Stuart was charged and the case went to trial but supportive testimony from John Coplans, then Director of the Pasadena Museum, and LACMA curator Jane Livingstone (who more recently resigned from Washington's Corcoran Gallery when the Mapplethorpe show was canceled) brought about a quick not-guilty decision by the jury, as Los Angeles lawyer Jim Butler, who represented Stuart *pro bono*, recalls.[2]

Since the Stuart incident in 1969, there's been hardly a ripple on the part of stalwarts waging war on obscenity/pornography in this community, but sexual reference — explicit or not — was only one object of suppression. Social and political subject matter continued to be diligently monitored.

Back in the 1930s, nothing like Bernard Zackheim's mural in San Francisco's Coit Tower, showing a worker with a copy of Karl Marx's *Capital*, surfaced on the walls of public buildings in L.A. Even so, Stanton MacDonald-Wright, who directed the Federal Art Program in Southern California, had to defend thoroughly benign Hall of Records murals against charges of Communist content leveled by civic officials. Indeed, Depression-era artists in Southern California tended to "understand" what was acceptable and what was not when submitting proposals to the Federal Art Project.

The Mexican master, David Alfaro Siqueiros, however, was not using federal funds nor was he in any way intimidated by the powers that ruled the local scene during the six months of 1932 he spent in Los Angeles as a political refugee. One of his three murals undertaken here, *Tropical America*, was executed on a wall on Olivera Street, downtown Los Angeles's block-long Mexican bazaar, as a declaration of his outrage against American exploitation of migrant Mexican workers and their mass deportation. Bearing an image of a crucified Mexican Indian just below a predatory American Eagle, the work infuriated civic leaders.[3] As a result the mural was shortly thereafter whitewashed; its remains have defied efforts at restoration in more recent years.

When local artists tackled Social Realism, the results were usually no more than tepid. Barse Miller's witty confrontation of Aimée Semple MacPherson's self-serving tactics with his Regionalist-style *Apparition over Los Angeles* (1952) portrayed the evangelist floating amid money-bag clouds over Angelus Temple — her monument to herself. As a result it was withdrawn from the annual exhibition of local artists at the Los Angeles Museum of History, Science and Art, LACMA's forerunner in Exposition Park.

In the 1950s, the rise of Senator Joseph McCarthy and the House Un-American Activities Committees cast new shadows on the Los Angeles art scene. Art critic Jules Langsner reported in *ARTnews* in 1951 on the City Council's removal of work from the city's annual exhibition at the Greek Theater in Griffith Park. Even the conservative artist Rex Brandt had to defend himself against charges of creating "subversive, sacrilegious and abnormal" pictures. On Brandt's painting of a sailboat, *First Lift of the Sea* (n.d.), the insignia for "Island Class" was interpreted as a hammer and sickle.

Los Angeles City Councilman Harold Harby led the proceedings, provoked, according to some, by disappointment in his son's desire to become an artist. Others thought he wanted publicity, and, according to Langsner, "thought (correctly) that he could get some cheaply by accusing the modest exhibition at the Greek Theater of being red."

Although Langsner subsequently reported that the Council ultimately relented in their condemnation of modern art as a "tool of the Kremlin," here he described how "hundreds of respected, sober citizens present at the hearing heard a Sanity-in-Art witness testify that Modern Art was actually a means of espionage, and that if you know how to read them, modern paintings will disclose the weak spots in U.S. fortifications and such crucial constructions as Boulder Dam."

Recalling the Siqueiros incident of 1932 was the *affaire Orozco* in 1953. This referred to an exhibition sponsored by the Municipal Art Commission but cancelled by UCLA, where it opened and almost immediately closed, when a political science professor charged that José Clemente Orozco "definitely incorporated Communist symbols" in his paintings, although the work hung without complaint in Boston, Toronto, Wilmington, and Detroit.[4]

Then in 1955, critic Henry Seldis wrote in *Art Digest* that the City Council had voted to melt down Bernard Rosenthal's *The Family*, an abstract sculpture commissioned for the entrance to the Police Facilities building, as soon as it was installed.[5] Intended to show that the L.A.P.D. was dedicated to the protection of the family, this stylized if unexciting bronze was viewed differently by Councilman Harby. "This is a shameless soulless, faceless, raceless, gutless monstrosity that will live in infamy."[6] Despite his allegation, the work still stands.

Indeed, the view that "modern" art had links with left-wing politics also impacted on the County Museum. James Byrnes, Curator of Modern Art,

1946-1953, described attacks made on his annual exhibitions of Artists of Los Angeles and Vicinity. He recalled in an interview that a painting of chickens in a coop was interpreted by a "professor" lecturing to a group in front of it as "the great American Eagle, stripped of its pin feathers and feeding on the seeds of Communism"; that a canvas showing a circus tent with a white horse being led by a black man was a matter of "the blacks taking over"; and scenes of ruined, bombed churches were considered to reflect what Communists thought about churches.[7]

Museum trustees let Byrnes buy an Albers and a Pollock, but solely for educational purposes — their spokesman asserting, "All right, I will agree that we buy them with the following proviso: that you don't hang them on the walls!"[8]

Evidence since that time suggests that a more tolerant museum audience has emerged, but civic officials appear slower to change their views.

As late as 1982, Barbara Carrasco's mural, *History of Los Angeles: A Mexican Perspective*, commissioned a year earlier by the Community Redevelopment Agency, was cancelled by the same organization on the grounds of its subject matter, especially two scenes: one referring to the massacre of Chinese railroad workers in the late 19th century, the other to the internment of Japanese-Americans during World War II. This incident recalls the whitewashing of the Siqueiros mural, an inspiration to the Chicana artist, and included as a vignette on her work. In this case, the decision was finally reversed when the Los Angeles Festival Committee commissioned the completion of the mural and it was hung at L.A.'s Union Station during the Festival in the fall of 1990.[9]

Not only did the completion of the Carrasco mural reflect a change of position in the social-political arena, but another situation which should make Angelenos stand up and be proud. Robbie Conal's 1990 billboard portraying "Artificial Art Official" Jesse Helms was returned to its Santa Monica Boulevard site in West Hollywood one day after its hasty removal by the billboard company, the result of rethinking on their part.

Indeed, for Conal, 1988 was a banner year. Only two years earlier he had been charged with defacing public and private walls by the Public Works Department, which vainly tried to have him prosecuted by the City Attorney's office, but wound up only billing him for the removal. Conal paid $1,300 to remove posters such as *Men With No Lips* (1985-87), and satirical portraits of Ronald Reagan, Donald Regan, James Baker III and Caspar Weinberger from the walls of buildings. In 1990, however, the

Tom Otterness, *The New World*, 1982-91.

Department of Cultural Affairs awarded him a grant, to confirm that at least in L.A. one branch of its officialdom and the target of his satires had turned around!

Post-Congress Update:

L.A.'s recent stature in relation to sexual reference in works of art may have been tarnished when Edward Thomas, regional head of the General Services Administration, ordered two components of Tom Otterness's sculptural ensemble, *The New World*, removed. A stylized figure of a woman in a squatting position and a newborn baby girl lying on its back with its legs up and holding a globe were part of an installation presenting, according to critic Christopher Knight, "a powerful symbol of liberty and triumph over tyranny," on a new federal office building named for Representative Edward R. Roybal early in December, 1991.[10] Roybal observed two young boys touching the baby's genitals, which prompted him to declare the nudes "an attractive nuisance" appropriate for a museum but not for a public courtyard.

Since the incident, Otterness and Thomas have issued a joint statement advising that the work will remain intact but the artist will design an appropriate means to keep the public "at a slight distance" from parts of the work.[11]

The author is grateful to James Butler and Janet Dominick for their assistance.

NOTES:

[1] Door of Life can be viewed at Advance Door Hardware, 1001 E. Slauson Ave., Los Angeles, CA.

[2] Conversation with author, September 1991.

[3] See Shifra Goldman, "Sequeiros and Three Early Murals in Los Angeles," *Art Journal* 33:4, Summer 1974, pp. 321-326. See also Goldman, "Tropical Paradise: Sequeiros's L. A. Mural; A Victim of Double Censorship," *Artweek*, July 5, 1990, p. 21.

[4] Langsner, "Art news from Los Angeles," *ARTnews* 54, September 1953, p. 48. In this instance, the Pasadena Art Institute took the show.

[5] Seldis, "Art News from Los Angeles," *ARTnews* 56, February 15, 1955, p. 15. See also J. Marshall, "Something is Rotten in Los Angeles," *Art Digest* 29, April 1, 1955, p. 5.

[6] Ibid.

[7] Stated earlier to Professor Julius Kaplan, confirmed by Byrnes by telephone to author, February 20 1992.

[8] See George M. Goodwin, Los Angeles Art Community: James Byrnes. (Los Angeles: UCLA Oral History Program, 1977), Vol I, p. 98.

[9] See Schipper, "A Matter of Pride," *Los Angeles Times*, Calendar Part II, "Festival '90," Aug 26, 1990, pp. 22-23.

[10] Knight, "Path of Disillusionment Leads to Royal Site," December 9, 1991, *Los Angeles Times* Calendar section, p. 1. The incident was originally reported by Laurie Becklund, December 5, 1991, *L.A. Times* Metro Section, pp. 1,3.

[11] Suzanne Muchnic, "Tom Otterness' The New World: Perils of Public Art," *ArtScene* (Los Angeles), February, 1992, p. 26. The artist has since designed a bronze railing to surround the work.

Art and Censorship in Cuba Today

by Samuel B. Cherson
(Puerto Rico)

A few days ago the prominent Polish film director Krzysztof Zanussi told me about a revealing experience which occurred during his 1975 trip to Cuba in connection with the premiere of his film, *Illuminations*. Although the movie was produced in a fraternal communist country, it was still necessary to obtain the approval of the Cuban authorities. A private screening was organized for that purpose at ICAIC (the government film agency), with the director unexpectedly present. To his surprise, Fidel Castro showed up at this session to personally assess the work. Zanussi said that Castro used to wear glasses in private — an image he wanted to conceal in public — and was slightly annoyed to have a stranger see him in that guise. This caused Zanussi to worry, since a rejection of his film would have brought on serious problems in his native country.

Several months ago the international press reported the sudden withdrawal in Cuba of the film *Alice in Wondertown* (produced by ICAIC) after four days of screenings in movie houses filled to capacity (and with enormous lines outside), because the public identified the military lead character with Fidel Castro, in sheer delight. This negative perception was considered extremely alarming in the highest government spheres. The suppression of this feature film has not only occurred at the national level but at the international as well. When the Latino Festival of New York tried to show it in 1991, the official Cuban reply was that "the film was not finished," an incredible excuse given the fact that it had already been shown in last year's Berlin Festival. In view of Castro's blatant act of censorship, all the ICAIC members, from the directors to the humblest employees, delivered an energetic protest letter to Fidel.

These incidents reflect to what degree Cuban arts have been and continue to be subjected to the personal dictates of Castro. At the outset of the Revolutionary Regime (in 1961, when the documentary titled *P. M.* was suppressed), he personally decreed the controlling dogma for artistic creation: "Within the Revolution, everything, outside the Revolution, nothing." This dogma has been incorporated into the Constitution now in force, which proclaims that "artistic creativity is free, as long as its content is not contrary to the Revolution. Forms of expression of art are free" (Article 38d). The constitutional level of this precept has had an overwhelming weight in the plastic arts.

Some analysts of the Cuban artistic panorama, with excessive ingenuity or good will, want to view, this distinction between form and content as a sign of official liberalism, as if it were possible to separate one from the other in the creative process, especially in a country where art and ideology are inseparable. If it is true that the Revolutionary regime has given a free hand to artists with regard to their stylistic leanings (not imposing, for example, a "Socialist Realism" in the old Soviet mold), it is no less true that the content of the work of art has been subjected to capricious and arbitrary interpretations about its ideological message. When, at a recent meeting between a group of young intellectuals and Fidel Castro, he was asked to define what is inside and what outside the Revolution, he replied astutely: "All of you know." As could be expected, this climate of doubt and indefiniteness about the acceptable content of a work of art has on many occasions curtailed creative freedom, either through official censorship or self-censorship.

It is not possible to enumerate here the many instances of censorship or coercion in the arts during the Revolutionary period. May it suffice to point out that artist Antonia Eiriz, a painter of distorted figures in an Expressionist style distant from the optimism that Cuban art "should" project, was asked years ago in an accusatory tone, "what secret purposes were hidden behind her monstrous images." Repression has not only been aimed at contents considered to be non-Revolutionary in the work of art per se, but also at "non-orthodox" artists' lifestyles (identified as snobbism, extravagance, homosexuality and others), to the extreme of proclaiming in 1971 at the First Congress for Education and Culture that "those tendencies whose criteria originate in libertinism, whose aims tend to hide the counter-revolutionary venom and which conspire against the Revolutionary ideology on which the construction of Socialism and Communism is based should be condemned and rejected."

Nevertheless, censorship and repression have not been a monolithic obstacle to creative freedom. Within the system that controls the arts there have been signs of more liberal and permissive stances, openings that a new generation of artists has jumped upon to produce an art of bold content, guided by a critical and irreverent attitude toward the inefficient and hypocritical socio-political tenets which have prevailed in post-Revolutionary Cuba. This is evident in the exhibition titled "Art and Cuba Today," shown at the University of the South, Sewanee, Tennessee (as well as in Boston and New York City), paradoxically, organized with the assistance of several official Cuban entities.

Many of the participants in this show, and Williams Carmona, an artist of the same generation I interviewed recently, seem determined to produce a confrontational art which tests the limits of permissiveness within a system that has consistently negated freedom of expression and which controls totally the exhibition spaces and the communications media. This exploration of the limits of governmental tolerance must be cautious by necessity, being careful not to aim too high, toward the supreme echelon of the ruling hierarchy or at the fundamental principles of the regime, so as to avoid triggering the repressive mechanisms available to the government. But even if the art of these young artists remains on peripheral grounds and posits dialectically, from within the system, corrections and reforms to some of the ills and problems, it is not risk-free, as shown by incidents of censorship and even more severe reprisals in recent years.

Tomás Essón, one of the participants in "Art and Cuba Today," has challenged the canons maintained for years by the Revolutionary government through his grotesque figures and his sexual and scatological references, aspiring to connect these elements with historio-patriotic themes. This aspiration got him into trouble with the government some years ago, causing him to "voluntarily" take down an exhibition considered to be offensive. One of the works, *My homage to Che* (1987-88), showed one of his monsters copulating in front of the guerrilla leader's portrait. The painter insisted that this was a comment on the hypocrisy and double standards of some government officials. After visiting the United States in connection with "Art and Cuba Today," Essón has decided not to return to his homeland.

Another exhibition of recent years, "Cultured Objects," was closed down by the Cuban authorities a day after its opening, on the instructions of the cultural censors in the Central Committee of the Communist Party, as reported by Carmona. Some of the participants were accused of being counter-revolutionaries — a very serious charge — and painter Angel Delgado was jailed because of his work. Not only artists suffered the rigors of cultural repression. Even a high official of the Ministry of Culture, Vice-Minister Marcia Leiseca, was dismissed because she encouraged an acceptance of these young artists. Although Carmona does not know of any artist now in jail because of his or her work, he assures us that

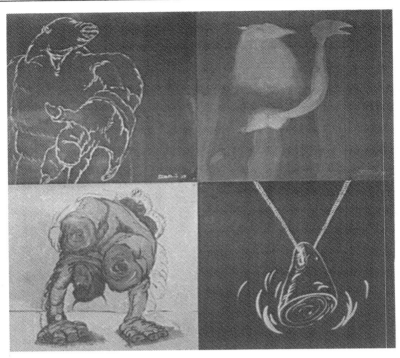

Tomás Essón, *Spoulakk*.

a list of artists who are permanently forbidden from exhibiting in Cuba was prepared by the Ministry of Culture following this incident. Other past incidents involving jail or repression, mentioned by Carmona, were the "body art" event on 23rd Street, ending with the arrest of the authors, and an event in the Thalia Hall, where a giant portrait of Che, spread on the floor and walked upon by the spectators, caused Fidel Castro's direct intervention. Although Carmona himself has not suffered this kind of repression, his bold "performance" criticizing fetishism and the cult of monuments earned him a call from the Ministry of the Interior; he had to explain to the Minister the motivation of his piece.

But censorship and reprisal do not always occur by means of the visible intervention of high officials. Sometimes it happens indirectly and at a lower level, through minor obstacles to the preparation or mounting of the artistic event. During the performance titled "Today's art . . . is an ass," watched last year by 400 spectators in the René Portocarrero silk-screen atelier, Carmona complained about the difficulties created for his work plan by minor officials; he painted the title on the behind of an actor who played the part of a dead military officer, as part of an elaborate wake. The title was exposed when the "corpse" lowered his pants.

Notwithstanding this and other repressive incidents, it is surprising that Cuban authorities have tolerated the sprouting of the kind of protest art that I have mentioned. Has there been an opening in the Cuban creative climate? The phenomenon lends itself to diverse interpretations, depending on the color of the glasses looked through. Some believe that the intellectual incompetence of the bureaucrats in charge of regulating the artistic activity makes it possible to wrap message-art in a metaphorical or oblique cloak, which bypasses the watchdog's eye and mind. Others see the existence of an ideological battle within the government ranks, between the proponents of greater artistic freedom and the hard-liners. But, in my judgment, it could well be a matter of sheer political calculation allowing the government to refute accusations of artistic repression repeatedly made abroad, while inside Cuba the unrest in the plastic arts arouses minimal repercussions, limited to an intellectual elite. There is almost no diffusion through the controlled mass media. It is a strategy that seems to be confirmed by the statement of a Latin American essayist living in the United States, who affirms that, "it is a remarkable triumph of the Cuban Revolution that this generation of artists exists in Cuba."

The Stars and Stripes: Johns to Burkhardt

by Peter Selz
(United States)

When Jasper Johns first appeared on the New York art scene with his *Flags* in 1955, the art world was provoked by the rich vibrancy of his encaustic technique, by his handling of the flat picture plane, and by the cool, detached and neutral attitude toward his subjects, which seemed to some like a respite from the impassioned canvases of the Abstract Expressionists. In the mid-'50s a few of us were bewildered, however, by the indifference to the meaning of the Stars and Stripes at the time of the greatest expansion of American economic and military power. When the Castelli Gallery exhibited these paintings in the late '50s, just as American art too was becoming dominant in the Western world, people might have seen more in these paintings than merely the "integrity of the surface."

Some five years later Claes Oldenburg made rough fragments of the flag in muslin, soaked in plaster and then painted with tempera. They were irreverent renditions of the Stars and Stripes. Like all the items which he had in his Store at the time, they were meant to "attach materialistic practices and art" and can be seen also as parodies of the highly touted flags by Johns. Oldenburg questioned, not only the values of the art world, but, beyond that, the attitudes of mass culture. "I am for an art that is political-erotical-mystical, that does something other than sits on its ass in a museum," he began his Statement of Purpose for the Ray Gun Theater in 1962. It's a lengthy statement, very worthwhile reading. It also has sentences like: "I am for an art that takes its form from the lines of life itself, that twists and extends and accumulates and spits and drips, and is heavy and coarse and sweet and stupid like life itself."

By the mid-'60s, with the Vietnam War in full gear, politically engaged artists began to use the image of the flag more seriously, employing it symbolically to protest the total immorality of that war in innumerable anti-war posters. Some were very powerful in their message, asking questions such as, *Are We Next?* Or presenting the *Napalm Flag*, or, again, the *Genocide Flag* of 1967. Even Mr. Johns, when prevailed upon, made his negative green, black, and orange flag, *Moratorium* for the environmental movement in 1969 — pretty mild compared to the other posters, but beautifully painted.

As the War continued and intensified in its mass killing, the messages in the anti-war movement also became more intense. One of the most effective anonymous posters of the period was called *Stars and Stripes Forever*. It consisted of a large number of wooden matches with their heads painted in red, white, and blue and ready to burst into flames momentarily. In 1970, also, Sam Wiener made his powerful image: *Those Who Fail to Remember Are Condemned to Repeat It*. It is a small box lined with mirrors and with flag-draped coffins expanding infinitely into endless rows, much as the body counts seemed to increase *ad infinitum*. This piece had the effect of a surreal dream of horrors, terrifying in its cool attitude toward death. Later, during the years of overt U.S. aggression in Central America — in Grenada, Nicaragua, Panama, El Salvador — Wiener made posters for mass distribution of this image.

The Chilean artist René Castro, now living in San Francisco, contributed to the San Francisco Art Institute 1990 Annual Exhibition, "The Flag" — a show which opened in the fall of that year at the time when American troops were rallied around the Stars and Stripes, protecting the oil wells of the Arabian desert. Castro's work, called *Burn, Baby, Burn* consisted of a Posada-like skeleton of a man draped in a mutilated American flag and wearing a large John Wayne-type Stetson hat. A vulture with a G.I. helmet is perched on his shoulder and a frieze of similar carrion birds decorates the top. The poignant message on the side reads: BY THE TIME YOU REACH MY AGE, YOU DON'T NEED TO BE FUCKING AROUND WITH THE FLAG.

In the same show was a strong image by Mason Byers, entitled *One Hundred Eleven Instruments of Counter Intelligence, Social Mobility and Selective Survival*, which was an assemblage of nine steel-jawed animal traps fixed to three large American flags. In the place of the bait, the artist placed ten-dollar bills and fake bags of cocaine. The phrase "Selective Survival" refers to the profits made by the drug dealers in cahoots with the CIA. The traps are for the victimized underclass. Byers stated the unfortunate truism that "through complacency, greed and misinformation the population does not question these actions." This work, like so many others in that provocative show, questioned the government's manipulation of the populace under the guise of patriotism. In a piece by Bernadette Ann Cotter, the flag was deconstructed, literally, that is, into thread, hanging from the wall and in little balls on the floor.

The organizers of that show also brought Dread Scott's work, *What Is the Proper Way to Display the U.S. Flag?*, from Chicago where it had caused a great uproar when exhibited at the School of the Art Institute in 1989. The piece consisted of photomontage, text, a shelf, a ledge and the flag, spread on the floor. The photos showed some South Korean students burning the U.S. Flag, one of them holding up a sign, saying "Yankee go home, son of bitch." On the shelf was a ledger where visitors could write their responses to the question: "What is the proper way...?" The way it was displayed, people naturally had to walk on the flag on the floor, thus "desecrating" the national symbol with their feet.

But are feet really so inferior to arms which are lifted patriotically to salute the piece of cloth? Why is no one troubled by the cancellation machines that besmear the paper representation of the Stars and Stripes millions of times each day at U.S. post offices? The Veterans of Foreign Wars attacked the Scott piece, demonized the artist, and provoked some members of Chicago's City Council to demand that the Institute's board resign to be replaced by "honest Americans and veterans." The School of the Art Institute had its city and state funding cut. Demonstrations with as many as 2,500 veterans took place, but many of Scott's fellow students made it difficult for them when they painted flags on the grounds where they were about to march. A great deal of public debate was caused by this work and even President George Bush took notice of a work of art. There were also a number of flag burnings while we were "cleaning up" Panama. The enraged President managed to bring the issue of flag burning to the Supreme Court resulting in Justice Brennan's memorable decision: "We are aware that desecration of the flag is deeply offensive to many, but punishing desecration of the flag dilutes the very freedom that makes this emblem so revered and worth revering." With Brennan, and Thurgood Marshall off the Court, men who are being replaced by individuals of the extreme right, will the Court rule with similar wisdom in the future?

In 1990, during the period designated by Mr. Bush as Operation Desert Shield and Operation Desert Storm, the Los Angeles artist Hans Burkhardt painted an astonishing series of paintings based on the flag. Paintings of political commitment have been consistent in the work of the 87-year-old painter. He had painted works protesting General Franco's bombardment of Spain's civilian population; he had made paintings of the concentration camps, and works protesting the bombing of Hiroshima.

During the Vietnam War he infused human skulls into large canvases of thick, heavily painted textured greys, which Donald Kuspit counted

Hans Burkhardt, *The Desert*, 1990.

"among the greatest war paintings — especially modern war paintings: summarizing the brutality and inhumanity not only of the Vietnam War, but also of the 20th Century as a whole."

In most of the current Desert Storm paintings, Burkhardt juxtaposed the image of the Cross to the U.S. Flag. In *The Desert* he has nailed an old Mexican crucifix on top of a painting of the flag. Into the field normally reserved for the stars he glued a piece of old burlap, and some additional lengths of rotten burlap are placed below the flag. The stripes are painted with great care and consummate craftsmanship, and a sensuous surface creates a drastic visual contrast to the crucifixion in the center. In a variant, *The Lime Pit*, a fragment of a crucifix with a headless Christ takes up the center of the painting and red paint is stained into the black burlap.

In *Tar Pits*, Burkhardt simply nailed two pieces of raw board together and additional black crosses, made of pieces of cord, appear in the star field as well as in the blackened area below. In *Silent Storm*, the largest of the works in the series, he again made two crosses out of rope and placed them in the upper left field, while the white spaces between the black bands are sensitively brushed, creating shimmering chromatic surfaces, which again seem in total opposition to the message of death. The bands of color in these works dialectically transfigure the suffering expressed by the dark crosses of death and suggest late medieval woodcuts of the Dance of Death. Burkhardt's works are executed with a masterful craftsmanship comparable to Goya's magnificently etched *Disasters of War*.

Jean Baudrillard asserts that our overstimulated world, in which "television is the ultimate and perfect object," signals the end of interiority and authenticity, threatening the self with becoming only a screen upon which networks of influence are projected. Such a condition suggests the end of creative originality and the construction of a simulated space of appropriation and pastiche. Jasper Johns's series of flag paintings can now be seen as replications, depicting material objects, as codified images without significant content. But some of the works mentioned here contradict Baudrillard's pessimistic stance vis-à-vis authentic art in our time. Hans Burkhardt's "Desert Storm" paintings raise many of these issues, not as theoretical problems, but in the form of major works of art. Now achieving an *Altersstil*, so rare in time, he has created these truly extraordinary paintings. I am reminded of Theodor Adorno, who formulated a tragic — rather than pessimistic — aesthetic in which he observed that, "The need to lend a voice to suffering is a condition of truth."

Pluralism, Balkanization and the Revenge of the "Primitives"

by Serge Guilbaut

In 1956, as France was just beginning to savor the benefits of a consumer society, Charles Estienne, an influential and popular French art critic, decided to give up his career in the art world and devote himself to writing popular *chansons*. In order to justify such a radical change, Estienne, who had heretofore believed that art criticism was essential to the development of a public consciousness, said that, faced with the growing meaninglessness of art criticism in its collusion with the art market and politics, he preferred to walk away humming one of his own street ballads.

The hopes and aspirations Estienne had held since the war had crashed against the wall of the reality of the art world. He found that the meaning of art was indeterminate and that he controlled so very little of his métier, that the image he had always believed in — that of the critic as the annunciating angel of the modern era — was in reality transformed into that of a small shopkeeper with nothing to sell. He could not escape the unenviable fate that transformed art critic into publicist. Switching from art for the elite to popular art was surely problematic, but at least, Estienne thought, his new position didn't carry with it the illusions attached to fine art.

If it was difficult to be an art critic in 1956, it would seem to be even harder today. The avant-garde has indeed disappeared. The authoritarianism of formalism has been undermined by pluralism which embraces practically all cultural voices, but the role of the critic is as problematic as ever because of the fragmentation of critical discourse. If art criticism is to embrace everything, even subjective criticism which ignores the social role, the relationship with the market, publicity and narcissism, how can it avoid dissolution into corporatism or balkanization?

In focusing on issues of multiculturalism, the 1991 Congress of the International Association of Art Critics demonstrates that art critics are finally ready to discuss the social and political challenges of the profession. This has not always been the case. This is why I would like to make a comparison between the present post-cold-war situation and that of the post-World War ll years in order to explore the impossible dream art criticism has to discover its *raison d'etre*.

The first Congress of art critics in Paris was held in 1948, when the new post-nuclear world order was being formed by the Marshall Plan and the Cold War. This Congress, however, is shaped by the thaw in Eastern Europe and the victory of international capitalism — whose cohesive power is somewhat overrated — as well as by the effect of divisive nationalisms.

The comparison between these two periods is fascinating when one considers that the first art critics' Congress attempted in vain to promote a universal and humanistic criticism capable of defining a global aesthetic linked to the past, despite portents of antagonistic cultural forces. 1948 was indeed the year in which the Western world, after several years of universalist hope, recognized that a new and complex world order was about to be conceived. It was the year in which Churchill somberly announced the descent of an Iron Curtain upon Europe, henceforth symbolizing the two antagonistic political ideologies in the race for global supremacy. Such a supremacy was quickly understood to be defined in territorial, ideological, and cultural terms.

The two new superpowers, the United States and the Soviet Union, after emerging victorious from the war, began, not nuclear warfare but a Cold War that left no field untouched. In this confrontation, a weakened and impoverished Europe ironically became the stake in this battle of titans. This old Europe served as a fulcrum for the two superpowers in their attempts to unseat one another. Though it may have been cold, the war was bitter. It was the beginning of a time when Russia, supported by European intellectuals, forcefully championed peace in Europe; America, with no less enthusiasm, guarded the concept of liberty. Each superpower managed European cultural debates via remote control, especially in France and Italy. These were the two least stable countries, whose volatile and divided electorate was capable of voting in either of the competing systems. Therefore it was in these countries, and in the heart of their cultural institutions, that the most decisive battles of the cold war would be waged.

In June of 1948, Paris welcomed art critics from around the world for the first International Congress. After the years of barbarism, one might have expected some consensus and preliminary evaluation of the international cultural scene, or at least an acknowledgement of the preeminent cultural achievements of the time. This was, however, not the case. In fact, any expectation of a relatively objective evaluation of the international art scene was quickly dashed, for the critics actually invited to Paris were not truly representative of the vital trends of the time. Instead of Clement Greenberg or even J. J. Sweeney, the United States was represented by the venerable Walter Pach; and France invited Jean Cassou to present contemporary French art (about which he knew almost nothing) in the place of Charles Estienne, Michel Tapié, Louis Degand or Georges Duthuit, who were all very active at that time.

Despite a rather limited theme — contemporary art criticism — the Paris conference was unable to go beyond the stale clichés that characterized the pre-war era. Reported in great detail by *Arts*, the conference revealed that in the face of a myriad of aesthetic and political options, art criticism could not come to terms with, let alone even define, the essential issues facing a growing number of young artists.

In greeting this international gathering, Jean Cassou could not refrain from celebrating the glory of the past School of Paris and the universality of its influence. For Cassou, Paris was still the center of the art world, an inextinguishable source of humanism among Parisians, contrary to Clement Greenberg's assertion that same year that New York City was the new art mecca. Not for a moment did Cassou doubt that the young painters of Paris would continue to be the epitome of vitality and energy envied by the whole world. The past was still so vivid in Paris that it obscured the present and blocked the future: "The momentum and energy of so many years cannot be extinguished so suddenly. Our recent past in which our present is rooted, a past so ingenious in its discoveries and resolutions, so quick to produce masterpieces, bespeaks profound and vital virtues deeply ingrained in our people which cannot be lost overnight."

In New York City, already institutionalized avant-garde facilities (magazines, galleries, and museums) zealously championed the most advanced modern art, even as they defused it. The critical institutions of Paris, however, bewildered by the experimentation of the New York avant-garde, tried to preserve the old principles that had made Paris the capital in its heyday. Jean Cassou continued to assert that French genius unified "the spirit and the mind" as a synthesis of "mathematician and philosopher" as well as craftsman. Indeed, for Cassou in the post-war era, the integrity of the common man and his taste for "a job well-done" was an essential component of the greatness of the Parisian artist. These virtues, asserted Cassou, "are ever-present and endow upon each of our artists a natural inclination for mastery. One can always learn from them, for they are rich in knowledge, the kind of practical knowledge that is immediately relevant. It is in this sense that the School of Paris is truly a school, and it is why our friends and colleagues abroad are able to continue to have faith in it."

This passage is quite remarkable when one considers that is was precisely these characteristics — the métier, the finished *objet d'art* — that Americans would attack. Jean Cassou was not alone in defending the pre-war golden age and a rationalist humanism mixed with the uplifting sentiments of the *front populaire*. Indeed, as curator of a national museum, it was not easy for Cassou to navigate the perilous political and aesthetic debates rocking the Parisian scene. Yet in spite of his intent to promote modern art and the French image, Cassou, like many French cultural officials, was incapable of accepting any ideas that challenged the classical notion of France and her culture. Therefore an air of unreality permeated the discussions. The aim seems to have been to connect the pre- and post-war periods as if the years of conflict had not changed anything. By reviving its old muse, Paris daydreamed of conquests, and could not establish in the present the kind of critical discourse that would be relevant to the art community.

The United States, on the contrary, convinced of being the vital center of the art world (and thanks to its private cultural institutions), championed the new abstract art that the public institutions of Paris were unwilling to acknowledge. Whereas the liberalism embraced by American museums propagated individualism as a sign of the new world order, Europe, mired in its political divisions and humanistic traditions, could not assimilate these notions into its frame of reference in the crucial year of 1948. This incapacity to formulate a theoretical defense of individualism, as well as to even imagine an art world whose center would not be Paris, would cost Europe cultural hegemony for years to come. The European blindness to this shift was almost total.

Today, the end of the Cold War, together with the breakup of the modernist monolith, should bring about an open and decentralized art, as well as critics capable and ready to evaluate their own aims amidst the proliferation of discourses. This is, however, seldom the case.

In the new world order yet to be born, it no longer seems possible to envision the renascence of a coherent, centralized art scene that could impose a unique and centralized direction like that of the past, much to the chagrin of critics like Hilton Kramer or even Clement Greenberg. Today, in contrast to the 1940s and '50s, the postmodern world, distrusting and rejecting mainstream discourse, is increasingly engaged in the horizontal proliferation of discourse rather than in vertical, hierarchical authoritarianism. It had seemed for a while that with the resurrection of painting in the 1980s, the role of the "rear-guard" would be played by postconceptual art, posing the social and aesthetic issues at the core of what Frederic Jameson called "Late Capitalism." What seems in retrospect to have been the most interesting development, despite some pathos, is the critical thinking of a group of artists who still believed in the potential of a subversive critical discourse amidst the hypercommercialization of art during the Reagan Era.

The struggle was taken up by art critics (those of *October* and *Art in America*, in particular) who still believed in the possibility of engagement in the culture. They succeeded in formulating a critical theory in radical opposition to mainstream thought, an attitude occasionally encountered in the work of certain contemporary artists, as well. That these critics eventually abandoned art criticism in favor of art history testifies less to the institutionalization of art criticism than to the painful realization that the art they had fought for was not always as radical nor as politically correct as they would have liked to believe in their avant-gardist enthusiasm. Their retreat from criticism also pointed to something new: so commercial had the cultural milieu become, Russell Jacoby notwithstanding, that the American university became, paradoxically, the only place where scholarship and criticism could escape from the hypertrophic market. Even after the latest recession in the art market, the collusion between criticism and consumption persisted. The traditional role of art criticism as defined by Greenberg, Rosenberg, Fried, and Krauss gave way to pawns of the market pushing the old-fashioned intellectuals into history or philosophy.

Likewise the work of Jeff Wall or Louise Lawler, who define the two most interesting poles of postconceptual art, never truly manages, despite its intelligence, to go beyond that which is circumscribed by the international art world. Though the coldness and ironic or analytical distancing shows a deep understanding of the implications of artistic representation in our postmodern world, it cannot break the silence that endows works of this generation with the voice of a witness, albeit for the prosecution, incapable of engaging in the social struggle it describes. In their profound understanding of the ethical and moral issues which face the contemporary artist, these spectators (*flaneurs*) of the 21st century so guard themselves against suffering that they speak only through looking-glasses. This in no way diminishes the value of their work, but shows how little leeway is left contemporary artists who wish to engage in any kind of criticism regarding our "society of the spectacle" without losing too many feathers. Between the forces of the market, and the co-opting of institutions and art history, neither the thought nor the voice of the artist has much of a chance.

A strange numbness has descended upon the Western art world. It no longer has that "something to fight for," as Americans had during World War II. It can no longer conceive of worthwhile challenges. It is not my intent to defend political art *per se*, certainly not latter-day Socialist Realism, but rather to illuminate the type of art which analyses the structure of visual expression and the structure of the art world to unveil the mechanisms of canonization and so forth, which Hal Foster has in fact termed "cultural resistance."

The extremely negative symbol of this implosion can be found in a brute state in the work of Jeff Koons who, just like Madonna, plays all his cards at once, mixing genres, ironically exploiting to the maximum the gamut of spectators' expectations, with a dash of critical discourse added. They denounce, indirectly yet ferociously, the various exploitations and corruptions of popular culture; at the same time they exploit themselves in their notoriously lucrative careers. One must concede that Koons's pornographic film and photography depicting Koons and Cicciolina copulating in a rococo setting (a blatant pun on classical prototypes in the history of art) are indeed devastating in their ironic criticism of the relationship between art and politics. The triviality of the political realm, epitomized by the election of the porn-star to the Italian Parliament, is introduced to that of the art world, whose current star is a former investment banker. In inflating the metaphor, the extremism of this position situates the work outside the acknowledged parameters of the art community. However, it reintroduces and continues Marcel Duchamp's gesture. It is the sexuality of the urinal rendered in hyperrealist guise. Sex-shop art replaces the urinal sculpture as a critique of the politics of art and the art of politics. At the same time, such interpenetration of genres points to how difficult it is not only to conceive of an oppositional art engaged in social and political life, but even to hope that strategies of representation can escape the radical erosion of meaning brought about by super-capitalism. These works leave behind them a devastated landscape in which critical and analytical works lose their gravity, but not their tragic significance in an absurd battle. Koons's success reveals, in the delirium of exhibition and exploitation, a society devouring its own image. This strange curse distinguishes our era from that of the post-war era, when the Abstract Expressionist generation truly believed in the possibility of expressing and transcending the existential anguish of the nuclear age.

Now as then, America seems in need of the periphery to revitalize its artistic core. This time, however, it is the revenge of the so-called "primitive" that has come to the rescue. In contrast to the cynicism and trendy pessimism of the contemporary scene, the tactics favored by marginalized groups (feminists, gays, "First Nation" Canadians, and Native Americans) seem the only viable voices capable of articulating a discourse of a different order: to propose another reading of everyday life. The stakes are crucial for these artists, and their work proves to be of vital and unquestionable importance in the context of the emerging "new world order" that is, however ironically, so furiously intent on copying the old.

Ironically, several American-Indian artists have begun to appropriate Western art forms in order to revivify their culture while freeing it of its image as an exotic craft of the past. It is an attempt on their part to situate themselves in the center of living culture, playing the game of postmodern diversity with an aggressiveness necessitated by their political aims. Traditional contemporary art, in its self-referential discourse, its cynicism, its disbelief, its intolerance, no longer seems to make sense to a culture awakening after years of exploitation. The work of these young artists is the product of a new social and cultural awareness, sometimes inspired by feminist discourse.

The works of Native Americans, however diverse, internalize the urgent problems of their daily life. Likewise, by defining, analyzing and reconstructing their autochthonic consciousness, such works have become important points of interrogation directly linked to another central issue: the repatriation of ancestral territory. Without romanticizing such art, one must admit that in these works (painting, photography, installation, or performance) there is something intractable: the exorbitant, perilous, even unacceptable demands upon the white establishment intent on maintaining the status quo. Yves Michaud asserts that this subversive disobedience is the consequence of the heterogeneity of such complex communities.

> These are a people profoundly engaged in actions and creations that cannot be taken out of context, whose aesthetic sensibilities cannot be

universalized, who come from a world which remains static, even as it approaches our own.

And it is necessary to acknowledge this, because finally, it is the only thing truly relevant to us: not the creators, the magicians, the innovators, nor the fabricators of 'the spiritual in art,' nor postmodern exhibitionism, in sum, not the great string of contemporary clichés inflated to a global dimension, but rather the fact that there are still, here and everywhere, works whose necessity challenges us like an enigma, provocative works which introduce a process of communication not necessarily successful, but which we, like they, are willing to risk.

After exploiting their exotic image for a while, these so-called "primitives" are now putting it to use for political and historical action. As Charlotte Townsend Gault has explained, "This art cannot be separated from the recognition of cultural identity and the reinterpretation of history in the face of discrimination, marginalization, and ignorance." It seems to me that, far from the prevailing cynicism, our contemporary culture would have the best chance of producing the kind of works that might shake up old habits, for the issues at stake are dangerous yet crucial for these communities. In fact, the stakes are so crucial that this revolt of the "primitive" will be difficult for our governments to deal with. Their demands seem to come straight out of a bad movie. The irony of the fact that these territorial demands emerge *en masse* the very year of the 500th anniversary of Christopher Columbus's "discovery" of America is loaded with both irony and danger, as recent events such as at Oka (Québec) testify.

The diversity, the social and political contradictions, challenging "First Nations" must not be overlooked. It restores to them another dimension, that of "the soul" or the "primordial condition," which has long been obscured by "rational" Western thought. Works like Ed Poitras's ritual environments (a species of Pan-Indianism as Charlotte Townsend Gault has termed it), as well as the political performances of Rebecca Belmore, or the ironic canvases commenting on the history of "Cowboys and Indians" by Cree artist, Gerald McMaster, testify to the vitality and complexity by which these indigenous people defy the federal administration.

The most striking example of cultural reappropriation is without doubt the work of Salish artist Lawrence Paul whose canvases are influenced — as one used to say — by Surrealist painting, particularly that of Dali in the '20s and '30s. In these canvases, Paul's experience on Indian reservations is translated via the demented idiom of Dali's melting watches, replaced by

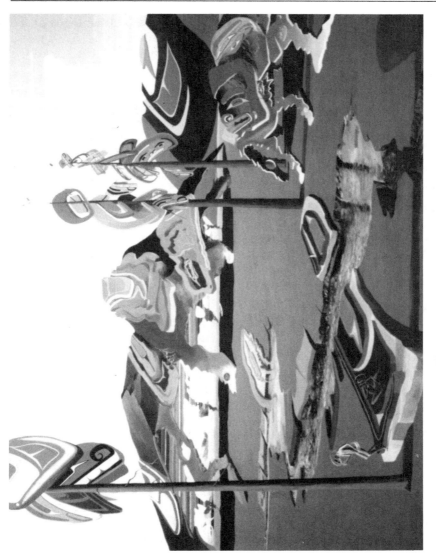

Lawrence Paul, *The Universe is so big white man keeps me on a reservation,* 1988.

totems or the Salish or Tlinglit motifs which have become logos of the "Indian" community. These surrealist landscapes are transformed into a critical discourse, turning the strategies of Picasso and the surrealists against themselves.

I am not completely convinced that this type of art or even this body of issues will not in the end succumb to the gallery system. The resistance may not last, but it is at the moment acute. The work of Lawrence Paul for example is intransigent and profoundly oppositional in its interpolation. I can speak of his work thus because I am a viewer of his work, which specifically addresses the clichés of my own culture, retrieving the dead images of my tradition to shoot them back at me.

In a fascinating role reversal, Western culture has unexpectedly become for indigenous cultures the "savage" which must be exploited: a moribund, bizarre, and exotic culture that must serve to pep up the other. The Persian Gulf War changed nothing, but underlined the new North-South relationships as well as the unending problems of all those marginalized who can now recover their voices.

The Western world no longer has the power to keep playing the role of a cultural Dracula; only to offer a tender throat, incessantly rerunning old films of past glories or watching *ad nauseam* the pornographic skits in which Jeff Koons and Cicciolina, breathing hot and heavy, repeat the never-ending representation of generalized corruption. There is, of course, no moral to this story, It's only a loop, a film without end in which one cannot even say "cut."

Translated from the French by Lara Ferb and Monique Fong

About the Authors

Esmé Berman was born in Johannesburg, South Africa, and as of 1987 lives in Los Angeles, California. She is the author of *The Story of South African Painting* (1975) and *Art and Artists of South Africa* (1970), and has curated exhibitions in South Africa.

Luchezar Boyadjiev of Sofia, Bulgaria, is a Lecturer at the National Academy for Fine Arts. He is a Fellow of the J. Paul Getty Program for research on the Bulgarian-born artist Christo and was the Bulgarian curator for several exhibitions including "Europe Unknown," Krakow, Poland, 1991; "Third International Istanbul Biennial," 1992, and "End of Quotation," Sofia, Bulgaria, 1990.

Samuel B. Cherson, a native of Havana, Cuba, now lives in San Juan, Puerto Rico. He is cultural critic for *El Nuevo Dia*, and contributor to other art magazines. Mr. Cherson has written many catalogue essays for exhibitions of Puerto Rican artists. He has also received the Bolivar Pagán Journalism Prize of the Institute of Puerto Rican Literature.

Calin Dan is an art critic in Bucharest, Romania. He was the Romanian curator for the "Third International Istanbul Biennial," 1992.

Gloria Inés Daza was born in Tuluá-Valle-del-Cauca, Colombia, and resides in Bogotá. She has curated a retrospective of the work of Jorgé Elias Triana and "New Directions for Emerging Artists." Publications include *Art & Artists of Colombia*, as well as other publications on contemporary Colombian art.

Adelaida de Juan lives in Havana, Cuba, where she is Director of the University of Havana Art Gallery.

Márcio Doctors of Rio de Janeiro, Brazil, is the curator of IBEU Gallery of Art, a professor of Aesthetics at the Federal University of Rio de Janeiro, and an art critic for *O Globo*. He is also a member of the cultural board of the bi-national center Instituto Brasil-Estados Unidos.

Shifra M. Goldman was born in New York City. A professor of Art History at Rancho Santiago College, Research Associate with the Latin American Center at UCLA, she is the author of *Contemporary Mexican Painting in a Time of Change* (1981), *Dimensions of the Americas: Art and Social Change in Latin America and the United States* (1993), and *Chicano Art: Continuities and Changes* (1993). She is also the 1992 recipient of the Frank Jewett Mather Award.

Serge Guilbaut, native of France, is currently professor at the University of British Columbia, Vancouver, Canada. He is the author of *How New York Stole the Idea of Modern Art* (1982), and *Reconstructing Modernism* (1991).

Alexander Jakimovich is a Moscow art critic whose most recent book is *The Late Soviet Civilization* (Moscow, 1992).

Amelia Jones of Los Angeles is an Assistant Professor in the Department of Art History, University of California, Riverside, and writes for *ARTFORUM* and *Art Issues*. Her book, *Postmodernism and Marcel Duchamp*, will be published by Cambridge University Press.

Mart Kalm is a native of Tallinn, Estonia, and a senior lecturer at Tallinn Art University. Dr. Kalm was the recipient of a J. Paul Getty postdoctoral Fellowship (1990-91). He has curated several major exhibitions.

Hassan Kamal lives in Damascus, Syria, where he is Director of the Museum of Modern Art.

Liam Kelly, a native of Belfast, Northern Ireland, is Senior Lecturer on the faculty of Art and Design at the University of Ulster, Belfast, and director of the public art center Orpheus Gallery. He is the author of *Art in Ulster* (1993), as well as a monograph on Clifford Rainey (1987).

Katalin Keserü lives in Budapest, Hungary, and is lecturer at the University Eotos Lorànd. In 1992 she received the N. Ferenczy prize from the Minister of Culture and Education of the Hungarian Republic. She is the author of four monographs on 19th- and 20th-century Hungarian artists, and a book on the Hungarian secessionists.

Elaine A. King was born in Oak Park, Illinois. She is professor of Contemporary Art and Critical Theory at Carnegie-Mellon University, Pittsburgh, and a freelance curator and critic. Dr. King is the author of *Barry Le Va: 1966-1988*, and curator for many exhibitions including "New Generations: New York & Chicago," "Elizabeth Murray: Drawings 1980-1986," and "Abstraction/Abstraction."

Vasif Kortun is a critic and freelance curator in Istanbul, Turkey. He is the organizer of the 1992 International Istanbul Biennial and the co-author of *Cãgdas Düsünce ve Sanat* (1991).

Želimir Koščević of Zagreb, Croatia, is Senior Curator of the Museum of Contemporary Art. Publications include monographs on Julije Knifer and the essay collections *Ispitivanje, Exat 51*, and *Meduprostora*. Mr. Koščević has curated numerous exhibitions including his country's exhibit at "The Venice Bienniale," "Yugoslav Modern Art 1995-1988," "Photojournalism in Croatia 1920-1940," and "World Masters in Yugoslav Collections."

Altti Kuusamo is an art critic living in Finland.

Bohumila Milena Lamarová, of Prague, Czechoslovakia, is Curator of the Museum of Decorative Arts, Prague, and has curated major exhibitions in Philadelphia, Montreal, Prague, Madrid, and Paris. She is the author of *Der Tsechechoslowakische Design* (1984), and the co-author of *Cubismo Cecoslovacco* (1982).

Joe Lewis was born in New York City and teaches at the Art School and the Critical Studies Division of the California Institute of the Arts. He is also administrator of the Los Angeles Public Art Program.

Silvano Lora is an art critic and professor at the University of Santo Domingo, Dominican Republic.

Beral Madra is a native of Istanbul where she is Director of BM Contemporary Art Center. She co-curated "Sanat Texnh: 14 Greek & Turkish Artists," and both the 1987 and 1989 "Istanbul Biennial." Other publications include *Cagdas Sanatin Kimigli* (1987), and catalogues for exhibitions of Turkish and foreign artists.

Linda McGreevy was born in Savannah, Georgia. She is associate professor of Art History at Old Dominion University, Norfolk, Virginia, and author of *The Life and Works of Otto Dix: German Critical Realist* and *Ida Applebroog*.

Alexandre Morozov is an art critic in Moscow.

Gerald Needham, born in London, England, is associate professor in the Department of Visual Arts, York University, Toronto, Canada. He has published a volume on 19th-Century Realism and curated the exhibition *Japonisme* for the Cleveland Museum of Fine Arts.

Amadou Gueye Ngom of Sokone, Senegal, now lives in New York. He is an associate editor of *Etc. Art Magazine*, Montreal, and a chronicler for several major Senegalese papers. Mr. Ngom is the recipient of awards from PCTV and the Black Filmmakers' Hall of Fame.

Tineke Reijnders was born in the Netherlands. She lives in Amsterdam where she is Editor of *Art & Museums Journal* and teaches at the Gerrit Rietveld Academy.

Anda Rottenberg was born in Novisibirsk in the Soviet Union, and lives in Warsaw, Poland, where she is director of the Soros Center for Contemporary Arts. Ms. Rottenberg is the author of *Van Gogh - Nuene-Paris*, and *Magritte, Kandinsky, de Kooning and Rauschenberg;* and has curated exhibitions in Italy, Germany, and Poland.

Kimmo Sarje of Helsinki, Finland, is Chairman of the Exhibition Committee for The Artists' Association of Finland. An independent artist and critic, Mr. Sarje has curated numerous exhibitions including "Erosion: Soviet Conceptual Art & Photography of the 1980s." *Archaeology of the Forms of Thought in Finland*, and, with composer Juha Haanperä, *Mini Opera Nostalgia for Avant-Garde* are among his published works.

Merle Schipper of Santa Monica writes for a number of California newspapers and magazines. She is currently completing a book on the art history of Venice and Santa Monica, 1945-1975.

Bernhard Schulz, a native of Berlin, Germany, is senior editor of the cultural pages of *Der Tagespiegel*. He has curated several major exhibitions at the Akademie der Kunste, Berlin, including "Amerika — Traum und Depression" and "Grauzonen — Farbwelten 1945-1955," as well as the exhibition "Ich und die Stadt" at the Martin-Gropius Bau.

Peter Selz was born in Munich, Germany. He lives in Berkeley, California where he is Professor Emeritus of Art History at the University of California. He has curated exhibitions at the Museum of Modern Art, New York and the University Art Museum at Berkeley, including "New Images of Man" (1959), "Futurism" (1961), "Jean Dubuffet" (1962), "Mark Rothko" (1960), and "Max Beckman" (1964). Professor Selz is the author of *German Expressionist Painting* (1959), *Art in Our Times* (1981), and *Art in a Turbulent Era* (1985).

Rebecca Solnit is a California-based freelance writer, the author of *Secret Exhibition: Six California Artists of the Cold War Era* (1991), and the essayist for numerous exhibition catalogues including *Kingdoms* (1992), *Landscape as Metaphor* (1993), *Ann Hamilton: Accounting, War After War* (1992), and *Compassion and Protest: Recent Social and Political Art* (1991).

Branka Stipančić of Zagreb, Croatia, is Curator at the Museum of Contemporary Art where she has curated "Ivo Gattin " (1992), "The Ukrainian Avant-Garde" (1990), "Goran Dordevic: Moscow Portraits" (1990), "Goran Petercol" (1987), and "Vlado Martek" (1986). Other exhibitions include "Dubravka Fakoci" (1985), "Geometries" (1986), and "Branko Lepen" (1987) at Gallery HDLUZ, Zagreb; *Art & Criticism in the Mid-'80s*, Collegium Artisticum, Sarajevo (1986); and the travelling exhibition of Ivan Mestovic's work. Publications include monographs on Ivo Gattin and Dimitrije Basicevic Mangelos.

Brandon Taylor is an art historian and critic who teaches at Winchester School of Art in England. He is the author of *Modernism, Postmodernism, Realism* (1987), *Art and Literature Under the Bolshevics* (two volumes, 1991 and 1992), and has co-edited *The Nazification of Art* (1990) and *Art of the Soviets* (1993).

Marcel van Jole is an art critic in Brasschaat, Belgium.

June Wayne was born in Chicago, Illinois, and has lived in Los Angeles since 1945. She is an artist and printmaker, whose works have been shown in major museums in Australia, California, Japan, and New York. Ms. Wayne was the 1990 winner of the National Association of Schools of Art and Design Citation for Distinguished Contributions to the Visual Arts.

Petr Wittlich was born in Ceské Budejovice, Czechoslovakia, and lives in Prague. He is associate professor at Charles University, and the author of *Prague: Fin de Siècle* (1992). Most recently, Mr. Wittlich curated an exhibition entitled "Situace 1992" in Prague.

Ann-Sargent Wooster was born in Chicago, lives in New York City where she teaches at the School of Visual Arts and the New York School of Interior Design. She writes for *ARTFORUM, ARTnews, Art in America*, and *High Performance* magazines.

Philip Zidarov is an art critic in Sofia, Bulgaria.

PHOTO CREDITS

Paula Pape (Brazil), p. 49; Jira Putta (Czechoslovakia), p. 64; Alfredo Jaar (United States), p. 71; Edo Kuipers (Amsterdam), pp. 94, 95; Boris Cvjetanovic (Zagreb), pp. 120, 174; G. Murza (Berlin), p. 132; Seppo Hilpo (Helsinki), p. 138; Gabriel Urbánek (Prague), p. 167.

Grateful acknowledgement is made to the following for use of their photographs:
Zabriskie Gallery, New York City, p. 17; Adrian Piper and the John Weber Gallery, New York City, p. 44; Jennie Livingston, p. 102; Warner Tübke, p. 132; and Robert Miller Gallery, New York City, p. 200.

typographic design: Barbara Bergeron
cover: MOG

typographic design: Barbara Bergeron
cover: MOG

Beyond Walls and Wars: Art, Politics, and Multiculturalism is the complete collection of the papers presented by art critics from 28 countries at the 25th Congress of the International Association of Art Critics held in the United States in 1991. Many of the critics also hold academic positions and work as curators or museum directors.

The book has been edited by Kim Levin, an American art critic who is a regular contributor to The Village Voice and other publications and author of *Beyond Modernism* (HarperCollins, 1988).